Dominican
BASEBALL

ALAN KLEIN

Dominican BASEBALL

NEW PRIDE, OLD PREJUDICE

TEMPLE UNIVERSITY PRESS
PHILADELPHIA

TEMPLE UNIVERSITY PRESS
Philadelphia, Pennsylvania 19122
www.temple.edu/tempress

Library of Congress Cataloging-in-Publication Data

Klein, Alan M., 1946–
  Dominican baseball : new pride, old prejudice / Alan Klein.
    pages cm
  Includes bibliographical references and index.
  ISBN 978-1-4399-1087-0 (cloth : alk. paper) — ISBN 978-1-4399-1088-7
(pbk. : alk. paper) — ISBN 978-1-4399-1089-4 (e-book) 1. Baseball—
Dominican Republic. 2. Baseball players—Dominican Republic. I. Title.
  GV863.29.D65K54 2014
  796.357092'2—dc23
  [B]

                                                          2013032930

♾ The paper used in this publication meets the requirements of the American
National Standard for Information Sciences—Permanence of Paper for
Printed Library Materials, ANSI Z39.48-1992

Printed in the United States of America

2 4 6 8 9 7 5 3 1

Contents

Preface

In a brief May 31, 2013, press release, Major League Baseball (MLB) publicly declared that its efforts to contrive an international player draft directed primarily at the Dominican Republic (DR) and Venezuela would be tabled for the foreseeable future. Few baseball fans took note that discussions between the Office of the Commissioner of Major League Baseball and the MLB Players Association bore no fruit after it seemed that MLB would steamroll the legislation through. As if to further bury the story, the announcement was worded in the usual cut-and-dried corporate-speak: "While both parties discussed an international draft, an agreement was not reached on some of the mechanics and procedures related to such a draft. Thus, an international draft will not be implemented in 2014."[1] Why did the two sides disagree? In the MLB Players Association's press release, the executive director maintained the vague tone: "At this time, the players are not prepared to accept an international draft."[2] A boring non-story? Not really.

On that same day, I got a brief phone message from Astín Jacobo, an influential Dominican player developer, which opened with, "We beat them! They just declared that the draft is going to fail!" American baseball followers had no idea that the draft story was a stand-down by the United States. Dominicans knew, and they declared a victory in the little-known baseball war that pitted the all-powerful MLB against a small, mostly unorganized group of Dominican player developers, or *buscones*. For Jacobo and others, that war has been a long guerrilla campaign involving direct and indirect confrontations with MLB, in addition to appeals to their compatriots. At issue is whether Dominicans will be able to gain a measure of sovereignty and continue to grow in influence in the future of baseball in their country.

Despite what it says publicly, MLB is determined to continue its free rein in the DR, tolerating only those who move through MLB channels. In recent years, Dominicans have seen the rise of influential compatriots and agencies capable of flexing a degree of autonomous muscle, at least some of whom—Jacobo, for instance—have not moved through approved channels. I have come to view Jacobo and others as insurgents in a struggle against MLB Commissioner Allan H. (Bud) Selig and his organization. The battle is low level, behind the scenes mostly. It consists of legal and policy chess moves, with occasional overt altercations, and it mirrors global relations between those with power and subalterns.

Insurgents are usually depicted as visually lacking in terms of hygiene, weapons, resources, and approval. In contrast to the crisp, clean, well-appointed look of legitimacy of their adversaries, insurgents appear disheveled, marginal, and lacking in credibility. Jacobo looks and acts like an insurgent. He wears no uniform (no operative does); his players look ragtag; he has no logos or business cards; and although he is successful, he lacks the visual markers of authority borne by members of MLB. However, Jacobo has fought long and hard to gain a measure of legitimacy, and his efforts and those of three of his fellow player developers (two Dominicans and a Venezuelan) were the forces that fostered a reversal of the international draft initiative. In the spring of 2012, this small band took the fight to MLB by fanning out to visit every MLB spring training site to seek out Latin American players on major league teams' forty-man rosters. They presented a spirited argument against MLB's plans to extend the draft to Latin America, and the players responded viscerally and instantly, swearing that they would strike before letting MLB have its way with their compatriots. Of 165 Latinos, 164 signed the petition that Jacobo and his fellow player developers presented. A year later, when the MLB Players Association met to review MLB's plan, those Latino major leaguers voiced opposition that helped squash the amendment. The chapters that follow chronicle this baseball battleground.

Acknowledgments

S aying good-bye to twenty-five years of research involves thinking of and thanking so many people. Hundreds have kindly given me their time and shared thoughts and information and are, of course, too numerous to name, but if they read this, I hope they know who they are and accept my sincere gratitude. Through the years, however, there have been a few people who have profoundly influenced the course of my work and whom I want to mention.

Milton Jamail and I began our journey into Latin American baseball as young scholar-pioneers. Over the years, he has supported me, instructed me, and generously shared with me. I cannot imagine my work without him. Ralph Avila, a historic figure in Dominican baseball, helped mold me as a scholar and as an anthropologist. He provided me with a father figure of sorts, and I will forever be grateful to him. Larry Dovalina was a godsend for my work on the Mexican League Laredo project. He not only paved the way for me in terms of establishing a network on the Texas-Mexico border but also had more insights than almost anyone I have ever met. The core of my work derived from a casual comment he made in one of our first conversations. That was also the case in subsequent research on baseball and globalization. Jim Small of Major League Baseball International happened to mention casually how he understood international baseball marketing and wound up determining the essence of my project. He was there at almost every phase of the work and, like Dovalina, Avila, and Jamail, guided my inquiries selflessly. They trusted me, and I, in turn, was buoyed by it. Finally, Astín Jacobo and I forged a bond through his father, with whom, we jointly discovered, I had done one of my first Dominican interviews back in the late 1980s. Connected as I was to Jacobo's late father and to the socially progressive views that both Jacobos hold dear not only made for an enduring connection but also helped frame the central theme of the present study. To all of these friends who were so influential in my research, I am ever indebted and so very thankful.

And one final shout out to my four sons, Jedediah, Cody, Benjy, and Jordan: when all else failed, there was always you guys.

Dominican
BASEBALL

Introduction

Dominican baseball has changed so much over the past twenty-five years that it is hardly recognizable. In the baseball world I first encountered in 1987, when I began my fieldwork, the sport had essentially been ignored—one could argue, "spared"—by Major League Baseball (MLB) for a half-century. Garnering no special interest (MLB was busy in Cuba, and before that, it was racially segregated), baseball in the Dominican Republic (DR) had barely any neocolonial disruption to contend with. Instead, it enjoyed ample cultural breathing room. Even into the 1980s, only a handful of teams thought enough of Dominican baseball to have a full-time scout in DR.

By 2000, however, the relationship between Dominican baseball and MLB had evolved into something neither party could have imagined. Dominicans were a regular feature in every major league clubhouse and were winning every baseball award. The game came to rely on a steady infusion of Dominican talent. With this, the relationship between MLB and Dominican baseball morphed into a distinct and unstable system of player development different from anything either had ever known. The genie had been let out of the bottle, and it looked, at different times, like Pedro Martínez, Sammy Sosa, Manny Ramírez, and any number of others. Back in the DR, thousands of youngsters redoubled their already extravagant efforts to clamber aboard the MLB wagon. How had the relationship changed each party? And how had the relationship itself changed?

In its first century (1890–1990), baseball in the Dominican Republic had been ignored or dismissed by Major League Baseball but not by other baseball-rich circum-Caribbean environments. Dominicans were regularly playing against teams from Cuba, Venezuela, and Puerto Rico, as well as U.S. Negro Leaguers, busily crafting a distinctive playing style, a pantheon of heroes, and mythic dramas. The baseball being played in Dominican cities of the 1920s, at the sugar refineries of the 1940s, and in the makeshift fields at all times was woven into a tapestry of sound, aroma, music, and emotion derived from daily rhythms of Dominican social life. Sporting rivalries as intense as those found anywhere were followed by whole communities; the games themselves became mass social rites replete with folklore. It did not matter whether the games were between small refineries or professional rivals in the capital. Local heroes, little known outside the DR, became heroes as folks in the smallest towns retold their feats. Early on, Dominican baseball was the game of Enrique "El Indio Bravo" Hernández and Tetelo Vargas; later, it was the game of Felipe Alou and Juan Marichal; and later still, it was the game of Tony Fernández, and Sammy Sosa, followed by Albert Pujols and Robinson Canó. Anonymous youngsters always watch and follow.

Baseball in today's Dominican Republic has to be characterized as a subsidiary of Major League Baseball and as a growing Dominican industry. Just about all aspects of the sport as it now exists on the island are directed toward the production of players for MLB: amateur and professional play, microenterprise and major facilities alike. The MLB Commissioner of Baseball has only one office outside of the United States, and it is in Santo Domingo. But while MLB structurally has become part of the woof and warp of Dominican baseball, Dominicans have emerged and entered the game at all levels of the industry as a potential harbinger of Dominican presence—their drive to do more than just supply talent. This new system is the outcome of the consensus and conflict between North America's and the Dominican Republic's notions of who should control the sport and for what end. Major league teams occupy state-of-the-art academies dotting the Dominican landscape that rival the baseball facilities of any minor league team in North America. These academies oversee all facets of player production. And the size of the revenue stream that flows into the Dominican economy (conservatively some $75 million–$80 million annually) is not lost on anyone either.

At the same time, within the Dominican baseball community one now finds a growing sense of pride and entitlement—people who want a more equitable partnership than MLB has offered. They are more than up for pushing their agenda. A Dominican has served as the general manager of an

MLB franchise; Dominicans have financed and built baseball academies and are now landlords to major league teams; and a score of young Dominican administrators who hold positions with major league teams could, if given an opportunity, run any enterprise in the game, including the Commissioner's Office itself. Perhaps, most importantly, Dominicans have gained control of the flow of talent that eventually forms the core of players on which MLB relies—against the wishes of MLB.

This book describes and examines the new system as informed by local culture, transnational links, and global forces. In this chapter, I set the table, so to speak, by laying out the context for and telescoping the study. The place settings at this table are as much about ideas and models (e.g., the informal economy and global commodity chains) as they are about the ethnographic details revealed through years of study, interviews, and observations.

Global-Local Confluence

A globalized world is all about understanding quickened connections among disparate people, ideas, places, and things that have reached the point of straining conventional boundaries while pointing to new formations. Understanding Dominican baseball is no different, and grasping the Dominican game through its links to Major League Baseball enables us to gain a sense of what a dynamic and seamless transnational system it has become. The symbiotic nature of this evolving relationship has benefited both partners. North America's game has continued to remain healthy, while Dominican baseball has emerged as a major domestic industry, rivaling agriculture.

Oddly enough, this dramatic expansion is the outcome as much of serendipity as of design. Sociologist Robert Merton's sense of *unintended consequences* is particularly well-suited to not only understanding the trajectory of events over the past two decades but also framing the widely disparate interpretations of what is going on in the DR.[1] In MLB circles, a perception has been created of Dominican baseball as an incoherent mélange of maladaptive practices. The media regularly report about a "Wild West" environment surrounding the signing of players and include exposés of players who are dying from the use of animal steroids or committing identity fraud. Such reportage provides both explanations of and a rationale for MLB's intrusion into the DR and fuels outcries from the U.S. and Canadian public to protect innocent young Dominican players from becoming victims of unscrupulous compatriots.

Dominicans hold a very different—even contrary—view. They see an MLB-driven world that gives them very few formal opportunities to gain entry and one that fails to consider the manner in which Dominican life makes it almost impossible to comply and succeed at the same time. The practices seen as legally and morally corrupt in the United States are regarded by Dominicans as essential—at times, laudatory—within a world they at once respond to and seek to circumvent. The old colonial Latin American maxim "*Obedezco pero no cumplo*" (I obey but do not comply) serves to underscore this very contemporary Dominican response to MLB's presence in their midst.[2] Understanding baseball in the Dominican Republic as both fractured and still coherently part of a global system is the primary aim of this book.

At the most general level, one needs to be mindful of the role that modern neoliberal economics plays in Dominican events. The anthropologist Steven Gregory's ethnography of tourism and globalization in the Dominican city of Boca Chica illuminates these connections. While visiting the shuttered sugar refinery of Boca Chica, Gregory was told that it was being left to die. "Ingenio Boca Chica and other government-owned sugar mills had been recently 'capitalized,' that is, leased to private corporations, which were expected to invest in them and enhance their profitability," he writes. "As yet, the factory's new operator—a Mexican multinational corporation—had not begun the renovations needed. . . . As a result some three thousand workers had lost their jobs. Once a bustling, albeit poor sugar settlement, or batey, Andres was now a community without an economy."[3] Neoliberal economic policies had destabilized the local economy, forcing more and more people to seek a living—in this instance, on the periphery of the nearby tourist trade. Because they exist on the margins of that economic sector, with no opportunities to gain formal entry, their futures remain in doubt and their legitimacy as genuine citizens of the state is further weakened. The global-local links are as undeniable as they are tragic.

In a very real sense, Dominican baseball is susceptible to the same forces. The former Cincinnati Reds pitcher José Rijo's sense of the links between neoliberal economic flows and baseball in his town echoes Gregory's assessment. Defending the lengths to which Dominican players will go to gain a foothold in North American baseball, which includes identity fraud, he pointed out, "We used to have [a factory] with 5,000 jobs. It's gone. We used to have the gun company. Gone. Duty-free. Gone. We used to have a hotel in this town [San Cristóbal]. We don't have one anymore. We used to have three movie theaters. We don't have movies anymore. All the job opportunities here are gone. What's people going to do? Be honest? And get a job where?"[4] The Dominican player developer Astín Jacobo said essentially the same thing when he lamented the loss of jobs in his city, San Pedro de Macorís: "Look, there's no more *ingenios*. When the *ingenios* left, we lost a large working population. Right now, all we have is baseball with a large number of people making a living from it."[5] These comments point to how North American baseball interests simultaneously align and malign—that is, they align with neoliberalism and malign Dominican society. It was this link among Dominican economic travails, internationalizing forces, and baseball that prompted the title of my first book on Dominican baseball, *Sugarball: The American Game, the Dominican Dream.*[6] In the ensuing years, those links not only have grown stronger; they also have driven the transformation of the relationship between MLB and Dominicans.

The booming industry that Dominican baseball has become is built on the production of baseball players. The sense of "new pride" Dominicans feel refers to the American acknowledgment and the Dominican exaltation associated with the remarkable numbers of players the tiny country supplies to Major League Baseball. In the 2010 season, the Dominican Republic—a country of 10 million—had 139 players in the major leagues. In that year, the United States—a country with more than 300 million people—had 982 players. These numbers indicate that, per capita, Dominicans are 4.3 times as likely to make it to the major leagues as Americans. The number of Dominicans in the U.S. minor leagues is even more impressive: It is now estimated that Dominicans make up anywhere from 25 percent to 49 percent (depending on how they are counted) of all minor league players.[7]

Being understood simply as Dominicans supplying labor to an industry, however, should dampen their pride. Defining success in terms of a neoliberal commodity chain wherein Dominicans supply either partially or wholly assembled ballplayers to Major League Baseball merely continues a century of Americans' extracting Dominican resources cheaply for profit elsewhere. It also misses important new developments.

Less flashy, and hence not as visible, has been the mosaic of Dominicans moving up the baseball commodity chain into positions of responsibility and power—a development that, while still small, has begun the process of reconfiguring relations with MLB. Some of these emerging relations have been consciously fashioned, while others are unintended consequences of a system in flux. Dynamism often comes with tumult, with contestation, and Dominicans have fought with MLB for access to the chain. This book describes the most important of these changes. They include high-profile advances in which Dominicans have risen to key administrative positions in the sport—most notably, Omar Minaya's becoming the first Dominican general manager of a major league team. Other changes are less obvious but even more important. They involve the emergence of Dominicans in key positions farther down the chain. Most significant of these is the rise of a sector of Dominican independent trainers (also known as player developers or *buscones*), who are responsible for producing the youngest ranks of players. Together with entrepreneurs and power brokers such as Junior Noboa (see Chapter 5), Dominicans no longer provide just a talent base; they are vying with MLB to work as equals in the industry. At best, MLB has been lukewarm about this prospect.

Changes in Dominican baseball include much subtler shifts, such as in how talent flows up and down the chain of player development and how players feed back into baseball-related activities after their careers. For instance, the widely known one-way flow of Dominican talent from the DR to the United States has begun to change. Dominican trainers, so successful at finding Dominican youth and developing them as players, are now being sought out by an international clientele. Consider the case of Javier (a pseudonym), who was born and raised in the heavily Dominican Washington Heights area of New York City and who opted to repatriate to the DR after failing to garner any interest in the MLB's annual draft. There he entered one of the many programs run by Dominican trainers for Dominicans. Or consider the efforts being made by Dominican player developers to sign their players with countries other than the United States. All of this is part of an emerging seamlessness associated with the transnational process that has come to define Dominican baseball.[8]

Twin Conditions Driving Dominican Baseball

Understanding Dominican life in general, and baseball in particular, includes a number of key realizations, but two stand above the others. First, foreign presence on the island—particularly, the presence of the United States—has always been of a boot-to-the-throat nature. Following this, as both precondition and consequence, is the chronic realization that for the vast majority of Dominicans, life is truly hard, and survival hinges on the ability to move deftly and creatively in and around institutions. If these sound like harsh or overly simple pronouncements, one need only peruse Dominican history and observe Dominican society to sense how these twin realities have resonated in all sectors, baseball included. The majestic swing of a bat or the grace of an infielder can find links to acts of guile and desperation one sees on city streets in San Pedro de Macorís or the oft-resented imprint of corporations, the U.S. military, or the U.S. State Department on the soul of Santo Domingo.

For Dominicans, the passion and beauty associated with baseball simultaneously represents the steel hand inside the velvet glove and a well-trodden path out of poverty. But while these tendencies form a compass that reveals the magnetic and political North of the transnational baseball world, they do not completely define the topography of the game in the DR. As indicated, that terrain has been shifting in the more than two decades since *Sugarball* first appeared, but the direction events are taking remains far from clear. As far as MLB is concerned, the Dominican game has matured from an afterthought into a rich player-producing industry that helps alleviate a chronic player shortage occurring in the United States.[9] Thus, haphazard recruiting of players has metamorphosed into an established commodity chain that begins in Dominican communities, moves into U.S. cities, and ends up back home. Dominicans take genuine pride in this, particularly because baseball is the only area of Dominican-U.S. relations in which they can feel on par with Americans.

However, MLB has continued a burnished tradition—or, more accurately, an old prejudice—in which foreign interests have entered the country as conquerors or colonists in search of resources, demanding authority and subservience. Consider that the DR government agency charged with defending Dominican players in their dealings with MLB has never been able to stand up for those who have been victimized by MLB's policies and operatives. Dominican Commissioner of Professional Baseball Luis Rosario has lamented, "This office should be able to defend cases like this, but . . . [MLB is] a monopoly, and it's their monopoly. They're the ones who govern the business and make the rules of the game. People take advantage of poverty."[10] Rosario is referring not only to the manner in which MLB historically has operated in the DR but also to Dominicans' ignorance of how MLB's operatives work, their resulting compliance, and the government's inability to alter the conditions of this relationship.

Resented Foreign Presence

Dominican baseball institutions, such as Dominican Baseball Commissioner Rosario's Office, have long been seen as nothing more than a rubber-stamping institution for MLB, but this is only the latest example in a long history of Dominican-U.S. relations. In 1869, Dominican President Buenaventura Báez lobbied the U.S. Congress to officially annex the Dominican Republic. He had the support of U.S. President Ulysses S. Grant but narrowly lost in a congressional vote. Relations with the United States have resulted in virtually complete dominance over the Dominican economy and politics, prompting at least one scholar to conclude that the Dominican Republic is "the most unsovereign sovereign country in the world."[11]

In 1904, the United States drew up the "Roosevelt Corollary" (an addendum to the Monroe Doctrine of the previous century), a list of Caribbean countries that would be shielded from potential European threat. If needed, U.S. Marines would be dispatched immediately to "protect" these nations, thus ushering in America's most imperialist phase. The Marines actually did occupy the Dominican Republic twice. The first time, for eight years (1916–1924), they ran all of the DR's major institutions in an effort to stabilize what Americans interpreted as chaotic political and economic systems that made the country vulnerable to European intervention. The second time (1965–1966), they occupied the DR again to "stabilize'" a government that the U.S. decided was unstable (this time, the freely elected government of Juan Bosch, which had strong populist programs and friendly relations with Cuba). These occupations had lasting effects on the nation and on the Dominican soul. Thirty years later, a Dominican friend of mine pointed to a hotel window that he proudly remembered driving by and shooting at during the 1965–1966 occupation.

Life Is Hard; Baseball Is Easy

World Bank data indicate that through the first decade of the twenty-first century, the Dominican poverty rate was higher than 50 percent, with poverty defined as living on $1.25 or less a day. That comes to more than 5 million Dominican men, women, and children having difficulty finding food to eat.[12] If they were given an additional 50 cents a day, that number would certainly be lower. But is it any more acceptable to have 4.5 million people struggling to survive than 5 million?

The case of Alfonzo (a pseudonym) illustrates these conditions—and a reason that so many people in the DR consider baseball a lifeline. Alfonzo was a prize prospect working with Astín Jacobo, one of the country's most successful buscones and was on the verge of being signed by a major league team. Jacobo said:

> His mother gave him away when he was three days old. He doesn't know who his dad is. . . . [He was] left with his grandmother, who would come and go, leaving him alone. . . . The kid went to school for the first time when he was about nine. He said that ever since he could remember, he was working—cleaning backyards and things. When he was eight, he was put to work in a bicycle shop. During baseball season, he would sell water and oranges at the fields. When he came to my program, all he had was a pair of shorts and two T-shirts [and]

a towel that looked like someone had cleaned the floor a thousand times with it. When he came to my *pensión* [dormitory], he watched TV with the other players, and when we turned it off so they'd go to bed, he went to sleep on the floor. . . . [H]e was used to sleeping like that all his life.[13]

Dominican humor, though dark, both highlights and dampens this kind of pain, as related by the former Cincinnati Reds pitcher Mario Soto: "An American boy grows up eating hamburgers, but in our country there is a saying: 'When you come home hungry and there is no food in the house, don't worry. You can never overcook a rat.'"[14]

For the poor, few options exist, and baseball as a path to upward mobility looms large because it values only skill, not patronage, race, or social position. Baseball has always been more democratic than Dominican society at large. Most Dominicans personally know someone who has played professional baseball. That is even more likely among the poor. Any Dominican can articulate the path out of poverty provided by the sport. Take, for instance, the pitcher Francisco Cordero, a major league closer, who said, "I don't know if I've ever seen a guy who's been rich since he was little playing baseball."[15] Enrique Soto, perhaps the most successful (and notorious) player developer in the DR, made a similar statement: "A person who cuts sugarcane should earn $80 a day but gets only $7. Who's going to cut sugarcane when he sees Alex Rodriguez [of the New York Yankees] get $252 million? It's very clear: You play baseball."[16]

Virtually every young player signed by a major league team beams at his newfound ability to build a better life for his family. But the elation associated with saving one's family, and oneself, fades into guardedness when one faces the sheer number of needy people who radiate out in all directions. With hands outstretched, these people remind the newly minted player of his obligations at every turn. "Remember all of the times I bought you breakfast?" one neighbor complained to a newly signed ballplayer. "You bought me some eggs once," the player corrected, but he wound up giving the man a small wad of bills anyway.[17] Still, for most young signers, the receipt of countless acts of kindness along the road to success causes less a sense of burden than one of gratitude that they can repay that kindness—a television set here, a roomful of furniture there, and baseball equipment for just about every kid who plays the game.

The possibility of going from worthless to worthwhile can take oblique, somewhat sad turns, as well, as it did for one young man whose family had been too poor to care for him. He ended up living on the streets and under the grandstand at the local baseball stadium for years. Miraculously (or maybe not), he found solace in honing his baseball skills and signed a contract with a U.S. team at sixteen. His family invited him back home to take up residence in the chicken coop behind the shanty they inhabited—an opportunity he leaped at. He spent his bonus freely on their needs. Rather than resentment, the boy felt elation at being deemed worthy to move into the chicken coop.[18]

Talent, while crucial, is not always sufficient, and escape from poverty commonly demands that one find ways around obstacles. Lying about one's age or identity, for example, has become identified with Dominican baseball. Even the MLB's threat of banning for a year does not stop the attempts. In 2002, the Los Angeles Dodgers signed Jonathan Corporán, a seventeen-year-old Dominican pitcher, for $930,000. His was among the first wave of big signings. What the Dodgers saw in Corporán was a wonderful combination of size (he is six-foot-two) and velocity (he threw regularly in the low 90s). The Dodgers needed only to verify his age. In a post-9/11 world, however, increased vigilance stirred questions about his identity, and soon the U.S. Embassy had enough evidence to determine that fraud had been committed. Overnight, seventeen-year-old Corporán turned into twenty-one-year-old Reyes Soto. His skills had not changed, however, so after nullifying his bonus, the Dodgers decided to re-sign him at the much lower figure of $150,000. "I'm glad we have closure," Jeff Shugal, the Dodgers' head of international scouting, wryly commented. "He's the same guy we thought was Jonathan Corporán. He just wasn't Jonathan Corporán." In a rare show of humor in such matters, Dan Evans, then the general manager of the Dodgers, quipped, "He just truly is 'the player to be named later.'"[19]

Why, if his skills remained the same, would a seventeen-year-old be so much more valuable than a twenty-one-year-old? Major League Baseball viewed Corporán/Soto as having committed an offense and concluded that he had intentionally set out to defraud. (If his deceit had been detected a few months later, he would have paid by losing a year in signing.) More recently, in January 2012, Fausto Carmona, a pitcher and All-Star with the Cleveland Indians, was charged with identity fraud. His name is actually Roberto Hernández, and he is three years older than his fake identification indicated. When pressed, Dominicans openly justify these attempts as responses to a market that wrongly skews age—independent of skill—to an extreme that ignores players who would be of ideal age in the United States. "You want sixteen-year-olds? We'll give you sixteen-year-olds" is their reasoning. Dominicans contend that it is wrong to be punished for an irrational market fetish for young boys spawned in North America.

Linking Dominican History to Baseball

Baseball played a valuable role in the imperialist spread of American influence throughout the world. No less a luminary than Albert G. Spalding, America's first baseball superhero, toured the globe in 1888–1889 with a team playing exhibition games in Hawaii, Australia, Ceylon (now Sri Lanka), and Egypt and making stops in Europe along the way. In his book *America's National Game*, Spalding boldly articulated the notion that the role of baseball was "to follow the flag"—that is, to lay the groundwork for early, or soft, imperialism.[20]

Americans held a naïve view of baseball as working for their benefit, whether by promoting admiration of the U.S. way of life in foreign lands or ameliorating rancor that might be directed at them. Even State Department officials bought into the belief that baseball served the United States in resolving cultural or political tension. In a communication to Secretary of State William Jennings Bryan dated November 1, 1913, James Sullivan, dispatch minister to the Dominican Republic, opined:

> The manifestation of resentment toward Americans, this is merely on the surface, I believe, and will disappear if the American Government makes any attempt to win the good will of Dominicans. . . . I deem it worthy of the Department's notice that the American national game of baseball is being played and supported with great enthusiasm. The remarkable effect of this outlet for the animal spirits of the young men is that they are leaving the plazas where they were in the habit of congregating and talking revolution and are resorting to the ball fields. . . . [Baseball] satisfies a craving in the nature of the people for exciting conflict and is a real substitute for the contest on the hillsides with the rifles.[21]

Sullivan, however, miscalculated the depth of Dominican resentment toward the United States. Had he remained at his post another decade, he would have seen baseball fueling both anti-American sentiment and Dominican nationalism. During the occupation itself, Dominicans viewed competitions against U.S. teams as surrogate warfare. When Enrique (El Indio Bravo) Hernández, a standout pitcher, defeated a team of U.S. sailors in 1914, the torrent of Dominican nationalism was overwhelming—Dominicans' equivalent to the U.S. hockey team's victory over the Soviet Union in 1980. "The [U.S. Marine Corps] teams will not win even one baseball challenge here, as they are simply inferior to our players," one editorial gushed. "The physical fitness of our underfed boys is superior to that of the chubby, ruddy-faced whites."[22]

Major League Baseball formally began its relationship with the Dominican game in 1951 when it laid the groundwork of what came to be known as a "working relationship." With no regard for the integrity of Dominican baseball, MLB simply decided that Dominicans should change the season in which they played, from summer (where it conflicted with MLB's season) to winter. In exchange, MLB would send some of its coaches and players to the DR to share their expertise. The assumption that Dominicans played an inferior brand of baseball that needed to be enlightened is, itself, rank ethnocentrism.

In the past quarter-century, MLB has further entrenched itself in how talent is developed in the DR and where that talent goes. Producing Dominican players has become a particular kind of global commodity chain, and while the concept is in serious need of revamping, it remains heuristic.[23] People in Dominican baseball circles initially had no response to this, simply gloating each time one of their native sons got to the major leagues. But over time Dominicans have managed to ascend to positions of power within, alongside, and outside official MLB circles. Those developments are what I examine herein. Perhaps most important, *Dominican Baseball* argues that we can no longer really think of Dominican baseball and Major League Baseball as separate, even as we chronicle them as distinct. They have become a system, but not as either has intended or would like. The result is a system that is simultaneously rational and irrational, collegial and acrimonious. It is a system that requires an anthropologist's touch to be fully understood.

Chapter Outline

Understanding how MLB and Dominican interests intersect and affect each other requires a perspective that is simple enough to be utilitarian yet sufficiently nuanced to get at subtleties. The global commodity chain (GCC) is offered as well suited, but in need of modifications. There is no simple way to grasp the transnational nature of what MLB-Dominican relations have come to be. So while I apologize for digressing into the realm of political-economic models, I believe it enhances the subsequent analysis. I have tried to avoid unnecessary arguments and controversies, as well as arcane language.

The GCC model has been used primarily by sociologists but also by some geographers and anthropologists. While it has serious limitations, it can be modified to be useful. In Chapter 1, I frame the way in which I look at Dominican baseball. Exploring labor as a "neoliberal exception" affects how the GCC, in this case, should be treated. I critique the GCC, modifying it to allow for a more critical and ethnographic perspective. Another key conceptual ingredient in this work is the informal economy. This concept is particularly well suited to providing understanding of global-local interconnections and disjuncture.

Defining the modern era of Dominican baseball is open to interpretation. Some would cite 1950 as the onset, when structural relations between MLB and Dominican baseball began in earnest. Others would argue that the modern era began when the first Dominicans reached the major leagues in 1954. Others still would claim it started when significant numbers of players began to enter the major leagues. In Chapter 2, I argue that the modern era began when MLB established a structurally significant presence in the DR in the 1980s. This presence is defined by the baseball academy system, and it took yet another decade for that system to fully take root. The rise of the academy system is part of a long, historic transnational string that dates back to the origins of the sport. What is potentially troubling about the academy system is that Dominicans' ability to have any impact on it is in doubt, and it has had pernicious effects on the Dominican game. I also look at the academy system ethnographically as a key production site in the commodity chain, examining the range of practices it uses to produce players. An account of the academy in terms of the social structure (e.g., players and coaches) sits at the center of the chapter.

The emergence of buscones, or independent trainers, has proved particularly vexing for MLB's system of signing talent in the DR. While their rise came about unexpectedly, buscones must be understood as having developed as part of the game, and they have gone on to form the only sovereign Dominican presence in the system of player production. Chapter 3 looks at the range of buscones operating in the DR today and how they have evolved into the most potent force confronting MLB's domination. The full range of their work is explored, and their essential links to the Dominican social fabric are described.

Chapter 4 focuses on five cutting-edge Dominicans who have had an impact on the game from a contemporary Dominican perspective. Astín Jacobo is a well-known trainer of talent who has emerged as a leading force in the counter-hegemonic push that the buscones represent. He occupies the lion's share of the chapter (and has a commanding presence in the book) because he is unique. He is at once respected and feared by MLB and heeded by other player developers; thus, there is no one who commands as much social space as he does.

Most people regard the Dominican legend Felipe Alou as a pioneer rather than someone who is currently at the forefront of Dominican baseball. Alou is a man of "firsts": the first Dominican from the island to make it to MLB and the first Dominican to manage a major league club. He is also the most consistent and poignant voice for Dominicans even after forty years in the public eye. Omar Minaya is well known to North Americans as the first Dominican general manager in the major leagues. After a successful stint as general manager of the Montreal Expos, Minaya took over at the helm of the New York Mets. He proceeded to create the first and most transnational organization in the industry, one that drove the cause of Dominican identity. Junior Noboa, following his journeyman career in the major leagues, returned to his homeland and launched a career as a broker in building full-service baseball academies. Success breeds more success, and soon Noboa was the man everyone sought when building state-of-the-art facilities. And Rafael Pérez is one of the most dynamic young administrators in the sport. Were baseball truly a meritocracy, Pérez would be in line to become the MLB's commissioner himself one day.

The academy represents MLB's most strategic production site in the DR (its way structurally to pursue its ends). As a system, the academy's cultural and ideological rationale for operating as it does in the DR "demonizes" Dominicans. By presenting Dominican baseball as inept and corrupt, MLB justifies creating policy. Chapter 5 looks at the anthropology of difference, or the manner in which organizations or societies maneuver around intractability between parties by diminishing one while inflating the other. This is particularly the case in intercultural dealings. Dominican practices are interpreted in this manner by MLB, and Chapter 5 explores how MLB has diminished Dominican claims to legitimacy.

In the past few years, the vitriol has reached unprecedented levels. Several crises have rocked the MLB establishment. For example, a kickback scheme was uncovered in which MLB employees were caught receiving illegal rebates from scouts in the Dominican Republic, and identity fraud has continued at disproportionate rates among Dominican players. As its "go to" guy to stop this, the baseball establishment chose Sandy Alderson, who, before going to the Mets in 2010 as Minaya's replacement, was arguably the second most powerful man in the MLB Commissioner's Office (after Bud Selig himself). Alderson brought experience to his charge of getting Dominican affairs in order insofar as MLB was concerned. He also brought an attitude that many in the Dominican Republic considered unacceptable, and resistance against both Alderson and MLB was mounted by outraged buscones. Chapter 6 looks at that tussle.

The conclusion, an epilogue of sorts, is built around the latest issues and how the two sides are currently poised to respond to each other. One outcome—again an unintended one—has the system that is now in place shoring up a vacuum that was created by that same system twenty-five years ago. I refer to the withering of amateur baseball, a casualty of the rise of the academy system, which is now, oddly enough, being resurrected by the buscones in their efforts to respond to the latest restrictive policies of MLB. This is truly ironic, yet oddly poetic.

1

Thinking about
the Global Commodity Chain

Between the time I first saw a skinny little fifteen-year-old named Pedro Martínez trailing his older brother at the Los Angeles Dodgers Dominican Baseball Academy and fifteen years later, when I saw him as a poised, two-time Cy Young Award winner eloquently handling the media in the Boston Red Sox locker room, a transnational baseball professional had been produced. Back in 1987, the undersize teenager was not on the official radar of anyone except the director of the Dodgers' academy, Ralph Avila, who was already raising an eyebrow at his pitching speed. Martínez was crude—small but smart—and driven. In the years between these two points in time, he moved through the Dominican system and the U.S. minor leagues, proving himself at each level until he broke into and dominated the major leagues.

These nodal points form the ends of a chain that links young athletes on the back roads of Dominican baseball to MLB, and for most fans and followers, it is one long, invisible apprenticeship. Fans in the United States have no idea that by the time a Dominican gets to the Rookie leagues in Florida, he has already been battle tested many times. Player development has always been considered a matter of honing skills already imbedded in the player through a series of escalating stages. There is no sense of this operating as a social and cultural proving ground, as well.

Dominican baseball and Major League Baseball are now so structurally integrated around manufacturing players that in many ways they function as a single unit, but one that has been around only since 2000. Before that, and going back to the early 1950s, MLB simply skimmed those players who were impossible to ignore, brushing off the rest of the Dominican sport. By 2000, the number of Dominicans in professional ball had so swelled—and their accomplishments were so widely acknowledged—that it became apparent even to the most ignorant owners and general managers that investing in the Dominican Republic was worthwhile. Academies were the new baseline. Whereas in the 1990s one could get away cheaply with leasing a *pensión* and a field somewhere in the DR to house and train young rookies, by 2000 no self-respecting prospect would have considered a team that did not have a first-rate facility. For major league teams, it simply was not competitive to operate cheaply anymore, because if they could not attract the best raw talent, in most cases they would not be able to develop the best players. And the name of the game (industry) is just that: finding and developing major league players who can help the team win it all. For MLB teams, this began at the academies and moved to the United States and the step-like minor league system. At each stage, players would become more refined and, if successful, move up to the next stage or be released either to return to the DR or to flee into U.S. cities.

As a production chain, the Dominican end is very different. Of course, the vast majority come to it as players working their way up, but increasingly large numbers of people enter into this budding industry in a variety of ways—some directly, others obliquely. Some former players return as coaches. Many non-players, however, also come to the academies: as elderly night watchmen, cooks, outside vendors for the academy, or buscones trying to sell the team a player. Then there are people who sell or service the people who sell to or service the academy—for example, a vendor might employ several people in his business, which, in turn, depends on the academies. The ability of Dominicans to break off increasingly tiny pieces of economic opportunity may seem remarkable ("Why bother?" one might ask. "They get almost nothing from it"), but it is not regarded that way in the developing world. According to MLB 2010 estimates, this synergy generates more than $75 million, but given all of the ancillary activity, it is likely that the figure is now much higher. All of this growth occurred in a cultural, economic, and political environment that was virtually open-ended, by which I mean that for fifty years, MLB had been able to operate however it saw fit. Dominicans were grateful for anything MLB handed to them. The striking overall growth of the past twenty years, however, resulted in opportunities never before considered, developments that Dominicans and MLB have responded to quite differently.

A general model is needed around which to fully assemble and comprehend this quickly changing study of transnational baseball. It should be structural yet flexible enough to allow for a variety of inputs and outflows in multiple sites. It should be direct enough to grasp the differences between Dominicans' and MLB's expectations and behavior that regularly come up. It should be nuanced and cultural enough to accommodate the fact that what is being produced is a certain kind of person in a social setting, with a particular history and proclivities, not a commodity that needs assembly. The model should also be capable of allowing for close observations at points where different acts of production are taking place. It should be sensitive to power, culture, and feedback. This chapter asks questions of these concepts and models at the very same time that it incorporates them.

Single Global Commodity Chain or Multiple Commodity Chains?

The global commodity chain (which is currently referred to as the global value chain) has been used by sociologists as a model to comprehend how commodities are manufactured and move transnationally. Following a short history of the GCC, this chapter critiques the concept with an eye toward reshaping it to understand how baseball players are produced. Because of the unique nature of what is being produced in this chain—elite professional athletes—the GCC concept, from the outset, must alter the way it conceives of what it does and how it operates. This begins with understanding that the nature of baseball as labor is unique.

Man Makes Himself, the title of the archaeologist V. Gordon Childe's magnum opus,[1] is my way of pointing to one of the most unusual features of baseball players as commodities. As "labor," baseball players' are unique in three very important ways: (1) They are both the commodity being produced and the producer of the commodity; (2) they constitute a radical departure from conventional views of Third World labor in that foreign labor is typically characterized as abundant, unskilled, and cheap, but Dominican players are the converse (i.e., relatively rare, skilled, and very well paid); and (3) the commodities that typically are considered in these kinds of analyses are not human beings. The player as a commodity is a cognizant human, aware of the operations being performed around and on him. He has a history that is in constant interaction with his present state, and he is capable of altering the conditions under which he is being produced. These attributes have the effect of changing the political calculus of how the commodity chain has been conceived.

Karl Marx long ago characterized the alienated relationship between workers (labor) and the commodities they produce as follows: "Labor's realization is its objectification. Under these economic conditions this realization of labor appears as a loss of realization for the workers . . . as loss of the object and bondage to it; appropriation as estrangement, as alienation."[2] The relationship between labor and what it produces, according to Marx, was inert and estranged—that is, labor is increasingly fractured into pieces and is less and less connected to craft. The commodities produced, then, are not considered in any way integrated into the workers' inherent sense of worth. But ballplayers are not alienated in this regard, and they do not have the same objectified sense about themselves as the one to which Marx alluded. The Dominican case is even more of a departure in this sense because baseball is so linked to economic salvation for self and family, and being a professional athlete is so self-driven and coveted that it cannot readily be thought of as alienated. Albert Pujols is no sluggish and unmotivated drone; nor are the yet unproven Dominican rookies at the academies. A different sense of labor emerges that more closely resembles self-actualized labor.

In addition, rather than being inert like cars, clothes, or electronics, the commodities produced are sentient beings who, as noted earlier, are cognizant and capable of altering the very conditions of their own production. A ballplayer is brought into the production cycle as a boy (a prospect) and becomes a man by the time he reaches completion as a professional. In the course of his production, he is maturing physically, emotionally, and, in this instance, cross-culturally. Through this process, he can take an active role in his own production in proportion to how he, his coaches, and others understand themselves and engage one another. The trajectory or production path is never wholly predictable, as the player who is being fashioned may move forward in the projected path or may deviate—for good or bad—in any number of ways. He may also leave the chain at one place and return to it in another and in some partially altered way.

In its simplest form, the movement through the baseball chain consists of jumping over a series of hurdles made up of increasing refinements in skills and overall psychological makeup. Three broad areas need to be considered in terms of moving up the chain. The first is compliance with the expectations and norms in the chain: Dominican players as employees are expected to demonstrate the requisite development of physical capabilities and talent at each level, but they are also expected to demonstrate a series of psychological attributes—referred to as maturity or coachability—that convince MLB coaches that they are indeed ready to be promoted. Those who fail to do so are eventually released, purged from the chain, and redeposited into Dominican society at large. Second, the larger social context (the social background and history) in which the athlete is being produced is a social and structural condition that may accelerate or retard the degree of fit within the organization that is working to fashion him. Finally, the athlete takes an active role in his own production, which can ease or hamper the transitions that lie in his path. This results in a complex network of potential and actual conflicts that can disrupt or even derail the process.

What would help in comprehending Dominican-U.S. baseball relations is a core model fitted with some useful concepts. The social sciences have no shortage of both models and concepts that purport to analyze relationships between developed and emerging economies, nations, and regions of the world. The problem is to find some that are useful and do not bore people to death. What follows is a brief (half-apologetic) assessment of one model that, while simple and useful, has been kidnapped by academic practitioners and rendered almost unrecognizable—that is, it has been transformed into something dry, politically neutered, and lacking in subtlety. Still, it offers a way to look at the complex relations in MLB-Dominican baseball.

Retooling the GCC

Global commodity chains are essentially international skeletal production sequences. The chain is little more than a series of events and sites that begins with the assembling of raw materials and ends with the finished commodity. Scholars derive meaning from the chain by welding their ideas, variable preferences, and disciplinary proclivities to it. As a result, the chain can privilege certain variables (e.g., labor, governance), regions (e.g., lead firms in the developed areas of the world or the margins of the chain in the underdeveloped areas), or ideologies (e.g., radical political economy or neoliberal economics). By itself, then, the chain is mute; it says nothing. *We* bring meaning to it. Its value lies in stripping it down and using it as a simple framework around which to assemble the materials (Dominican rookies) and producers (MLB employees, coaches of major league teams, and so forth).

History of the GCC

The term "global commodity chain" has consistently been attributed to Immanuel Wallerstein and is understood as part of his world-systems analysis. It was actually born as a sidebar in a 1977 article in which Terence Hopkins and Wallerstein laid out their version of Marxist-based dependency theory.[3] The "world system," Wallerstein's name for global capitalism, that emerged in the sixteenth century divided the world between nations at the "core" (the powerful center of the economic system) and those at the "periphery" (the powerless and dependent margins). For Wallerstein, the commodity chain concept was a different and more meaningful way to discuss national versus international relationships: "Let us conceive of something we shall call for want of a better term, 'commodity chains.' What we mean by such chains is the following: take an ultimate consumable item and trace back the inputs that culminated in this item—the prior transformation, the raw materials, transportation mechanisms, labor input into each of the material processes, the food inputs into the labor. This linked set of processes we call a commodity chain."[4] There we have it: simple, unadulterated by ideology or disciplinary preference, and waiting to be inscribed.

The debt to Marx's notions of production is implied in the division of the world into owners of capital and workers. As conceived by Hopkins and Wallerstein, the GCC is a means of looking at a global division of labor and power according to which developed nations—"core nations"—dominate those at the "semi-periphery" and "periphery." The notion of the commodity chain never evolved to the same degree, however, that Wallerstein's view of inequality and power in the global economy did.

By the 1990s, the commodity chain model had been picked up by the sociologist Gary Gereffi, who with Miguel Korzeniewicz edited a volume on the subject.[5] Gereffi would become the most notable figure in global chain research. Beginning with this initial collaboration, Gereffi embarked on an ambitious research agenda comparing industrial development in various areas of the world and in a range of industries. Using the GCC and an optimistic view of globalization's benefits, Gereffi and his students came to dominate this research area.

For Gereffi, the relevant areas of study were (1) "input-output," which refers most directly to the production process; (2) territoriality, which examines the geographic features of production chains; and (3) governance structures, or the ways in which the chain is controlled from the top. He would later add "institutional context," the rules that are lived by. The role of governance of the chain received a disproportionate amount of attention from scholars.[6] In his initial sense of governance, Gereffi distinguished between producer-driven and buyer-driven commodity chains. The former refers to industries in which dominant manufacturers own or control much of the vertical linkage. Buyer-driven chains reflect a more decentralized structure dominated by disparate retailers and others. Decentralization does not spill over into the governance realm, however; rather, it reflects neoliberal flexible production schemes.

Within a few years of the appearance of Gereffi and Korzeniewicz's anthology, attempts had already been made to refine the GCC model. For instance, the sense of "commodity" itself was being questioned as referring to only basic production (e.g., agriculture) and to low-value-added goods.[7] Also, some scholars were growing dissatisfied with Gereffi's binary scheme of producer-driven and buyer-driven chains, which also served as a template for governance of the chain. Timothy Sturgeon, for instance, pushed to supplant the sense of "commodity" with "value," reflecting a much broader international business view (with an emphasis on value-added) of global chains.[8] "Global value chain" was now the operating system for this area of research.

Anticipating the shift, Gereffi, in conjunction with John Humphrey and Sturgeon, expanded the view of chain governance into a five-part scheme that showed greater sensitivity to the types of relations between lead firms and their subordinates farther down the chain.[9] These efforts had the effect of pushing the structural orientation of the chain model along, and in economic sociological terms, it seemed that the model was evolving.

Critique of the GCC

Gereffi and his colleagues built a very successful fiefdom. Graduate students were cultivated and sent out to spread the word that global value chains constituted a relevant school of thought. Grants were won. Publications proliferated. Influence spread. From my small corner of the academic world, I found the research uninspired and unenlightening, not because the scholars were not saying anything big enough, but because they were not saying anything small enough. They were not ethnographically engaged. But there was more.

To begin with, Gereffi neglected the commodity chain's historical link to world-systems thinking and seriously watered down its reliance on power and inequality in a global context. What he concocted instead was a structural analysis of the manner in which firms based in the developed world organize and govern the chain of production. He did this by fixating on so-called lead firms and privileging their ability to control the chain ("chain drivers" was the term he devised). Gereffi also ignored the full possibility of agency on the periphery. This is oddly interesting, considering that he has been credited with integrating power into his examinations.[10] Insofar as he has, for instance, discussed "downsizing" or barriers to the entry of lead firms, Gereffi has indeed opened his analysis to views of power. But as his thinking evolved, these notions of inequality were increasingly swamped by an interpretation that emanated from the top of the chain and by an all-too-static view of structure. Gereffi's jargon—"governance," "chain drivers," "moving up the chain," and so on—also reflected his top-down view of the chain. Coupled with indifference to views of resistance, labor relations, or agency in general, which facets of power Gereffi employ matter little.

Jennifer Bair has cited other critiques of Gereffi—most notably, that his model is too simple to convey the complexity of networks as they exist on the ground.[11] Others argue that the emphasis on verticality in the chain downplays the importance of horizontal links (e.g., place or gender).[12] Gereffi also has been taken to task by those who claim that he pays scant attention to the complexity and nuance of labor relations.[13] A particularly strong reaction has come from those who have studied resistance to governance. Their complaint is that Gereffi's models make light of, or ignore altogether, human agency and the state.[14] Gereffi's contention that globalization in the full package production of apparel in Mexico would result in economic upgrading, for instance, has been shown by Marcus Kurtz and Andrew Schrank to be overly optimistic, if not wrong.[15] Using Gereffi's variables, Kurtz and Schrank examined the Dominican apparel industry and compared it with that of Mexico and other developing nations. They concluded that, contrary to Gereffi's optimistic view, the shift to increased full package production in the country would result in significant upgrades, and overall economic benefits were not forthcoming at all.

A disciplinary shot has also been fired across Gereffi's bow from the fields of geography and anthropology. The geographers Neil Coe, Peter Dicken, and Martin Hess take commodity and value chain models to task by uncovering the "linearity" within the global value chain's facile links between processes and organizations.[16] Coe and his colleagues prefer a much more nuanced global production networks model, "a multiplicity of linkages and feedback loops rather than just 'simple' circuits or, even worse, linear flows."[17] The geographers' critique of the GCC is well deserved and a long time coming, but they still lack qualitative ways to move beyond the dependence on structural arrangements.

The anthropologist Robert Foster took Gereffi and GCC research to task for ignoring the micro-interactive capabilities of ethnography.[18] The methodology that ethnographers employ excels at uncovering not only how meaning is imbedded in place but also the articulation of parties/agents and institutions at every node of production, distribution, and consumption. George Marcus, who is also an anthropologist, claims that "multi-sited research is designed around chains, paths, threads, conjunctions and juxtapositions of locations in which the ethnographer establishes some form of literal presence."[19] He, too, is singling out ethnography as up to the task of dealing with how meaning is negotiated in complexly interactive sites such as those in global commodity production. That is a path that the study of Dominican baseball needs to pursue.

I could not put my finger on it, but in looking at the commodity chain research—especially at nodes of production—I had a gnawing sense that I had seen it all before. Then it came to me: These chains were watered-down versions of Marxist political economy, particularly the works of the French anthropologists Claude Meillassoux, Maurice Godelier, and Étienne Balibar of the 1970s.[20] They had influenced my dissertation, an examination of the buffalo hide trade of the nineteenth century.[21] As disappointing as GCC studies were to me, my dissatisfaction was not so great that I would consider abandoning the concept. The GCC's utility lay in its simplicity as a skeletal framework to array the production scheme and as a mechanism to initiate discussions of production around multiple sites. Anthropologists have forged some wonderfully effective and simple tools to use in understanding these transnational production schemes.

The Informal Economy

Insofar as it illuminates behavior associated with power disparity, the informal economy has been an elegant and valuable concept. The term gives us a way to see how those who are systematically denied access to legitimacy and power fashion a wide range of practices to gain what they require. It has been widely used by scholars to grasp the world of the dispossessed in developing nations. In Dominican baseball, the informal sector is also useful when one considers the sizable number of people who earn a living through their proximity to MLB.

The social anthropologist Keith Hart has been credited with coining the term "informal economy."[22] His study of Ghanaian urban markets chronicled how a disadvantaged sector survived outside the formal labor market; he showed that Ghanaians who were unfortunate enough to be denied access to "wage employment" were carving out a living through a patchwork of self-employment schemes. Moreover, Hart's use of the term allowed us to include skills and services gained and performed on the outskirts of the formal economy in our overall analyses.

Most scholars of development today see the informal economy as a socially undervalued yet significant contributor to the overall economy that enables large numbers of workers (the majority, some argue) to earn a living. Alejandro Portes goes as far as to argue that the informal economy fosters capital accumulation and thus benefits the formal sector by lowering the cost of labor reproduction.[23] The informal economy has also grown considerably in direct proportion to the global expansion of neoliberal economic policy. Looking at the Dominican Republic, José Itzigsohn notes that neoliberal policies such as the privatization of state-held industry have increased the ranks of underemployed and unemployed people as the state has reduced the funds it once spent on social-security programs.[24] Foreign corporations that set up operations in the DR may have increased the number of people in the workforce, but they did so while reducing local wages. As a result, more Dominicans became refugees in the informal sector.

The case of Dominican baseball follows along parallel lines. Informal workers (here defined as those unable to gain official status or blocked by official policy from taking full advantage of opportunities) often circumvent the official mechanisms of the government or MLB to get at resources and subsistence opportunities. In a move that is directly applicable to Dominican baseball, a cottage industry has grown up in countries like the Dominican Republic to supply false identities and other quasi-legal and illegal acts. Since official identity is often too expensive and too difficult for poor people to establish, the informal sector supplies an illicit path to obtain identity documents. The informal market also has a social context. Jan Breman mentions that "ease of entry" is a cardinal social feature of the informal sector, while others mention ease of survival.[25] Flexibility in all things is also a major feature of the informal economy and is fostered by, among many things, incomplete accounting or information.

The overall utility of the informal sector is that, by defining people as excluded, it promotes practices that imperfectly ape the official sector's behavior. The excluded are put in a place wherein however they move, they reproduce their marginality.

Steven Gregory's Dominican Work

Steven Gregory's study of the informal Dominican tourist industry provides a wonderful parallel to the study of Dominican baseball carried out here.[26] His critical orientation relies heavily on resistance: "I examine the ways in which the laboring poor circumvented, challenged and reworked [the formal and informal] distinction and in the process, exercised alternative, and often oppositional, conceptions of productive labor."[27]

Gregory clearly shows that the Dominican working poor who stand in an antagonistic relationship to the state are willing and able to fabricate their own strategies. Substitute "MLB Commissioner's Office" for "state authorities" and Gregory is describing what goes on in Dominican baseball. Once we move beyond the people who are officially and directly employed by Major League Baseball (the players, coaches, and employees of the academies), we

---

BOX 1.1. DOMINICAN BALLPLAYER COMMODITY CHAIN

MAJOR LEAGUES
AAA MINOR LEAGUE
AA MINOR LEAGUE
A MINOR LEAGUE
ROOKIE LEAGUES
ACADEMIES
BUSCONES
YOUTH AMATEURS

---

can make out a rather large sector who "nibble" (*picar*) an existence on the edges of the industry—for instance, vendors who supply produce and meat, linen services, and the many temporary laborers associated with the daily functioning of baseball academies.

Many of these people are *los olvidados* (the forgotten ones) who form the backbone of the informal economy. They struggle to survive and comply with the dominant structures, but they are routinely forced by their disadvantaged position to circumvent convention (i.e., disregard the rules). Because of this, the World Bank considers the informal economy a persistent and growing feature of developing nations and a destabilizing influence: "A high level of informality also can undermine the rule of law and governance. The fact that a large share of the population is openly ignoring laws, regulations and taxes can weaken the respect citizens have for the state."[28] Of course, institutions such as the World Bank also conveniently neglect to mention that people end up in the informal economy because they have been socially jettisoned, but the potential for opposition is clear.

The use of the term "informal" is particularly appropriate when examining social practice in the developing world because it suggests the duality of its opposite (i.e., "formal"). Hence, depending on where one sits, the behavior that one sees as wily and scheming can just as readily be understood as creative and open. This kind of duality is evident at many nodes in the commodity chain (see Box 1.1).

The Dominican Chain's Links

Creating a fully formed, modern Dominican baseball player involves the eight stages identified in Box 1.1. Each stage is a production site that brings together the player and various agents and agencies responsible for "building" him by imparting the techniques and information needed to create a level of accomplishment that can be measured in some fashion. Movement up the chain represents becoming more fully formed as a player. Like other global commodity production schemes, there are multiple sites in different parts of the world, but in the production of baseball players (or any high-end athlete), the sites are socially and culturally determined, not simply operations performed on inert objects. Rather, value is added by working through a socially formed person who responds to the process (training) in a complex and negotiated way.

Dominican baseball deals most directly with the three earliest stages of this commodity chain (i.e., youth amateurs, buscones, and academies). At each node of the chain, elements come together to work on crafting a future major leaguer. These nodes involve an articulation between the commodity to be crafted and an array of people (both related and unrelated to the sport), and the relations can become complex. What follows is a brief outline of this process, with a discussion containing more nuance and detail reserved for later chapters.

Stage 1: Youth Amateurs

The Dominican Republic is teeming with young boys and teens playing baseball, yet in contemporary Dominican baseball, the organized ranks of amateur baseball needed to cultivate them are relatively weak. Little League and other tiered, structured systems, from the local to the national level, have never been strong, and organized baseball is largely absent from the school system. What little there was has withered over the past twenty-five years. At the informal level, however, baseball is played everywhere. It is from these ranks that the most talented players are identified—usually between age thirteen and sixteen. While their playing is somewhat makeshift and erratically organized, these boys are nevertheless regularly scrutinized by men who seek to develop them into players who might interest MLB teams.

Stage 2: Buscones

The people who first spot talented young players are referred to as buscones (scouts plus trainers) or, as I prefer to call them, player developers (see Chapter 4). Over the past decade, buscones have become an essential part of the system because they have captured the role of gatekeepers for young talent. Boys with noticeable talent are brought into a program that seeks to develop their raw potential over a period of years. This stage usually also includes various arrangements of room and board for anywhere from one to three years.

This is the first production site to bring together disparate elements: specifically, buscón and player. But others who are only tangentially related to the enterprise may also affect the act of production. The parents, family, friends, and community of the young athlete, for instance, play a huge role in either stabilizing or destabilizing the player's development. How complete the development program is will determine the possibility of curbing deleterious influences.

The nature of the relationship of the player developer to the athlete has to be examined. Its intensity often goes beyond that of a coach or mentor. Because many of the boys have no father, the buscón may become not only an extended family member but also a surrogate parent to the player. The player's family and friends are also factors that may aid or hamper his development, so sophisticated buscones seek to eliminate as many of these diversions as they can. Training usually goes on for years, but the young player is picked and trained with the idea of shopping him at sixteen and a half, or what is known as July 2 (the date on which MLB allows teams to formally attempt to sign the best and youngest legal talent).

Stage 3: The Academies

The academies are the pivotal site on the island. Major League Baseball teams run the academies to get their rookies ready to play in the United States. Once a player has been signed by a team, he is immediately placed in its Dominican academy, where he takes up residence for up to three years. A full staff attempts to train him and build his skills to determine whether he will be able to move to the U.S. Rookie leagues and from there farther up the ladder.

The signed rookies train daily and play in the Dominican Summer League. They are regularly evaluated and instructed by a steady stream of coaches who come from the parent club. In addition to baseball instruction, they receive language and cultural instruction designed to help them transition more easily to life in the United States. The academy is a complicated space for the Dominican rookie because of all of the areas of change that are expected of him. External sources of distraction are more easily kept at a distance than in the previous phase, but culture, education, and family background can all affect his play and his ability to get along with others at the academy.

Stages 4–7: U.S. Minor Leagues (Rookie, A, AA, AAA)

The minor leagues in the United States consist of a series of graded stages through which players try to pass en route to their ultimate hoped-for destination: the major leagues. Each of these stages forms a production site where one's level of play, if successful, will result in promotion, release, or being held for another season. In the off-season, the player returns to the DR, where he is encouraged to train (perhaps even at the team's Dominican academy) or play in a winter league.

Successful development will land the player in the ultimate stage: the major leagues.

The Commodity Chain as Dynamic and Volatile

At its most structural, the athletic commodity chain is perfectly convention-al: a commodity is manufactured piecemeal until it is complete and ready to be used. However, I made the argument earlier in this chapter that this is a unique chain: the player is both the goal and the means of production. Thus, the commodity chain is highly dynamic and has a high degree of unpredict-ability.

Retrofitting Back into the Chain

At any point in the process, a player may be released. When that occurs, it may have a range of possible outcomes. Unlike other forms of commod-ity manufacture, in which a commodity that fails to meet specifications is ejected—ceasing to exist in the chain—athletic talent can change the condi-tions of its own manufacture. To that end, an athlete may persuade another team to pick him up, and he may then reach his potential. Or he may reinvent himself (change positions), thereby getting a fresh start. Even if his playing career has clearly ended, a player may reenter the chain in an entirely differ-ent capacity (e.g., working for the team as a coach, scout, or employee).

The commodity chain model, then, should include a detailed examina-tion not only of player-team encounters at each stage but also of what may take place once a player has been ejected at any level. This constitutes a dynamic attribute of the commodity chain model that is made apparent in an ethnographic context.

Other illustrations of the power of the ethnographic method to illumi-nate purely structural arrangements may include, for instance, the follow-ing from the buscón stage. Compared with the social relations found in the larger commodity chain, and certainly in the capitalist system, buscón relations resemble premodern forms, à la Karl Polanyi,[29] in that they build ties and social networks of dependence colored by a dual emphasis on social and economic conditions rather than by market principles alone. In some instances, buscones may once have been players, and they tap into their long-standing relations with former player developers or teams that they played for to enter the chain. An ancillary commodity chain has developed among these men that links them, from small to large, on the basis of social bonding rather than purely on the basis of economics. Gregory found this, as well, in the informal tourist sector of Boca Chica: "It was common among the working poor to loan, borrow, and make gifts of money, services and goods to address needs and cultivate exchange-based relationships with others."[30] The constant exchange and negotiation among people that he observed was built on intensive social networks, and the networks, in turn, were erected on an implied understanding that if any one person succeeded, they all succeeded. Pursuing individualism and self-serving behavior instead of cooperation dooms anyone in the informal sector.

By constantly looking to "ethnographize" (if such a word exists) the sites in the chain, we can humanize the structural relations. Moving up the chain is the only goal shared by all, but while everyone is aware of the variables that allow this—playing well and accumulating impressive baseball-related statistics—what is often missed is the social and cultural frame of that playing and of those statistics. For instance, a player who has been sent to the U.S. Instructional League (a rookie league) from the DR is being asked only to extend his play during the off-season, but a Dominican might understand it as having to try out all over again. Dominican players are socialized to try out and prove themselves. Every change of venue for them marks a new trial and thus typically adds to their stress level. Escalating stress levels is something Randy Smith, former vice-president of the San Diego Padres, often sees in young Dominican players: "For many of them, it's an out-of-body experience. . . . When they first get [to the Instructional League], they think they have to do everything better than what they did to get here. They try to hit the ball farther, run faster and throw harder. When you try to do that, you actually perform below your capabilities."[31] The player who experiences a tailing off of his performance often pushes himself harder, reinforcing the negative cycle. Such an experience is sufficient to derail some players' efforts altogether, while others survive only through a change of teams. Occasionally, proactive teams try to head this off by bringing the players' coaches from the DR to the Instructional League to provide psychological and cultural continuity.

Political Maneuvering within the Chain

Perhaps nothing typifies the informal economy more than the stain of illegitimacy that is left on so many of the people in it. Whether performed by the state, parties in power, or corporations, the blocking of access to an official identity and the requiring of formal documentation separates society into those who are granted permission to engage all institutions and those who are excluded from doing so. This process begins with having access to an official identity—a birth certificate or a *cédula* (an official certificate of identity for which one needs a valid birth certificate)—which is a challenge for those in the informal sector. It is, however, a challenge that often gets met. There is "a lively black market in authentic and forged documents in Boca Chica," Gregory writes, "ranging from foreign passports to Dominican birth certificates and cédulas."[32] The reason that large numbers of Dominicans cannot easily get access to documentation of their real identity is a function of archaic record keeping, civilian ignorance, and poverty. "For a variety of reasons, many people in Andres and Boca Chica did not have birth certificates which were needed to obtain other forms of identity," Gregory writes. "Many people, especially those in rural areas, delayed or neglected registering their children's birth."[33] Obtaining a false identity—an act punishable by law—has become an accepted industry because it gives those in danger of being completely swallowed up in poverty a chance to survive on the edges of the formal system. What is important here is understanding that obtaining a fake identity is perceived differently: The legitimate see it as immoral, while those in the informal sector understand it as essential and hence moral (i.e., as complying as well as they can with society's dictates). These are not wanton criminals but obedient, wayward would-be citizens.

As Chapter 6 and the Conclusion show, identity for Dominican ballplayers is also fluid. Their ages and identities routinely have been altered, causing one longtime expert on Dominican baseball to conclude, "You have no idea how old they are. Papers can be bought. You can create a person, whatever you want to be. If you have the money you can be that person."[34] The determined efforts of MLB to stem identity fraud is discussed later, but briefly, MLB generally views identity fraud as a straightforward legal violation; thus, the organization believes it should be treated in accordance with the law. However, when one adopts the informal perspective, purchasing an identity does not look black and white at all. For Dominican ballplayers it is even less so, because so much is at stake—much more than was at stake for the residents of Boca Chica about whom Gregory wrote.

2

The Rise of
the Academy System

In the thirty years they have existed, academies have gone from haphazard affairs to a full-blown system of player production that defines the nature of Dominican baseball. These baseball academies function as a sort of halfway house for players to ripen from bare to green. Players entering the academies have signed professional contracts and thus are no longer amateurs, but they are not ready for the American rookie system either. The academies will serve as an entree point into a world in which they simultaneously have proved themselves and yet still have to prove themselves. In fact, proving themselves will have become a constant theme in their young lives as they string together tryout after tryout to impress one person after another. Stress is present, and it is integrated into their psyche.

The academies also offer the young players a world of plenty, the likes of which they have never seen: as much food as they want, living conditions about which many could only have dreamed. They play with equipment that is second to none. With the material bonanza, however, comes a demand that they not only comply as they never have before but also perform at ever increasing levels of baseball excellence. They will be judged by their ability to excel both physically and mentally. They will be expected to learn new things and function in ways they cannot fully grasp to get to the United States, and no player gets to the United States without going through the academies.

This chapter chronicles the rise of the baseball academies and how they have become the pivotal institution in both Major League Baseball's international efforts and within Dominican baseball. The academy system is also looked at as a site in which players are forged, and that process is understood to be less one of industrialized mass production than one of crafting and negotiation. The modern academy system is physical and social testimony to MLB's realization that the Dominican Republic is critical to the health of the industry. Through the splendor and completeness of these sites for the creation of top-notch players, as well as the care taken to better understand the players who are there, MLB has formally brought the Dominican Republic into its family. In *Sugarball*, I likened the early academy to a colonial outpost, calling attention to both its invasive economic function and its cultural "foreignness."[1] The foreignness is neither new nor threatening to Dominicans because baseball has always been able, at least partially, to "Dominicanize"—that is, domesticate—foreign influences. Indeed, the way Dominicans experience and use the game outside the foul lines has been one of their most impressive intercultural accomplishments. Because the academy system is the latest iteration of Dominican baseball, it should be shown to be part of the game's overall historical flow. Below I outline the three most significant moments in Dominican baseball history—the game's origins on the island; the period in which it took root, and the rise of the academies—all of which illustrate both the transnational quality of baseball and Dominicans' acumen in domesticating foreign influences.

Historical Briefs

The transnational nature of how baseball moved into and developed throughout the Caribbean basin is impressive, both in how receptive cultures were to the sport and in how quickly they put their marks on it. In the Dominican case, three moments in particular are noteworthy.

Origins

One myth that needs to be reexploded from time to time has U.S. Marines introducing the game of baseball to the Dominican Republic. Even though reputable histories repeatedly point out that baseball was brought to the Dominican Republic by Cubans, Americans feel the need to retell the story in own their terms.[2] The migration of Cubans to the DR began in 1868, when segments of the sugar-planting class and others sought to escape their country's Ten Years' War. They ended up modernizing the Dominican sugar industry and brought with them their cultural affinities, among them an infatuation with baseball.

Cuqui Córdova, the preeminent Dominican baseball historian, has tracked down the two earliest sources of the introduction of baseball by Cubans. In the Dominican capital, Santo Domingo, the Cuban brothers Ignacio and Ubaldo Alomá organized the first two clubs to play baseball as early as June 1891. Córdova also notes that two years later, in the town of La Vega (north of the capital), two more teams were organized by a Cuban doctor, Samuel Mendoza y Ponce de Leon. These teams were composed of transplanted Cubans, a sprinkling of Dominicans, and a stray Puerto Rican or American. Meanwhile, the game spread to the eastern city of San Pedro de Macorís, with its surrounding sugar mills, where it took on a life of its own.

Laying Down Roots

Originating the game and establishing it are two different things. The way baseball took root in the Dominican Republic is fairly typical and similar to how it did so in other nations, such as Mexico and Cuba. There the sport grew popular among affluent members of society (who had access to leisure time) and in time trickled down to the less affluent classes.[3] In Santo Domingo, baseball initially found fertile soil among the sons of wealthy Dominicans. It received an almost immediate boost, however, from Dominican youth who attended schools in the United States and Puerto Rico, for whom the American game was a way to prove their class position and modernity. The desire to claim modernity and cultural independence was certainly at the root of Cubans' affinity for the game, as well.[4]

Baseball really took hold in the DR once it escaped its class confines, however, and this it did in short order. Rob Ruck's magnum opus, *The Tropic of Baseball*, mines the memory of the informant Báez Vargas, who explains, "Boys like José Sabino, Lulu Pérez . . . were the first to play, but we who were not from such affluent backgrounds were not far behind."[5] Vargas does not mention how the game actually leapt from one class to another, but one need only consider the speed with which youth culture is passed around to get a sense of how such a diversion can spread. The first and only baseball diamond in the capital was a crude one in a glorified lot on the Malecón (boardwalk), but once baseball took root among the working class, lots sprang up all over Santo Domingo. Introduced by Cubans and rooted in schools in Santo Domingo, Puerto Rico, and the United States, baseball quickly diffused to other areas of the country.

Outside the capital, the game grew in sugar-producing areas through the development of fierce rivalries among refineries.[6] Teams were goaded on by their fans, who were also their neighbors, so that the competition became deeply rooted in a shared sense of space. By the turn of the twentieth century, baseball was well on its way to becoming the DR's national sport.

Ruck's informants often characterized Dominican baseball of the late 1920s as *beisból romántico*, noting, "We played for the love of the game."[7] The absence of a monetary motive is often cited as the source of the sport's popularity during this amateur period. These tropes, of course, carry the condescending implication that being extrinsically rewarded to play contaminates the purity of the game and the fervor of the fans and players. People in the eastern part of the country, near the sugar refineries, might partially disagree with the *beisból romántico* perspective. While they might have appreciated the lofty and passionate level of play at the time, they also would have seen economic incentives as liberating rather than polluting (reflecting class differences). Players from the Consuelo sugar refinery, for instance, embraced getting paid while not having to work for the simple reason that baseball to them, and to others, was more than a game. Earning a living and escaping poverty were essential.

Fielding teams that included paid players from Cuba and Puerto Rico, as well as from the U.S. Negro Leagues, not only raised the level of competition among the most powerful teams in the DR (e.g., the Tigres del Licey and the Leones del Escogido, both of Santo Domingo) but also furthered the transnational character of the game. Foreign players and teams who came to compete in Dominican baseball were often measuring sticks for the accomplishments of Dominicans. Seeing their compatriots vanquish opponents from elsewhere was the stuff of lore and embedded cultural traditions around the game. The 1937 season was the acme of this kind of play. The capital city's team Escogido (Santo Domingo was renamed Ciudad Trujillo by the megalomaniacal dictator Rafael Trujillo) went on a wild buying spree in which it raided the Negro Leagues for stars such as Satchel Paige and Josh Gibson, forcing other teams to do the same. A dramatic and remarkable level of play characterized that year, filling the annals with stories of incidents and accomplishments but fiscally draining the league by season's end.

Dominicans made the foreign game their own, as readily identifiable as their national dish of rice, beans, and chicken (known as *la bandera*, or the flag). Whether the modern major league academy system will be similarly domesticated is a serious question, however. In many respects, the academy system represents a different sort of outside influence that is closer to the notion of Trojan horse than invading army.

The Academy System

To find the precursor to the Dominican baseball academy, you first have to look at the Kansas City Royals of 1970. The team's new owner, Ewing Kauffman, had decided to find baseball talent that perhaps had been overlooked in the social turmoil of American cities of the time by building an academy outside Sarasota, Florida.[8] Art Stewart, a longtime scout for the team, remembers holding the first tryouts; he also recalls that many people in baseball considered Kauffman's decision laughable. In the tryouts, Stewart discovered a number of remarkable players, however, including the second baseman Frank White, who, along with George Brett, would become the face of the Royals. The goal of the Royals' academy, like that of Dominican baseball academies, was to find and hone talent in places others had either missed or ignored—players who could move up the organization's rungs to the major leagues.

While the Kansas City experiment was Kauffman's brainchild, in the DR two men independently created the academy concept. Epy Guerrero, a Dominican and a successful scout for the Toronto Blue Jays, built the nation's first academy in 1977. Five years later, Ralph Avila, a transplanted Cuban (via Miami) built his academy. Avila's academy in time would morph into the Los Angeles Dodgers' first academy and the template for the modern academy system in the DR. It is Avila's role as the founder of the modern Dominican academy that has stamped him as one of the most important figures in the history of Dominican baseball.[9]

The Beginning of the Relationship

Because through the early 1970s only sixty Dominicans had made it to the major leagues for even the briefest periods, the need for academies was not immediately apparent. Larger political events unfolded to change this situation, however, when the Cuban Revolution and the subsequent U.S. trade embargo choked off what had been the main flow of Latin baseball talent. As the Cuban embargo deepened through the 1960s, several clubs envisioned the Dominican Republic as picking up the slack and providing significant numbers of players. This prompted a reworking of the relationship between MLB organizations and Dominican baseball begun in 1951, which came to be known as a "working agreement."[10]

The working agreement was more a loose arrangement than an actual, formal relationship. It consisted of major league clubs supplying key personnel (coaches and players) to their Dominican partners, while the Dominican partners acted as a sort of holding tank for Dominican players that the MLB club thought might have a future. It was formal only by contrast to the absence of any prior relations, but it nevertheless contained the hubris of MLB in that the latter insisted that Dominicans change their playing season from summer to winter so as not to interfere with MLB's season.[11] Ralph Avila remembers the Dodgers' working agreement with the Tigres del Licey:

> We [the Dodgers] had a working agreement with [the Leones del] Escogido for about fifteen years. Then in 1971 there was a disagreement about how to handle some of the ballplayers. [The Dodgers' manager Tommy] Lasorda was managing Escogido that year. He became good friends with Monchín [Pichardo, the owner of Escogido's rival, the Tigres del Licey], so he changed our working agreement over to Licey. They had me come down and check the facilities—clubhouse, training room, ball field. They were in need of some remodeling. They had to make these repairs for us to go ahead. Also, as part of the agreement, the Dodgers would supply the manager, pitching coach, and trainer. We had twenty-six players we signed, and Licey used them. Some played for Licey, and some played in other places that Licey controlled.[12]

Signing and Developing Players

The working agreement was partial, covering only the Dominican Winter League season (late October–January). It also did nothing to establish a systematic way to scout and sign players on the island. Before 1970, when the Dominican Republic was an afterthought, major league scouts might occasionally get a call from a Dominican contact (if they knew any) alerting them to a possible player of interest. More often than not, the scouts would mentally file the invitation in the trash, but if prompted enough times, they would stop in the country. Finding good players was more difficult in the early days than it is today. Only the San Francisco Giants, Pittsburgh Pirates, and Dodgers established contacts in the DR, and even then, they were erratic. (Whereas in the first forty years, 1950–1990, MLB saw its role in the DR as haphazardly skimming talent, the past fifteen years has seen a shift to thinking of the DR as a renewable resource. To that extent, MLB is no different from any other capitalist enterprise that seeks resources abroad. It has invested heavily and more rationally because it makes better business sense to restock than to clear-cut.)

Avila outlined the changes the Dodgers faced and their early efforts to find players. They began with the view that scouting would have to be thorough. The casual nature of finding talent depending on the occasional bird dog's report would have to give way to a systematic effort on the island. Few people in Major League Baseball were thinking of focusing on the Dominican Republic. Along with Epy Guerrero and Howie Haack of the Pirates, Avila roamed the island in the 1970s looking for talent on a somewhat permanent basis. Their searches were completely unregulated, prompting many to characterize scouting in the DR as the Wild West, where an American scout could do whatever he wanted.[13] Edy Toledo began scouting in the early 1980s for the California Angels and, later, the New York Mets. He described the free-ranging habits of the scouts: "We scouted all over the country . . . in the mountains, small towns, over bad roads, crossing rivers with donkeys. We had no phones, no cell [phones], no computers. If you see a player and you like him, you sign him right there. You bring him to Olympic Stadium in Santo Domingo and get him ready to go to the States."[14] The players signed in those early years were quickly shunted into the North American system of minor leagues, where the outcomes ranged from difficult to disastrous. Felipe Alou, one of the first players to be signed by the Giants in 1955, was sent to the United States in the spring of 1956. There, he ran headlong into a world in which a different lifestyle and different customs often took a back seat to racism. Alou (Rojas is his real family name) overcame these issues, but many Dominicans succumbed to their experiences, as did Chico Contón, who came to the United States to play in the Northern League in Florida in the 1960s:

> The manager said, "They're gonna yell a lot of things at you. Put cotton in your ears." Later, they took me to the black section [to live]. I introduced myself as a ballplayer, and the people said . . . "No, no, you make a mistake." . . . I told them, "You go tonight and you gonna see." . . . Still, I couldn't eat with my teammates, couldn't sleep with them. When I went home [to the Dominican Republic] they couldn't believe what I told them. I had to take over [news]papers to show them.[15]

Racist attitudes may have abated between the 1950s and the 1980s, but player preparation had changed little when Gilberto Reyes, who caught for the Dodgers throughout the 1980s, was sent to the United States as a sixteen-year-old. He had to learn the language and culture on the fly as an unsophisticated and naïve youth. Reyes was projected as being capable of making the cultural transition to the United States from his Dominican background. "He was a smart kid, and I knew he would pick up the language fast," Avila said.[16] No one thought to check closely on Reyes, who recalled how terrified he was at first, with no preparation and total immersion:

> I was really upset and lost in those early days. The first year I cried a lot; I think I cried every day for the first two months. I even missed my flight to the United States. I was in such shock. One time I remember trying to cook some rice, and I burned it. I called my mother in the Dominican Republic and cried, "Mommy, I burned the rice! What can I do?" She calmed me down and told me to put ketchup on it and mix it in. It worked. Everybody thought I did it on purpose. I used to sit between my American teammates watching TV, and I asked them all the time, "What does that mean? What's he saying?" I tell all these guys [young rookies], "You gotta talk. I don't care what you say; you can tell them to 'go fuck yourself,' but talk all the time."[17]

For many excellent prospects, the quick transition to the United States proved too difficult socially and psychologically, derailing their playing potential. Remediation in the DR was important. Avila could see the need for cultural remediation in these players partly because he experienced similar difficulties when he arrived in the United States from Cuba:

> I was scouting international tournaments, and I saw the Dominican team in the Pan American games. It was clear that they [had] really good ballplayers. They beat the United States. They beat Venezuela. They beat Nicaragua—all good teams. Then I saw some of those Dominicans come to the United States and get released. How could these guys have tools like that and get released? So I started taking notes and talking to players, and we decided that 99 percent of the time [a player was released] not because he lacked ability but because he lacked education and work habits. We made a report, and that's when I came up with the idea of a baseball academy to teach them and prepare them to go to spring training and a different culture.[18]

The idea of an academy was something Avila had toyed with as early as 1974 (three years before Guerrero opened his Blue Jays academy). At the time, the Dodgers brass was not open to the proposal, so Avila approached Monchín Pichardo, the owner of the Tigres del Licey. Because of the working agreement, Avila already had eleven players under contract with the Dodgers for the Winter League season. He was looking for a way to intensify their development and speed up their ability to transition to the U.S. minor leagues. Operating in the administrative vacuum that Dominican baseball constituted back then, Avila was able to work freely and convinced Pichardo that he could cut his costs and improve the quality of his players if he opened a baseball "school." This would allow Pichardo to keep the best players and cut those who had no future. (Pichardo had an unwieldy reserve system of more than fifty players.) It would also help solve some of Avila's concerns about getting Dodgers prospects ready.

Pichardo loved the idea and asked Avila to get the Dodgers' permission to head the "school," or academy. Avila recalled:

> I was in charge of Monchín's academy, but there was a problem. In the academy we had eleven players from the Dodgers and seventy-seven from everybody else. [Licey had quasi-agreements with other teams that allowed it to sign their players.] All the clubs that signed Dominican players wanted them to play for Monchín because he took good care of them. That was the problem: I was running the academy for Licey, not the Dodgers, and I didn't wanna waste my time with players who didn't belong to us. I was developing players for other teams.[19]

Within a few years, Avila again approached the Dodgers about an academy, and again there was mixed support. So in 1981, accompanied by his main scout, Elvio Jiménez, Avila built a makeshift facility:

> I moved from Olympic Stadium in Santo Domingo to San Pedro [de Macorís]. We didn't know if we could afford it. I convinced Monchín to pay players a little more. I told our players on Licey that for that little bit more that they [were] getting, we'd move to San Pedro and work their asses off. First we had a boardinghouse. We started with our eleven Licey-Dodgers players. Then we started signing new players. We had to house them, so we built two rooms in Elvio's backyard, and we put eight beds in each room, and Elvio's wife fed them. If she spent $150 on food, we'd pay her back. That's how we started.[20]

The Dodgers' owner, Peter O'Malley, would remain dubious about an academy until 1984. By then, seven or eight other organizations had entrenched themselves in the Dominican Republic. O'Malley slowly came around, and when he began looking for a site, he began to regret not having started earlier.

But two years (in 1986) and $400,000 later, the first fully modern academy, the Dodgers' Campo Las Palmas, was opened. It was spectacular by anyone's standards: fifty acres, two manicured baseball fields, modern dorms able to house sixty players and a staff, a spacious dining area, and a clubhouse. It was built away from the urban area and was walled off to discourage interference from the outside, as well as to promote its learning environment. Campo Las Palmas became the standard for a generation to come.

The initial phase of the academy system, with its ramshackle combination of leased *pensiones* and found fields, did not end with the establishment of Campo Las Palmas, however. Most MLB teams thought the Dodgers were being their typical extravagant selves. When I visited the Royals' academy in 2002, I saw an organization that had been active in the DR for fifteen years but was still in a transitional stage. Luis Silverio, who ran the Royals' academy in the early 2000s, recalled the transition:

> When we started in 1987, we stayed at hotels. We cooked over there. [*Points to a building near the field.*] We walked from the field to the hotels. A friend of mine told me about this place in Salcedo that had a government field. I went, and like most complexes here, no one took care of it. Then we started to build a dormitory setup under the bleachers here, and we put beds and ceiling fans in it. On this side of the bleachers, we built a kitchen. I don't know how we got players to come here and stay. It was bad.[21]

By 2002, the Royals' academy had a brand-new dorm and dining center tucked between houses on the side street and across from a field that had been brought up to MLB's rising standards for academies. Still, the Kansas City organization had only just entered the era of modern academies. It was undoubtedly hindered by its small budget, but it also took time to convince the team's owners that the DR was vital to their long-term interests. Three years later, a growing sense of the importance of finding Dominican talent had settled in among all major league teams. The "*pensión* academy"—dispersed and still in the city—had given way to the fully modern academy, and most organizations, including the Royals, were either leasing or had built full-fledged academies.

The Dominican Summer League

The Dominican Summer League (DSL) has come to be regarded as one of the better Rookie leagues. Consisting of thirty-five teams (with at least one representative of every major league team) and playing a seventy-two-game sched-ule, the league offers Latin American rookies a chance to show off their skills. Officially, the league was created in 1985 by Sal Artiaga, a former president of the National Association of Professional Baseball Leagues; Freddy Jana; and Avila. The seed was planted slightly earlier, according to Avila: "They say it started in 1985, but I started this in 1983. I got a four-team league started in the south and got MLB to donate 250 dozen balls and a bunch of bats. I took all of the Dodgers rookies and some players from other teams, and we had a season. The next year [1984] we moved north to the Cibao [region], and we successfully ran [the league], including an all-star game and champion-ship."[22]

The DSL has grown in importance since its official four-team inception. (The original teams were Santiago, San Francisco de Macorís, La Vega, and Puerto Plata). As the league evolved and academies sprouted throughout the country, the distance traveled became more significant. Divisions of the DSL were crafted around the geographic proximity of teams: Teams in the Santiago area, in the nation's midsection, formed one division, and teams to the west, east, and south of Santo Domingo formed the others. Because of the distance between divisions, there was minimal play between them until the playoffs.

The creation of the DSL, which officially is part of professional base-ball's minor league system, functions heavily in the remediation effort that is demanded in accurately projecting talent. Most baseball scouts and front-office personnel understand that Dominican prospects lack game-playing experience. Jesús Alou, the director of the Boston Red Sox Dominican Acad-emy (and Felipe Alou's brother), said, "Today you got kids that have been trained to run the sixty-yard dash in 6.6 or 6.7 [seconds], but when you put them in a game and at the plate, they are much slower from home to first because no one bothered to teach them how to hit and run to first. Too many kids prepare for tryouts, and not enough prepare to play the nine-inning game."[23] Louie Eljaua, an international scouting director with the Chicago Cubs, also made this point: "A Dominican kid has played a lot fewer games than an American. A kid in the United States probably started with T-ball at age six, so by the time he's twelve, he's played in hundreds of games. Kids here play baseball early but maybe haven't played a game until they're eleven."[24]

Whereas North American and many Asian players have a long paper trail that documents their baseball history from Little League through school years, Dominicans have nothing. Baseball statistics (e.g., batting averages, win-loss records, earned run averages) represent a currency that is heav-ily used in determining a player's worth. Dominicans are penniless in that world, a situation that was made worse by the gutting of the amateur system. Hence, there is little on which to base a decision regarding how to project a player other than what his tryouts show. The DSL represents the first time a Dominican player can gain currency that is in any way measurable, and from it a team can more accurately project his movement through the minor league system.

The DSL also provides opportunities for players who will not necessarily move beyond the academy but who are needed as roster fillers during the playing season. "Sometimes you find players who can help you fill out the Summer League team," said Alou. "You know they're not gonna go on, but you can use them for the team, and they get good money. They might stick around, too. Some . . . help warm up pitchers and work in the bullpen and throw [batting practice]."[25] As the rational gateway to evaluation (generating statistics on players), the DSL has become an essential component of player production. It has also become integrated into the economics of the academy and the baseball-intensive zone around Boca Chica, with its ability to provide employment to fill-in players, umpires, and the like.

Until 2006, the academies also functioned as a storehouse that would hold players until they could be moved legally into the United States. A visa quota system had been in effect for foreign minor leaguers that prevented teams from sending as many players to the United States as they may have liked. The H2B visa for foreign workers coming into the United States seasonally extended to minor league baseball players, as well as to the usual agricultural workers and those servicing tourism. Before 2006, H2B visas were granted in very limited numbers by the U.S. State Department, and MLB had to parcel them out carefully among teams. Each team then had to deliberate to determine which of its foreign minor leaguers it would send to the United States. The result was a backlog of people left in the Dominican academies. Foreign major leaguers, by contrast, are given P1 visas, which have not been in limited supply. President George Bush (a former owner of the Texas Rangers) signed the Compete Act of 2006, which opened up the supply of H2B visas.

Critical Mass around Boca Chica

One of the more remarkable and unforeseen outcomes of the formation of the academy system was the gradual relocation of academies to the Boca Chica area, on the coast between Santo Domingo, to the west, and San Pedro de Macorís, to the east. At present, only the San Diego Padres Dominican Academy, which opened in 2008 in San Cristóbal Province, west of Santo Domingo, is located at any distance from the concentration of clubs in this area. The critical baseball mass that has formed creates an environment that fuels hypercompetitiveness among the teams and programs.

The germ of this centripetal force came from Junior Noboa, a former major leaguer turned entrepreneur who built Baseball City, the country's first super-academy complex that could house multiple teams. He created the fully modern, state-of-the-art complex near Las Americas International Airport, a location he saw as essential to building ties between the team's front offices in the United States and their Dominican operations. "They could take a plane from New York, spend five hours on the ground, and go back the same day," he said. "It's easier and better for everyone."[26]

Noboa's sense was more accurate than he could have imagined. First, the convenient location encouraged more frequent interactions between U.S. and Dominican ends of the organizational chain. International scouting directors, general managers, and others started making the Dominican academies a regular monthly stop. As a result, the academies now are not simply isolated outposts but strings of offices and operations connected to the hub. Academies and their operations inevitably have grown in both visibility and importance to those at the American hubs, becoming a meaningful part of the teams' social fabric.

Some teams have experienced this in the form of promoting two-way flows of lower-level personnel. The Tampa Bay Rays and the Mets, for instance, regularly send small groups of their Anglo minor leaguers to the DR to visit with their Dominican teammates and experience their world. These "experiments" have been highly instructive to the Americans and foster transnational seamlessness. I traveled through Consuelo with some Rays players in 2009, when the Americans got a chance to watch—and then play with local boys—a game called *trapagas* (a version of street baseball played with bottle caps). Not only did the eight- and nine-year-old boys who challenged them humble these Americans, but in the course of the visit, the boys also increased the Americans' understanding of the difficult road their Dominican mates have traveled. Most important, the inability of the Americans to speak Spanish and perform even the simplest tasks (such as ordering food) gave them a sense of what their Latin teammates experience when they arrive in the United States. These experiments also have an effect on Dominican Rays, who appreciate the American players' taking the time to visit. "They came here, ate our food and saw how we live," a Dominican player said. "Not many Americans would do that."[27] Minor league coaches and interns also go to the DR more frequently to assist and learn about the Dominican operations.

As teams began to concentrate around the airport and in the Boca Chica area, the number and kinds of interactions among them increased. Dominican academies became more integrated into the parent clubs' networks. The economic impact is noticeable, as well. Vendors and support services of every kind (e.g., strength trainers) have moved into the area. The total number of people being hired in the vicinity of Boca Chica has reached significant levels. The kinds of services they offer to the academies (e.g., security, laundry, maintenance, education, and information technology) has also increased, which is having positive effects on nearby communities. In addition, public relations have been enhanced as players with certain teams have spent time working with youngsters in these communities. Mets players, for instance, have served as mentors to young boys in the communities near their academy. The Red Sox are also involved in community support though the Lindos Sueños program, begun by the philanthropist Charlene Eberhardt. Lindos Sueños sends American youngsters (and some players) to the DR to help build baseball fields in communities close to the Red Sox academy. The volunteers work in the community in the mornings and play ball with locals in the afternoons. "All I can say," noted Jesús Alou, "is that since we started [the Lindos Sueños] program, no one steals from us anymore."[28]

A small but growing presence of "baseball programs," or mini-academies that prepare younger boys for tryouts and in essence act as feeders to academies, has also been detected. More of them are found in the airport/Boca Chica area than anywhere else in the DR; some of them are located right next door to major league academies. The International Academy of Professional Baseball, financed and run in part by former members of the New York Yankee organization, for example, sits directly across the road from the Yankees' complex and develops players who in short order will try out with that neighbor, among others. Thirty minutes away, in San Pedro de Macorís, an array of such programs are run by Dominican player developers.

As the number of teams located in the Boca Chica area has grown, so has the transparency of their operations to other organizations. Since many now live cheek by jowl, in a loose sense, teams now know more about one another's situations than ever before. They encounter one another as neighbors, and not always as friendly ones. The Rays are immediately next door to the Dodgers; for a time as the Rays' academy was being built, the team's personnel rented or shared space with the Dodgers. Gossiping (a form of information peddling) and backbiting about neighbors goes on here, as well. When the two teams played each other, the Dodgers often derided Rays players by calling them "renters," which, in turn, triggered responses from the Rays. Predictably, a rivalry ensued and continues. In short, the concentration of major league facilities has partially transformed the area, socially and culturally, into a baseball zone that is not unlike the country's free-trade zones, with their unique interactions, economies, and social configurations.

The Social Structure of the Academy

Baseball academies as a site in which to develop and test Dominican prospects have grown from an ad hoc solution to a set of organizational problems (in the form of exclusive training sites) to become an integral feature of MLB teams' overall structure, ubiquitous and replete with preconditions and consequences. To look at baseball academies as a system is also to make generalizations about what their goals, functions, and outcomes are.

One should never lose sight of two things. First, academies and rookies have the same goal: to form/become major leaguers. Hence, the incentive to comply with the demands of the chain on the part of all parties is high. This is not a reluctant and guarded operation. Second, the lavishness and opulence of the academy, and the demands it places on them, generally overwhelm rookies when they first enter the academy system. Standing in stark contrast to their lives, the academies make a number of statements to the novices coming in. One is that if they succeed, this lifestyle can be theirs. Another is that they have entered an environment that commands respect and awe. And finally, they will be closely scrutinized and evaluated, so if they fail to impress, they will be released.

The rookie coming into an academy has entered a complete, self-enclosed environment that is radically different from anything he has known. The experience is designed to intimidate him enough so he can be remade into the kind of player the team is looking for. He faces the demand to constantly perform in a range of areas. And because only a few will succeed, he will find himself in an ultracompetitive environment. All of this is stressful. Thus, the entering rookie is frenetically trying to figure out the best way to maneuver— how to respond to all of this and play his best baseball. How does one understand the academy within the context of the commodity chain? What social negotiation goes on between the institution and the player? The first question calls for a structural assessment of political economy. The second should be looked at through what Arnold van Gennep and, later, Victor Turner called "liminal space."[29] In terms of how the rookie exists within it, the academy is poised between being and becoming. Liminality invokes a sense of dramatic change of status and a transformation accompanied by rites of passage. These rites of passage entail a range of physical, social, and cultural changes, and appropriate tools are needed to understand how this affects the individual and his world.

A baseball academy has the same characteristics as any educational institution: It is hierarchical and designed to educate, evaluate, and elevate those who go through it. It matters little whether what is being taught is baseball skills or language. The overwhelming direction is toward the resocialization of those who go through it. It is also tempting to frame the academy as an oppressive environment in which the rookie's resocialization is of a coercive sort. One can all too easily invoke Paul Willis's study of educating working-class kids.[30] The social structure of the academy provides a skeletal outline for how this is carried out and by whom.

The Director

Along with their critically important administrative assistants, the directors of academies are responsible for overseeing everything. The teaching of baseball skills and seeing to the welfare of the players form the core of their charge. Personnel decisions (hiring and firing the scores of employees) fall to the director, as well. Juggling coaching, administering a facility, and scouting on a daily, and sometimes hourly, basis begins as soon as the director arrives at work. Tryouts and negotiations with players seeking to sign (and their buscones) are enacted at almost any time of the day, as are meetings to evaluate players; to discuss room, board, and travel issues; and to consider miscellaneous behavioral problems. Behind every good academy director one usually finds a very efficient administrative assistant. Cinthia Ortiz of the Rays is an excellent example. She handles such critical functions as payroll, travel arrangements, and visas to and from the United States, as well as requests for paperwork and information from the team's base in Tampa Bay. Ortiz is even more knowledgeable in these areas than the director. She is also a person rookies feel comfortable talking with, and comfort is important in the context of an academy. Employees like Ortiz are essential in every successful academy.

To the dozens of players in his charge, the academy's director is the most important person in the world. He is their gatekeeper, so they must impress him to earn promotions. His coaches will teach the players the skills, and the players will get game experience. But the director is often the one who teaches them how to function as young men—and as young men in a foreign country. The rookies have to evolve at a rapid and constant pace, yet most often they lack the wherewithal to do so. As Jesús Alou summarized his role as the director of the Red Sox Dominican Academy: "You are more than a coach because you are the father figure, the big brother, the uncle, and the adviser. These boys need somebody they trust and somebody who will help them out."[31]

Changing Relations

There is no simple or single way to operate as the head of an academy. Some directors take a hands-on approach, while others remain at a distance, allowing the coaches to handle routine matters. Some are authoritarian and remote, while others are close and informal. The results will vary depending on such factors as the nature of the cohort of players, how the director reflects the style of the organization, and even changes within the organization itself. A quarter-century ago, I characterized Ralph Avila, the director of the Dodgers' Campo Las Palmas academy, as a blend of stern authoritarian and protector, weighted on the former side.[32] He ran Campo Las Palmas as a modified military school, and in those days, the approach worked for him and for the Dodgers. "I don't think we had more than four or five bad cases in all those years," Avila said.[33] This emphasis on instilling discipline in preparation for the demands of the future was probably more prominent in the past, when fewer players were reaching the upper ranks of baseball and were receiving minuscule signing bonuses. Avila's style also may have been effective because he was left pretty much on his own. The situation has changed considerably since then, and different management styles are now required.

Some academy directors have an avuncular style. During his ten-year stewardship of the Red Sox academy, Jesús Alou has dealt with the many changes that have come to the DR, but his manner has always been easygoing and modest. A humble man, Alou has always downplayed his playing skills—for example, he characterized his fifteen seasons in the major leagues and lifetime batting average of .280 by saying, "I was a horseshit player."[34] A man who is comfortable with himself can be generous with others, and Alou is. "There is a lot of insecurity in baseball," he said. "Even after one year or two years of being in the academy . . . the kid does not know what his future will be. He is worried. There is a lot of pressure, and that's [where] we try to help."[35] Edy Toledo, the former scout and director of the Rays' academy until 2012, who had a long career with the Mets and the Rays, also fits into this mold. According to Juan Henderson, the director of the Mets' Dominican academy, Toledo once signed a boy to the Mets for $30,000, who had been trained by three different buscones, all of whom expected a share of the bonus. "This boy lived at home with his mother, who was really old," Henderson said. "The buscones wound up threatening her, and the boy ended up giving all of his money to the men just to leave his mother alone. What a shame. The kid was depressed for weeks, but you know what Edy did? He promised [the boy] he'd send him to the United States. That really motivated the boy, and he worked hard, and now he's doing well in the United States."[36]

Henderson has headed the Mets' academy since 2005. He represents a younger generation of directors with a broader range of experience; some of them, including Henderson, attended U.S. schools, graduated from college, and played professional baseball. (Henderson spent five years in the Angels organization.) He has a developed sense of professionalism but is evenhanded in his dealings. His personal style is anything but authoritarian, informed by the need to handle players with large signing bonuses and a keen awareness that the Mets give their Dominican rookies the best of everything and thus they should be grateful.

Toledo, though older than Henderson, showed while he was with the Rays that one can retool to accommodate the modern practices demanded by today's academy. The Rays have all of the progressive qualities of the Mets organization but at a fraction of the cost. Still, like the Mets, the Rays have players who have signed for significant amounts of money (the highest bonus paid thus far is $800,000). "Kids today don't have the same passion for the game as they did twenty-five years ago," Toledo said. "They want the money and the fame now. We have to motivate them differently nowadays."[37]

Carlos Alfonso, former director of international scouting for the Rays, concurred: "These players have been getting bigger bonuses, and they feel that they've already taken care of their families. So they've already won. The result is that for more and more of them, their desire is gone and they feel entitled."[38] Players being signed today, then, require a more nuanced set of responses from academy directors than did those a generation ago. While conducting fieldwork in 2007, I took notes as I watched Alfonso deal with two Rays players who were not following the coach's instructions. "He's speaking to them quietly, and, most importantly, away from the others," I wrote. Later, Alfonso told me that streetwise kids see the world as a string of confrontations, all of which engage their street responses, but they often respond well to a measured, reasonable voice that others do not hear:

You have to know how to deal with different kinds of people and in different ways. A lotta times, I ask the boy to bring his family along to tryouts. It gives us a better opportunity to make a connection. [One player's] uncle brought him to the tryout we held. That day we had a couple of pitchers who showed up early, at 8:15 for a 9:00 A.M. start. So I had two pitchers already warmed up when I got there. [The] uncle, who had played in the States, came in, and when his kid wasn't the first one looked at, he got all macho on us and told the kid to take his cleats off and get back into the car. I calmly went over to him and said, "Look, I understand why you would be upset. Your boy is really talented, but I had two [pitchers] warmed up, and I couldn't shut them down when you got here. Of course, I would have had your nephew try out first." He felt better, and after some back-and-forth business, we wound up signing [the player].[39]

From 2005 to 2011, Rafael Pérez held a position similar to Alfonso's with the Mets. He viewed spotting talent and developing it as two very different tasks and said that there is a serious shortage of people who know how to develop talent as well as the men discussed here do. Handling players, their families, and player developers while avoiding situations that can cause failure and cost the team its investment is a key area in which today's academy directors must be skilled.

The academy director of yesteryear too often was the cultural interpreter and ambassador during occasional visits by people from corporate headquarters. Twenty-five years ago, Avila was operating a colonial outpost that was almost completely separate from the Dodgers organization in Los Angeles. At the day-to-day level, he was answerable to no one. The occasional visits from scouts or Dodger administrators, including Lasorda, to casually check on the academy broke up long stretches of functioning on his own. At times, the isolated academies might have posed challenges to infrequent visitors from the United States who were unfamiliar with life in Third World countries. During one such visit by an assistant general manager in 1998 at which I was present, the academy director prepared to take everyone back to the hotel after a wonderful meal and rambling late-night conversations. He left us on a patio and then returned with two handguns tucked into the waistband of his slacks. The U.S. visitor's eyes widened as the director handed one of the weapons to his assistant. Looking at the American, he commented casually and with a sense of playfulness for his foreign visitor, "It's for psychology, to let people know you mean business. At this time of night, you have a lotta people who are looking to do things."[40]

The emergence of a concentrated sector of academies near the airport that is closely linked to urban centers and to the United States, as well as the increasingly rational operation of the academies themselves, which includes heightened security, make such scenes less likely. The increased interactions between the U.S. and Dominican parts of the commodity chain create opportunities to solve problems in different locales. I have referred to a transnational seamlessness that allows disparate pieces of the chain to respond to one another more effectively and meaningfully. In 2012, the manager of a U.S. minor league team called the major league office to discuss a Dominican player whose father had had been injured in an accident in the DR. The player was worried and distracted. The manager, whose team was located in a relatively remote area of the U.S. Midwest, was directed to the head of the organization's Dominican academy, and arrangements were made for the director to visit the player's father in a remote area of the DR. The player's distress eased, and he regained his focus on baseball. Although they are not formally required to, astute organizations and their personnel (including academy directors) increasingly do this kind of thing to protect their investment and promote players' chances for success.[41]

Scouting by directors has also changed since the academies first opened. They used to be the conquistadors of the trade, traveling everywhere and rooting out talent at games being played all over the island. These days, their travel is more limited and usually triggered by their contacts with buscones, who now control the flow of young, unsigned players. "Everywhere a scout goes, the players have already got somebody [a trainer or player developer], because everyone has a program," said Luis Silverio, who ran the Royals' academy before he joined the team as a major league coach in 2002. "You go around everywhere in the country and you'll see three or four [buscones] with programs right there. [Former] professional players have programs; the guy on the street who has the energy, he'll have a program."[42] Still, scouts remain road-bound. If a scout receives a tip about a player from a buscón he relies on, he will make a point to assess the player, often more than once. And if he is impressed, the scout will invite the player to the academy for a tryout.

Infield, outfield, pitching, and hitting coaches have always been present at the academies, and they continue to form the backbone of day-to-day activities and drills. Scouts today, however, have to rely on a stratum of buscones to gain access to prospects, which gives those who have solid social skills and street savvy a distinct advantage.

The Players

Significant changes have taken place in how players are dealt with in the pressurized world of constantly having to prove themselves and seeking enormous signing bonuses. Other areas, though, have remained the same. Players continue to know that they represent their families' best hope for escape from difficult conditions. Signing that initial contract with a team, for most, continues to be the high point of their lives—even years later. As one player reported with an ear-to-ear grin, "Mostly, I used [the bonus] in my family's house for a construction project that, by the way, isn't finished yet. I used it to bring money to my family. I'm the man at home now because it's easier for me than for others."[43] Silverio summed this up nicely: "You gotta remember with these poor kids that when they sign, they become the biggest person in the family. They are the ones that travel and buy the family new clothes. The parents look up to this kid. The father is not the father anymore."[44] This perception of how the young player takes on a new role within his family has remained unchanged in the decades I have watched the academies.

In general, the players' education levels have remained low. (Most attain less than an eighth-grade education level.) This does not mean that ballplayers are less educated than the Dominican population at large. In my earlier study, I noted that 20 percent of the boys at the Dodgers' academy had either completed or almost completed a high school degree.[45] Most recently, the MLB Commissioner's Dominican office informed me that ballplayers slightly exceeded the national average in terms of graduating high school (17 percent versus 16 percent).[46] Still, 80 percent of a population that has not earned a high school diploma is hardly reason for celebration—and it inadvertently underscores how viable baseball is as an economic alternative.

Academies as Remediation

As in the past, many players need some measure of cultural remediation. For instance, in the 1980s, academy directors often mentioned that young players needed to be taught a basic sense of sanitation (e.g., how to use toilets). That may have declined over the years, but it is still fairly common.[47] Juan Henderson still encounters it, and Jesús Alou said, "Sometimes you wind up teaching these kids how to use the toilet—that you don't stand on it or that you put the paper in it, not elsewhere in the bathroom."[48]

Changes are definitely evident, however. Players who are now being signed tend to be younger; they are physically larger and stronger; and they have more impressive basic skills. It is no surprise that their signing bonuses have escalated. And with this have come changes in players' attitudes—and, in turn, changes in how they need to be handled at the academies.

Improvements in their nutrition and training while attending the player developers' programs have contributed significantly to making the players larger. "When I was young, I thought I was the tallest man on the island. I was maybe six-foot-two," Alou recalled. "Now most of these boys are my height or taller."[49] Although a very small minority may be using steroids, that is not the case for Dominican players in general. "The other day, we went after one of the kids we signed," Alou said. "While I was looking for his buscón, I [saw] a guy with this rubber band doing maybe three hundred pulls. Another guy was doing push-ups. They really push more to make them physically ready."[50] The same buscones who feed the young players better than, in many cases, they would be fed at home are also responsible for enhancing the boys' tryout skills. Tryouts consist of basic demonstration of baseball "tools," so from the time they enter most player developers' programs, the boys are trained in hitting, running, and throwing. "They are taught to show well at tryouts at the academies—things like pitching and hitting—but we don't know much about how well they can play the game," Alou commented. "We try to put them in game situations as part of the tryout by having them play our boys."[51]

And, of course, the bonuses paid to Dominican rookies by major league teams have kept pace with the increased competition to find and sign the best young players. Old-school academy directors lament this state of affairs. "A good signing bonus in those days [1980–1995] was $10,000," Avila said. "Today they're throwing figures out there that are crazy. They don't know anything about a kid. They watch him for half a day, and then they start making crazy offers."[52] Offers in the high six figures, and even seven figures, were becoming routine before MLB cracked down following the 2011 collective bargaining agreement. The guidelines for the July 2 signings in 2012 pared back the number of high offers but in no way ended them.

Young players have always been preferred in the DR, but until perhaps a decade ago, eighteen- to twenty-year-old players were also signed, albeit at a lower rate of pay. Now the emphasis is almost exclusively on signing players at sixteen and a half to seventeen (see Chapter 6). Because teams have to evaluate players entirely on the basis of projections, they assume it will take additional time to move them up the commodity chain. But as bonuses have escalated, the ideal age of a prospect has become more or less fixed at sixteen to maximize the amount of time the team can work with him to get him ready. The change in players' attitudes as an outcome of all this is to be predictable. Administrators at academies are taking note of these changes, which pose special challenges.

Making a Ballplayer

Habitus. The resocialization component of Dominican player development calls to mind Pierre Bourdieu's use of "habitus," in which society and individuals create day-to-day dispositions and bodily discipline that reinforce social norms.[53] These norms, attitudes, and bodily practices are typically inculcated in childhood or in the formative period of one's life. The baseball version of this process comes later in an individual's life, making it somewhat more difficult to achieve; still, the effort is entrenched and, for the most part, successful. Baseball people use terms such as "makeup," "coachability," and "muscle memory" to describe a fusion of disposition and bodily discipline in their attempts to transform raw prospects into legitimate talent. The academies also use an array of practices to erase undesirable traits and forge new, more desirable ones.

The cloistered environment of baseball academies enhances their ability to resocialize and implant a new habitus. Rookies are in residence almost year-round, going home only at Christmas and after the DSL season. If they live nearby, they might go home for part of a weekend. Some teams, such as the Mets, prefer to keep players at the academy even longer. "We only send them home for a couple of weeks instead of six weeks following the [DSL] season," Henderson said. "This way we can control their nutrition and training, and they don't go back to their bad habits."[54] Although they may complain about being separated from their girlfriends, it is imperative to understand that in most cases, the players are equally eager to stay at the academies. Genuine willingness on the part of the subjects gives the process an air of collusion: teams want to create a certain kind of player, and players want to do whatever the team requests. So can this ever fail, and if so, how?

The only factor that truly has the potential to spoil this baseball enculturation is a player's past. Rookies enter the academies in their mid- to late teens with a history, and even when they are motivated, they cannot always easily replace their old identities with a new one. To paraphrase a quote found among those who ran early twentieth-century Indian boarding schools in the United States, whose purpose was to eradicate the indigenous in favor of white assimilation, "You have to kill the Indian [read, *tigre*, or street tough] to save the child [player]."[55] Academies are attempting to do this, only with players generally pushing the agenda.

The findings from the study by Paul Willis of working-class youth who actively resisted their resocialization experience in the British school system are not operative in the case of Dominican baseball. Yet rookies often experience conflicts between their hoped-for futures and their entrenched pasts. In a sense, the degree of difficulty in resocializing these players can depend on how divergent that future and past are.

Training the Body. Dominican rookies at the academy must learn to play their positions in new and more professional ways. The skills that got them to the academy must be recast in accordance with a team's style, and in sports that is done through training and constant repetition. For instance, the free swinging of the bat designed to showcase a player's power at the plate has to be replaced by a more discerning eye that helps him swing at only the right pitches. "Muscle memory" is a sports euphemism for having learned a series of movements until that series is ingrained and unconsciously carried out. Learning to play one's position and doing so to a team's or a coach's satisfaction means doing something thousands of times. This is the first and most obvious sense of baseball habitus as it is found in the academy. The repetition to the point of fatigue is designed to be daunting. Pushing the body to exhaustion through repetition is intended to break down or remove old physical responses and replace them with new ones. This is reflected in one rookie's comment: "The work here is harder. Getting up so early, and the running, always the running, is hard. But I heard it's even harder up there [in the Florida Rookie leagues]. So we have to push ourselves more and more."[56]

Cultural Remediation

Baseball skills aside, to move up the commodity chain rookies are expected to show that they are amenable to instruction and possess a degree of cultural and psychological awareness that will enable them to navigate the cultural terrain in the United States. Some organizations understand remediation as bicultural—that is, they see a need to teach rookies how to read and write in Spanish as well as in English. Shortcomings in any of these areas can result in embarrassing cultural episodes that can distract and humiliate players, as was the case for one young, newly arrived rookie sent to play in a small U.S. town. He was put up in a boardinghouse but was so culturally paralyzed that he would not venture down the hall to the bathroom. Instead, he relieved himself out the window. He got caught, and the team had to intervene with the owner of the boardinghouse and with the local authorities. For his part, the player felt humiliated after being confronted about so private a matter by strange people in a barely comprehensible language.[57]

The remedial nature of the academies' work includes not only behavior that is new and encouraged but also counterproductive behavior that may be part of a rookie's upbringing. For instance, the casual—to the point of negligent—attitude of many Dominican rookies about keeping appointments and arriving at them on time may be an outcome of having little to plan for, but it is deemed detrimental to their future development. Its opposite—punctuality—is considered critically important. To erase the inclination to be tardy and replace it with a sense of responsibility, everything at the academy is scheduled and put in a time frame. What follows is a typical academy schedule for a day on which no game is being played:

TUESDAY, MAY 15

7:00	WAKE-UP CALL
7:00–7:45	Breakfast
7:45–8:00	Stretch
8:00–8:25	Early work
8:25–8:40	Team meeting
8:40–8:50	Pepper game [a warm-up routine of bat on ball]
8:50–9:15	Players' throwing program
9:15–10:05	Fundamentals (e.g., bunting with men on)
10:05–10:20	Fruit break
10:20–10:30	Long tee
10:30–11:30	Position players' offense routine
11:30–12:30	Conditioning
12:45–1:45	Lunch
2:00–3:45	Charla MLB
4:00	English class
11:00	CURFEW/LIGHTS OUT

In a discussion of Campo Las Palmas more than a quarter-century ago, I published a Dodgers' daily schedule that is virtually identical to this one, suggesting both that the basics of training have not changed and that the commitment to instituting respect for time and task has been unwavering.[58] The notion of "strictly" adhering to rules and timetables for waking and curfews irritates almost all rookies, even those who are relatively well educated, as shown by the following incident. Javier (a pseudonym) came from an intact family who had educated him. He was a high school senior when he signed with MLB, so he was no stranger to punctuality and schedules. Still he ran afoul of the academy's rules. "One time, I had to go to the bathroom, and it's past curfew, and if you weren't in your room, then you have a problem," Javier recounted. "You will have to wake up early, at 6:00 A.M., and run. So I went and got caught, and I said, 'I only had to go to the bathroom. Why should I be punished?' But they do what they do in the States [strict adherence], and I had to run. We have to adapt to the rules here so we don't make mistakes over there."[59]

Strict respect for time and the rules around it is a key part of a larger remediation project that includes adherence to a general behavioral code at the academy. Henderson's Mets rookies all have to make their beds, learn how to behave in the bathrooms, and show up on time for all of their appointments. "We make rules about everything they do. Everything," he said. "In the beginning, we're flexible, but soon they have to do it the right way all of the time or they get punished."[60]

Some rookies who grew up in the streets find themselves running afoul of the academies' rules. Being a *tigre* (tiger, or street tough) is the flip side of being "coachable" and is seen as counterproductive to advancement. Because it is an almost instinctual response to perceived threat, street behavior for many of these young men is highly adaptive and honed—in other words, it is the habitus of many Dominican rookies who come from backgrounds of poverty. In *Sugarball*, I described a Dominican minor leaguer who confronted his manager with a bat in his hand when, in the aftermath of a theft, lockers were being searched. The *tigre* in him kicked in. In the academies, this might also manifest itself as fighting among rookies over perceived slights, systematic violating of curfews, or forcing oneself on women, all of which are widespread violations.

At the academies, such behavior, while disruptive, is understood and acted on in Dominican terms, but in the United States, it can result in dismissal. In the United States, an "attitude" is rarely tolerated and is likely to be culturally mislabeled and to carry dire consequences, said Silverio. He cited an example of a player whose *tigre* demeanor almost got him released:

> We have a kid who was sent back here from the States three days ago. He was having a tough time. [There was] no understanding of what he's going through. They didn't get his body language. We do a lot with body language. If you say something, maybe we go . . . [*He strikes a quarter-turn pose with a defiant facial expression.*] So coaches say, "I want no part of this kid." We had a problem with this kid here, too, about his behavior, but we know how to deal with it. Over there, they didn't accept it. He had only three years of school. He may act angry and like he doesn't give a shit, but he does.[61]

Punishments for infractions at the academy actually are less harsh than the plethora of rules would suggest. "Only two things get to [academy rookies]: losing money—we fine them—and extra running," Henderson said. "But sometimes we have to do the final thing, which is to send them home."[62] Being sent home is akin to being suspended from school: it is less serious than being released and is generally intended to scare the rookies straight. Still, every academy can cite cases of prospects who were released because the remediation efforts failed. One international scouting director who had bawled out the staff at the Dominican academy for inadequately preparing rookies they were sending to the Gulf Coast League said, "They need to be more professional and disciplined than they are. We released a guy recently who we caught walking through the lobby in Fort Myers [Florida] with a case of beer under his arm, after curfew, and who had been in a fight already that night. We just sent him back [as an outright release]."[63]

Release conjures up the question of whether the organization or the player is at fault. Did the team really understand the player completely and were all possible remediation efforts attempted, or was the player flawed beyond redemption? Silverio recalled an incident in which the Royals almost released a player because they misread his behavior as a character flaw instead of giving him time to sort himself out:

> We don't have enough patience. I repeated this to the front office. They forget about the adjustment time that these players need, and they let them go [release them]. . . . We got a guy right now in AA. Some people thought he was too nonchalant. He didn't want to work hard, they said. We almost pulled the trigger on him. [He] was a tough guy to coach. . . . He came from a broken home, no education. He went through hell in the United States and was sent home. . . . Now he's back in AA. He matured and is a different guy. And we almost lost this good player.[64]

To prevent misinterpretation of the cultural behavior of their young players, teams offer instruction on American culture and language. The baseball superstar Pedro Martínez, one of the most culturally astute players to come out of the DR, routinely cautions rookies about situations that might prove problematic: "Sometimes you just make a mistake trying to be nice. Like you whistle at a girl. Girls don't like to be whistled at [in the United States]. In the Dominican [Republic], that's flirting with a girl. . . . Here, some of the girls will take that as sexual harassment."[65] There are so many areas of culture that foreign players have to navigate in addition to food, sex, and the authorities that cultural remediation must begin before they arrive in the United States. For example, navigating through U.S. airport security checks can prove hazardous for Dominican rookies who make comments that agents consider inappropriate: Joking about bombs is something academy instructors specifically caution rookies about. It can also involve the simplest situations, as Henderson explained:

> We do a lot of different things. We teach them about time—how to be on time for lunch. . . . [I]f they're a few minutes late, they miss it.

Also, they have to clean their tables after they eat. We take them to the mall. That's one of the first things we do. We teach them how to behave there, how to treat their money, how to treat people there: girls, cashiers. We had good feedback from people who had our guys in Rookie ball and A ball. They had no problems.[66]

Leading and Leveling. In the 1980s, the leaders in an academy's cohort typically were those who had been there the longest. Today, leadership continues to be based on seniority: "There are leaders—the guys that have been around long in the academy. If I've been here for three years, then I have to serve as an example so others see how things are done and what the rules are."[67]

In the wake of the developments of the past two decades, new kinds of leaders have emerged alongside the traditional ones. They are called *viajantes* (travelers), a reference to their status as signed prospects who have spent time in the United States and have returned to the academy to resume their careers. They have seen the "Promised Land," which gives a certain amount of credibility and social capital that others lack. "The *viajantes* are the ones who come back [from the United States]; they act as leaders," Epy Guerrero said. "When they're traveling and come back to the academy, they are examples for the kids. They lead."[68]

Players who repeatedly break rules or disrupt their group's cohesion are dealt with by their peers and the academy's administrators, who work to "level" the offending party—that is, bring him back into line with the others. This is not new; it was standard practice in the early days of the academies, as well: "If they have an attitude . . . [w]e turn our backs on them, the hot dogs."[69] Players continue to use these measures. "We usually ignore . . . those who think they can do what they want," said one rookie. "Sometimes we just tell them, 'Hey, stop this!' Some guys are more passive, and when you tell them to stop, they understand."[70] Along with rising signing bonuses, however, has come a growing sense of entitlement. This, combined with swollen egos, adds to the problem of leveling undesirable behavior among rookies. Yet shunning remains the most common response. "The most expensive [players with high signing bonuses] sometimes walk around all macho," a player told me "What we do is shut them out. We don't talk with them. It's not so bad [at this academy], but on some other teams, you see guys thinking they can do whatever they want."[71]

Competition as a Motivator. Academy life breeds stress, but the awareness that the players are all competing for a limited number of opportunities may be the most stressful aspect of all. They have a relatively short time in which to prove that they are worthy of playing in the United States. Hence, despite the friendships and mutual dependence created at the academy, a climate of serious competition is pervasive. The players recognize this when they refer to the DSL as "Vietnam" because of the combative competition not only among teams but among the players on a single team. One rookie articulated this philosophically: "I know there are only a few opportunities for us, but in my case, I try to work harder. If there's a limited number of people traveling, I want to be in that group, whatever it takes."[72]

Some internalize the stories told by returning players, which waver between grim determination and despair:

> [The *viajantes*] talk about what it's like over there. You go to the United States and think you're going to move up there, but there's even more competition than here, because really, the business [MLB] isn't for us, for Latinos; it's for Americans. You have to do double the work or triple the work that an American does to move up. And then the language is a problem that makes it hard, because if they are telling you to do something, and you don't understand and just say, "Yeah, yeah, yeah," and then they see you don't understand, they say, "Oh, Latinos are dumb."[73]

Players at the Dominican academies experience the same mixed emotions when they see teammates moving up and down that one would find in any competitive environment anywhere. As one rookie said, "I feel good because at least it's another teammate who's taking the first step. But at the same time, to tell you the truth, I feel a lot of envy."[74]

Learning to Speak English. Language acquisition is the most important cultural variable that determines whether and how fast a player will make it up the chain. Rafael Pérez, director of the MLB Commissioner's Office in Santo Domingo, is promoting the most recent incarnation of the organization's language program, which centers on enhancing language acquisition and overall educational attainment. Offering language programs has played some sort of role at the academies since the system's inception but has grown in importance very slowly. I was present at Campo Las Palmas in the early days when language instruction consisted of little more than learning the names of parts of the uniform and various baseball expressions, such as "I got it!" and "Slide!" Major league teams have now placed language acquisition on the front burner because they realize that, given the size of their investment in Dominican talent and facilities, anything less would be irresponsible. Still, most rookies are not highly motivated to learn English, which perpetuates the long-standing trend of facing difficulties when they arrive in the United States. Consider the following examples:

> The Minnesota Twins' Luis Castillo . . . once set off a fire alarm at a team hotel when he pulled what he thought was a shampoo dispenser in a bathroom. And . . . a group of [St. Louis] Cardinal minor leaguers were repeatedly late to team functions because they refused to get dressed beneath the security cameras in their hotel rooms—cameras that turned out to be smoke detectors.[75]

Recently arrived Dominican rookies playing in the Short A season, a truncated version of rookie-level play, readily attested to the shortcomings of the language programs they were given both on and off of the field: "It's hard here. The coach would say, 'Hey, . . . you gotta bunt' or something, and I would just look at him. The academy taught me phrases like, 'Hi, how are you?' but Americans speak fast and with accents, and we can't understand."[76] This extends to off-the-field encounters, especially in the classic eating situation that has always plagued foreign players: "I would just point to the picture on the menu or order what my teammate ordered. And we all know how to say 'Coke.' One day, I asked for a club sandwich. The waitress asked me, 'Lettuce and tomatoes?' And I said, 'Oh, yes, lemonade.' I laugh now, but I was embarrassed then."[77]

Sal Artiaga is a pioneer in the area of language instruction for Latin American players, created a pamphlet of English phrases that they need to know. The pamphlet was desperately needed when Artiaga began publishing it more than twenty years ago, and it has gone through several editions since then. Academies and the U.S. minor leagues have put together language-instruction modules—with varying degrees of success—that their players must complete. Campo Las Palmas had a fairly good language program in the late 1980s and early 1990s, when Avila ran it. The minor leagues, however, had far less to offer Latin American players. I remember attending an English-language class for minor leaguers in Vero Beach, Florida, in 2003. Instead of using relevant conversations, the instructor built the lesson around a taped song that she played to the assembled Dominican and Venezuelan players:

> *Harold wants to reach the top. Harold wants to be a star.*
> *Harold doesn't want to drive an inexpensive car.*
> *Harold has a cell phone. Harold has a VCR.*

> But Harold wants an MBA from Harvard.
> (Repeat three times "Harold wants to go to Harvard.")[78]

By the middle of the first decade of the twenty-first century, some organizations had made serious advances in language instruction. The Rays, for example, began to understand that, while language acquisition may start in the Dominican academy, it has to be reinforced through the earliest rungs of the minor league experience. The organization's administrators who deal with Latin American issues simply made an effort to find excellent instructors at all levels (as did several others) and monitored the program. This added a small layer on top of other efforts, such as finding bilingual coaches and other staff. The person in charge of the language program regularly traveled to the Rays' minor league affiliates to ensure that issues were being handled and the teachers and players were operating as smoothly as possible.

Social Production and the Education Initiative

In 2005–2006, the Cleveland Indians fused the idea of language acquisition for Dominican rookies with advancing their overall education. The idea that an educated player will be a more successful player is an interesting one. It also has the advantage of seeming self-evident. "Most of these players have [only] two to three years of school," noted Jesús Alou. "They don't know how to learn, and you know you have to 'teach' the game. So if these guys go to school, I think that they can learn how to learn the game, and that makes them better players."[79]

The ability to speak English is, of course, necessary to function on the playing field and in the clubhouse. Further, learning how to position oneself, how to make infield adjustments, how to strategize pitching to a particular batter or an entire lineup, and (as a batter) how to figure out a pitcher also make use of language. So the link between language acquisition and education is real and important. But learning "how to learn," as Alou put it, ties into a player's coachability, and that is a different tack in determining a player's success.

The link between language learning and general education has a second, ethical dimension—namely, that these Dominican "boys" are sacrificing a secure future gained through education to take a high-risk gamble on a baseball career. Such framing of the issue has made the MLB Commissioner's Office uncomfortable because it validates a view held by many in the United States that the baseball industry is fostering exploitation of Third World youth.[80] That position is unquestionably sincere but is simultaneously ethnocentric. The argument that educating minority youth is more important than encouraging them to pursue futures in sports is a North American one derived from studies of U.S. inner-city youth.[81] It is based on a demonstrated relationship between education and employment opportunity. Thus, experts such as Henry Louis Gates Jr. can legitimately point out that, because there are fifteen times the number of black doctors as professional black athletes, black youths should pursue education over sports.[82]

Employment and Education. Unlike in the United States, in many developing nations the link between education and employment opportunity is weak or nonexistent. While it may seem counter-progressive and counterintuitive to Americans to promote baseball over education, in the DR, the argument in favor of baseball, at the expense of education, is a credible one. This was brought home to me while checking in to a hotel in Santo Domingo during one of my trips. The bellhop and I were chatting in the elevator, and I asked him how long he had been in that line of work. He replied that he had been at the hotel for four years. After a brief pause, he said that he was a lawyer, as well, but could not make a living at it, so he supplemented his legal career with hotel work. A lawyer who has to work as a bellhop is guaranteed to raise eyebrows in the United States.[83]

In 1997–2002, the Dominican economy was robust, whereas in 2002–2004, it was in crisis. Yet opportunities for all sectors of Dominican society have been uneven in both prosperous and difficult times. World Bank studies show that even during the boom period of 1997–2002, for instance, there was no real improvement for the poorest Dominicans. The downturn of 2002–2004 brought deterioration in real income across the board, with 14–16 percent of Dominicans sinking into poverty.[84] Thus, even when it is running well, a weak economy does not benefit the poor, and when times are bad, the poor suffer disproportionately.

Dominican schools mirror this overall unevenness in that they are unable to deliver education systematically to everyone. Even when they can get the students into the system, they do not have the resources and teachers to graduate them.[85] As expected, those who are most in need (children in rural areas and girls) tend to fare particularly badly. Although some studies show that in general terms economic opportunities increase with education, other findings contradict this. "For men, unemployment rates are highest for those with vocational degrees (18 percent) and those with post-university education (10 percent)," according to a World Bank report. Also, the probability of being unemployed actually increases when completing higher education (tertiary education), going from .014 for those who did not complete tertiary education to .032 for those who did.[86] So the straightforward claim that education is linked to increased economic opportunity (career and employment levels) cannot be made. In this context, pursuing a career in baseball can be a rational alternative—or, at least, an acceptable parallel venture to advancing through education.

The Indians and the Mets were unaware of, and unconcerned about, these sobering figures. They were convinced that promoting language skills and education was efficacious. Rafael Pérez, who was one of the primary architects of the education initiative, declared, "Even if nothing comes out of it as far as developing better players, [the] bottom line [is] it's the right thing to do."[87] Valoree Lebron, the daughter of a former U.S. consular officer and director of a school in Santo Domingo in which several teams enrolled players, claims that the effects of education are transformative: "We take a close-minded animal and turned him into an open-minded person."[88] This is an argument that resonates with the MLB Commissioner's Office. Lebron claims that critical thinking skills learned in an educational setting contribute to the development of the most successful players (with success measured as an ill-defined combination of capabilities both on and off the field).

Lebron's school was the pioneering site for the Indians' educational programs: Three times a week, after a full day of baseball, a bus carted the Indians' Dominican rookies to Santo Domingo, where they were enrolled in courses that guided them toward graduating high school. Those who had little education were given remedial courses, while more advanced players were directed to courses appropriate to their educational level. Compared with the classes I had seen at the academies, Lebron's school certainly impressed me with its comprehensiveness and efficient operation. In short order, the program, which cost about $800 per player per year, spread from the Indians to the Mets, the Seattle Mariners, and the Red Sox. The Royals joined the following year, by which time all but the Mets had left. Currently, no teams are registered with Lebron. They prefer to offer language-based education on-site at the academies. Having to manage the logistics of the programs, however, appears to have dampened the teams' enthusiasm for them. At the same time, the MLB Commissioner's Office may be influenced as much by criticism of these efforts from certain quarters as by the intrinsic value of educating Dominicans.

While the players may, in abstract terms, recognize the value of education, they are driven first and foremost by the desire to become ballplayers. As a result, many are reluctant to fully embrace the educational opportunities provided to them. Gilberto Reyes, who coached at the Mets' academy, candidly admitted to me, "I had to fight with them just to get them on the bus [to go to classes]. They didn't wanna go. They [had] been out of school since they were seven or eight, and they just wanna play ball. They'd scream at me, 'No way, we're not going!' I'd tell them, 'Get on the fucking bus, or I'll break your legs!'"[89] The teachers at Lebron's school also encountered reluctance among players who came to class unprepared and were not eager to learn English. "They say they don't need to learn English because they're ball-players," I was told.[90] Long bus rides to the classes did not help. Jesús Alou expressed mixed feelings about the academies' education programs:

> What I don't like is that the players try to hurry their workouts so they can shower and eat and get to their classes an hour and a half away in Santo Domingo. This is their time to play ball. They need to focus their attention. What I like . . . is that they are busy. They play ball all day and go to school in the evening. Then they get back by 9:00 P.M. and work on their computers and go to bed. We don't have them breaking curfews. . . . That problem is 90 percent gone.[91]

The concern about the long bus rides was one factor that led to the creation of on-site education programs at the academies. But it did not erase the idea among players that learning English is not all that important. The rookies faced the grim consequence of that mistaken view when they arrived in the United States. Thus, adding a layer of general education to the language-based programs at the academies has not been embraced by many players and staff members. Not surprisingly, though, it has found support among players who take advantage of the programs to complete high school.

Performing Los Mets. Under Pérez's guidance, the Mets followed the Indians into the area of educating their players. Within a year, both teams had graduated players from Lebron's school in Santo Domingo. The Mets used the accomplishment to bolster their effort to become known as the baseball industry's most significant transnational brand. On August 6, 2007, Lebron's school held a graduation dinner at the Hilton Hotel in Santo Domingo with an assembled body of students, parents, and guests, all of them smartly dressed and full of optimism and pride.

The guests sat at round tables as the graduates—escorted by their parents—entered the room. The clapping in the banquet hall was significantly louder when the baseball players entered. The Mets were graduating four academy members who stood out because of their class, race, and general discomfort. They were larger and darker-skinned and were not dressed as well as the well-heeled and lighter-skinned, upper-class Dominicans. Normally this kind of race and class mixing would not have been countenanced in Dominican society, but the Mets managed to override the social code as they declared their twenty-first-century transnationalism. In the wake of this bold move, they nudged Dominican identity a little farther into the globalized world.

The evening's keynote speaker was none other than Rafael Pérez, who was working for the Mets at the time and put an organizational spin on the event even as he talked about how important it was for these boys to finish school and praised Lebron's institution. He pushed the brand at every opportunity, specifically linking what could be considered a purely local event (i.e., educating Dominicans in the DR) to its larger symbolic meaning to a major league team from New York, the most populous metropolitan area in North America. That he and the Mets' general manager, Omar Minaya, were Dominicans also was not lost on the crowd, further enhancing the perception of seamless local-global linkage. The message was that the Dominican Republic was becoming an important part of the global community, and that the Mets were aiding the effort. Education had become part of the performance of global branding and protecting the brand from external criticism.

Conclusion

As a site in the global production chain, the modern baseball academy system reveals many of the most important directions baseball will take in the Dominican Republic. Having begun as isolated outposts where players were haphazardly produced, the academies have grown into transnational hubs where a wide range of people, with different agendas, converge to develop future major league players. These academies are layered sites of production. Their primary function is to develop major league talent, but to do so effectively, they must address the young prospects' needs for cultural and social remediation. At this point, the production of baseball players has to include people and goals that have little or nothing to do with baseball itself. Thus, as a node in the commodity chain, the academy unquestionably brings the most sweeping set of inputs into the production scheme.

3

A Nation of Buscones

What do you call men like Enrique Soto and Astín Jacobo Jr., who look for talented teenage baseball players they can train and develop into viable major league prospects? After working with these boys for years, Soto and Jacobo will take them to MLB tryouts in the Dominican Republic, and if they are successful, the young players will become professionals and receive significant signing bonuses. As their developers, Soto and Jacobo will receive as much as 35 percent of that bonus. The baseball world has come to know people who do this work as buscones (sing., buscón). The term derives from the Spanish *buscar* (to look or search for)—in this case, baseball talent.

Jacobo and many of his colleagues dislike the word, which has taken on pejorative connotations. They insist on being called "independent trainers." Even as the word used to identify these people is contested, the buscones indisputably have become key nodes in the Dominican baseball commodity chain. They also constitute the most overtly challenging part of that chain.

And even though Jacobo dislikes "buscón" and feels it does not describe what he does, his own term, "trainer," is equally inaccurate. The people who engage in this activity do much more than simply "find" or "train" players. Jacobo finds, trains, houses, feeds, and financially supports prospects (and often their families); he educates them if they so desire; and he tends to the medical needs of the boys and their families, all while building and refining the prospects' baseball-playing skills. And he does this for years. He then shepherds the prospects through the long, labyrinthine, and stressful world of tryouts and negotiations en route to signing. Hence, as opposed to simply "finding" or "training," Jacobo completely develops players and launches them into their careers. I prefer to call him a "player developer." However, in deference to Jacobo and others, I also use "trainer," the term they prefer. Finally, the industry and the American public continue to refer to these men as "buscones." In this volume, I use the three terms interchangeably.

As noted earlier, the Spanish word *buscar* means "to look or search for." In the early seventeenth century, however, Francisco de Quevedo wrote the novel *Historia de la vida del buscón, llamado Don Pablos, ejemplo de vagamundos y espejo de tacaños* (literally, *The History of the Life of the Swindler Don Pablos, a Model for Hobos and Mirror for Misers*). Its protagonist, Don Pablo, embarks on a lifelong journey to escape his lowly roots, which wind up hampering his search for respectability. The cultural perception of the buscón as a charlatan originated in *Historia*. At the same time, however, the core meaning of the term as one who "looks for" something has persisted. In the 1913 Webster Spanish-English dictionary, *buscar* is defined as "one who looks for ore," or a prospector. This duality exists in how the term is used in Dominican baseball, as well. Inside the major league community, on the one hand, people tend to regard buscones as pimp-like hustlers of young Dominican baseball talent. Dominicans, on the other hand, see buscones as the discoverers and developers of talent who play an essential, positive, and increasingly powerful role. This chapter explores the differences in these views. It also seeks to provide a sense of how this stratum in the commodity chain has come to play such an important role in contemporary baseball.

The activities and processes associated with player developers follow a fairly generic sequence. The first phase in this sequence is the initial identification of a talented young player, followed quickly by negotiations with his family to establish an exclusive buscón-player relationship. This includes formal arrangements about what the trainer will provide and what he expects in terms of compensation.

The second phase takes place over the long time period—often years—needed to develop a player. The entry point is ill-defined, but the prospect typically is thirteen or fourteen years old, and sometimes younger, and the target exiting age is sixteen and a half, the youngest one can legally be to sign a professional contract. More often than not, buscones will continue to develop players until they are signed—at perhaps seventeen or eighteen. During this time, the player must receive daily instruction in the baseball skills that will impress scouts. He must be physically developed (in terms of weight, height, and strength), and he must be psychologically tutored in how to present himself well in the next phase.

The third phase consists of the complex process of securing an offer from a major league team. It begins with a series of tryouts at teams' academies, which are designed to showcase the players' "tools," or baseball skills, such as running, fielding, batting, and throwing. If a player is successful, negotiations will follow between the buscón and a team's scouts. Tryouts now consist not only of demonstrations of basic skill sets but also of arranged games, sometimes played over several days, in which a prospect can be evaluated under game conditions. If the prospect is successful, the team makes an offer to the buscón and the player. The buscón and player then make a counteroffer, and negotiations continue until a figure is arrived at, concluding this phase.

The fourth, and final, phase consists of verifying the age and identity of the prospect. The team and the MLB Commissioner's Dominican office check the birth certificate and other evidence presented by the prospect's family and the buscón; this may involve visits to the hospital where the prospect was born and the schools he attended. Often, this is a lengthy process. Once the prospect's age and identity have been verified, the paperwork is turned over to the U.S. Embassy, which conducts its own review. Then, if everything checks out, the team is cleared to present the money to the prospect at MLB's office in Santo Domingo, and the prospect becomes a member of the team's minor league system. The buscón receives a percentage of the signing bonus as his commission.

The process is now complete. The devil, of course, is in the details. At every stage, specific practices and relationships may veer off-course, causing misunderstanding or the breaching of conventional practices.

Origins of the Buscones

Buscones have been portrayed as uniquely Dominican, but they actually originated in the United States. In the era before the baseball draft, low-level scouts known as "bird dogs" (as in the canine aides to hunters) located talented youngsters who might interest full-time scouts from major league teams. If a tip sounded promising, the scout would travel to evaluate the player, and if the player was actually signed, the bird dog might receive a relatively small finder's fee. Bob Nightengale has called the bird dogs "baseball's oldest talent evaluators, a group of major league scouts born in the 1920s, whose observations remain valuable, even if their salaries have never adjusted for inflation."[1]

Buscones also were part of the Dominican baseball scene long before they became demonized. Ralph Avila and Edy Toledo, for example, remembered encountering buscones in the 1960s and 1970s. The buscón of today who figures so prominently in developing talent was originally a bit player, according to Avila. "There were always people like buscones in Santo Domingo, only we didn't call them 'buscones.' We called them 'bird dogs,' and they were there for the [major league] teams that came into the country. [Teams] would come to Santo Domingo and contact their bird dogs to organize a try out for them. They would pay these guys something to bring them players and more if they signed the player."[2] The first buscón Toledo could recall meeting was a Cuban man named Santín, who brought prospects to various teams and was paid small sums if the boys were signed.[3] These proto-buscones differ from contemporary player developers in that they performed only one function: finding talent. Structurally, they played a minimal role in the early U.S.-Dominican baseball relationship.

Twenty years later, however, buscones had evolved into the multifaceted institution that finds players, contracts with them, develops them, houses and feeds them, secures tryouts, and plays a role in the negotiations with teams. In terms of roles played, the buscón, as mentioned, has become scout, trainer, agent, surrogate parent, and adviser, and he plays these roles over a period of years to boys who come to regard him as the most important person in their lives. It is their position at the base of the chain that makes the player developers so important, however, because all major league teams are dependent on them for talent.

Three major trends converged in the early 2000s to facilitate the creation of modern buscones: (1) Amateur leagues weakened, (2) buscones began to develop players directly, and (3) major league teams stepped up their organizational and fiscal presence on the island. In this transformation, buscones went from little more than baseball versions of hotel bellhops to minority shareholders in the hotel. It was the uncontrolled growth of their power that triggered the ire of Major League Baseball. Ironically, buscones did not seek this powerful position. Instead, they came to it by filling a void created by the proliferation of MLB teams' academies. In *Sugarball*, I predicted that the academies would hurt amateur baseball, writing, "Most important, the academies contribute to the cannibalization of the Dominican amateur leagues. By signing players at the age of seventeen and courting them even earlier, the academies are weakening the upper echelons of amateur baseball."[4]

The pipeline of player development that relied heavily on an intricate series of amateur leagues and informal player development was short-circuited when fifteen-year-olds began to seek tryouts at academies around the country in the hope of bypassing the traditional amateur system. "The amateur leagues are almost gone now. [They're] very weak," said Jesús Alou.[5]

"Before, there were more leagues and not as many programs [academies] around. The players then were probably more prepared—played more—than they are now."[6] A void was created, and the trainers, who were already familiar with young player development, quickly stepped in. Enrique Soto helped pioneer this when he began training young players in his hometown, Baní, in the early 1990s. Soto, like others, had no boarding facilities and used local public fields to train the players.

Rising Bonuses

This proto-buscón period coincided with the rise of the modern academies. The overall economic footprint of MLB within the Dominican Republic dramatically increased from the late 1990s on, which resulted in, among other things, escalating signing bonuses for young players. Although many people affiliated with major league organizations would claim that buscones were responsible for the escalating bonuses, intensified competition among teams drove this as much as anything else, and the rise of the buscón was more of an effect than a cause. "In the 1990s, more Dominicans started getting to the majors," Louie Eljaua said. "They were helping [teams] win championships and accumulate all of the most prestigious awards, and you could sign Dominicans for a fraction of the cost of U.S. [players]. Then the competition started getting cutthroat, so some scouts or agents would say [to the buscón], 'Okay, they gave you $250; we'll give you $500.' That's how it started escalating."[7]

The perception that signing bonuses for Dominicans were spiraling beyond levels MLB considered acceptable is interesting. Even in the early 2000s, signing bonuses in the Dominican Republic were minute compared with what U.S. talent commanded. "It makes sense to sign ten seventeen-year-olds [in the DR] who throw 88 or 89 [miles per hour] and hope they get to 93 or 94 in four or five years rather than spend millions on one guy [in the United States]," said an instructor at the Philadelphia Phillies Dominican Academy. "Look at Miguel Asencio. We got him for $6,500 at seventeen. Today, at twenty-one, he'd be a first-rounder worth millions [in the MLB draft]."[8] Signing "on the cheap" was the original and primary lure for major league teams looking at the Dominican Republic. "What has changed is the value of the player," said Jesús Alou. "Not too long ago, the average bonus was $7,000 to $8,000. You could go out there and get a guy for $10,000 who would cost you $1 million today."[9] Sandy Alderson, one of the most powerful and astute men in baseball, has echoed this recollection: "I can remember when I used to go to the Dominican Republic, other places; we would sign ten or fifteen players. Might be $5,000 or $10,000 apiece. Today, you can spend $4 million on one player. That's not what investors like to do. They like to diversify; they like to spread their risk."[10]

Major league teams managed to stock their minor league systems for decades with cheap Dominican talent, with the occasional star rising through the ranks. By the start of the twenty-first century, however, the number of high-end Dominican players had grown, and major league organizations began to focus on securing this rising talent. As the competition for Dominican players emerged within MLB, the cost of signing players rose. Although the escalation simply brought prices more in line with those in the United States, MLB considered it pathological and blamed the buscones.

Vilifying Buscones

As early as 1996, Bill Chastain wrote an article about the Tampa Bay Rays in which he briefly mentioned buscones and the remuneration they received.[11] A 1998 article by Juan Forero provides a more textured description. "He cleared the beans and asparagus and other crops he grew in front of his house," Forero wrote about Andres James, a Dominican who had abandoned scouting for the Giants to pursue player development. "The small plot that once produced food for his family is now covered in red dirt. James is now in the business of producing players, with the hope that someone he produces will wind up on a big league roster."[12] The parallel between farming and player production is simple but clear, as is the link between player production and a livelihood strategy. It is notable that these early articles in no way implied that buscones were swindlers.

By the first decade of the twenty-first century, that had changed. In 2001, Steve Fainaru, a reporter with the *Washington Post*, wrote an influential—and very damning—article claiming that Enrique Soto had swindled his player, Willy Aybar, out of more than $400,000 of his signing bonus.[13] Fainaru depicted Soto as cunning and criminal and, in the process, ended up painting all buscones with the same brush. The article influenced subsequent perceptions of Dominican trainers, whom the media increasingly portrayed as underhanded and crooked.

As he has come to be understood in North American baseball circles, the buscón is a low-level street hustler, a villain of Dickensian proportions, and even an exploiter of children (if you use the United Nations' definition of a child as anyone younger than eighteen). Take the example of Rich Fairly (a pseudonym), the director of international scouting for a major league team. He is visiting the team's Dominican academy, as he does several times a year, and on this day he is watching a half-dozen young Dominican prospects (accompanied by their buscones) at a tryout. He takes a long look at the prospects as they go through their paces and asks the academy's director about one in particular whom he finds interesting. The buscón's asking price strikes Fairly as gouging, and he is incensed. Although he is shouting at no one in particular, Fairly's vitriol is directed at the buscón, who can hear him but does not understand English: "I'm not giving in to that little pimp! That's all they are. They're throwing figures around and think we're gonna jump at 'em. [The player] wants $1 million? What kind of horseshit number is that? We'll decide what the number will be, not them. Hell, most of these guys don't have a clue how to prepare these guys We'll make an offer based on what we think of the market and be prepared to walk away from it."[14] While directed at the buscón, Fairly's anger is a reaction to the new price of doing business in the DR. In the past, a major league functionary at his level announced the price, and the buscón took it, with little or no grumbling. That the trainers now have their own sense of the players' value can infuriate MLB scouts and scouting directors.

At a 2011 tryout in the Boca Chica area held only for major league scouts by one of the more established buscón cooperatives, the language was less vituperative but no less demeaning. The scouts in attendance represented five major league organizations, but they were not really taking the tryout seriously and had not seen any players of interest. "Hey Chuck, you got any buscón repellent in your bag?" one quipped. "I don't wanna get bitten [*laughter all around*]." Thus, even in lighthearted banter, they felt a need to insult the buscones. The players' uniform shirts bore the abbreviation DPL, for Dominican Prospects League. To generate conversation, I feigned ignorance and asked what the letters stood for. "Stands for Dominican Suspects League," I was told. "Blows my mind what these clowns think we'll drool over."[15]

Those who are closely associated with MLB tend to hold buscones in contempt, or worse. When I returned to Dominican baseball in 2002 after an absence of nine years, this attitude came to the fore. When I mistook an adult who accompanied one of the young players for a family member, one director of international scouting for a major league team said, "That's not his father. Trust me, you wouldn't want to have one of these guys over for dinner. . . . [T]hat's a whole other element now." Another said, "We don't even want them in the dugout. They're basically pimps."[16] At that time, the teams believed they could avoid dealing with the buscones, encouraging prospects to bring their parents rather than their buscones to tryouts. "Before, you could tell a player, 'Hey, we're not going to deal with your buscón,'" said Luis Silverio. "He might say, 'Okay, deal with me,' and he would deal with the buscón on his own. Not anymore."[17] This change in how business is conducted is what sits so poorly with MLB. It represents a loss of control to an unregulated sector of the Dominican baseball commodity chain.

Positively Dominican

In contrast to most Americans, Dominicans feel that, their flaws and transgressions notwithstanding, the player developers or trainers are essential to the health of baseball. The Dominican directors of major league academies, who deal with buscones more often than anyone else in their organizations, tend to view them positively, as the following quotes show:

> Most buscones are honest and try to follow the rules. Of course, the bad cases are more reported in the news, but, really, most are doing a pretty good job.[18]

> I believe the buscones are a very important part of what's going on in baseball in this country. . . . [T]hey are benefiting baseball even if some of them are crooked. They are getting kids interested in playing. . . . They might not always know how to teach these kids the proper way to play baseball, but they get them in camp and keep them away from life on the streets.[19]

> I hate to admit it, [but the buscón system] really does work in [the players'] favor. . . . We've got kids thirteen years old, fourteen years old, with talent. [The buscones] feed them, give them some better instruction, give them a chance to develop every day. If you go back to the old system, nobody would discover them, [and] nobody would help them.[20]

> I have to be honest with you, and I want to state for the record: Buscones, or independent scouts, are a very important part of the industry. They help fill a gap, because there's not a lot of organized baseball in the Dominican Republic. . . . [L]ike in any other big group of people, there are some guys—and I wouldn't say the majority of them, because there are a lot of hardworking people—but you will find some bad apples. . . . [T]hose incidents are the most publicized.[21]

Even non-Dominicans grudgingly praise buscones when pressed. Louie Eljaua of the Chicago Cubs, who is no friend of buscones, found something laudatory to say about Soto, whom many people regard as the epitome of the dishonest buscón: "Whatever else you say about Soto, I will give him this: With all the money he makes, he does put it back into his program. If you go to his field, he's got a better batting cage than we do. The kids hitting [batting practice], they've got brand-new baseballs. They all have uniforms."[22]

An American Buscón

The view of buscones as devious and Faginesque, once established, is not easily dislodged from the public's mind, and it may subtly become essential-ized—that is, viewed as part of the Dominican character. Aiding such a cul-tural construction is the assumption that American sports and culture stand in stark contrast to the corruption that goes on "down there." Nothing could be further from the truth. Take, for example, the Amateur Athletic Union (AAU), America's premier sports program. It is a case of an American insti-tution that fosters buscones.

In his engaging study *Play Their Hearts Out*, George Dohrmann studied the coach and players in an elite boys' basketball program from age twelve through high school graduation.[23] Elite AAU teams receive substantial financial support from sneaker companies, and Dohrmann chronicles how much of the system that grooms and selects the next generation of NCAA and NBA stars has filtered down to the twelve-year-olds. The men who organize and coach AAU teams—including Joe Keller, the coach of the AAU team Dohrmann studied—have access to considerable resources, which enables them to assemble teams made up of the most talented boys from disparate parts of the region and the country. They compete for national championships and through them amass more wealth. Coaches like Keller must convince the most talented kids to join their teams rather than their rivals. To accomplish this, they use every known ruse to entice the boys and their parents.

According to Dohrmann's study, Keller manipulates players and their families in ways that are reminiscent of the tawdry, one-dimensional pimp tropes one often finds in the portrayal of Dominican buscones. Consider what Dohrmann quotes Keller as having said to one young recruit's finan-cially struggling single mother: "Your son is going to be in the NBA someday. He's going to make you millions. . . . [He] will stay with me during the week but can come home on the weekends and stay with you. . . . You shouldn't worry. . . . [He] will be like a member of my family."[24] In reality, once the boy was on board, Dohrmann reports, Keller rarely engaged him and often undermined his confidence. Eventually, the player left Keller's program.

Another prize recruit to whom Keller had acted as a surrogate father, and who was being "groomed" for the NBA, was abandoned once Keller realized he was not going to make it. The boy "felt betrayed, used, suddenly aware that the man who often claimed to love him like a son had only exploited him to get rich," Dohrmann writes, quoting the boy as saying, "Man, I'm not gonna lie, it does hurt. I looked at stuff like he was my pops, you know. I don't have a pops and he was like my pops."[25] Keller is portrayed as so reprehensible that one expects him ultimately to get his comeuppance. But in the book, he doesn't.

Most important, however, is that while readers may come away appalled, Dohrmann's study does not lead them to believe that all AAU coaches are like Keller. He is understood as an exception, a malevolent figure who represents the rogue in a world of upright and respectable coaches. When similar behavior is reported in the Dominican Republic (e.g., in Fainaru's article on Soto), American readers effortlessly accept the characterization of all buscones as deceitful and corrupt. As Soto commented, getting right to the heart of the anthropology of difference, "If [American] teams invest, they're organized. If the buscones invest, we're thieves."[26]

A Continuum of Player Developers

A new definition of buscones would have to include a more complete appreciation of the range of their functions, their role in the larger chain, and an awareness that they are struggling to claim a position of their own in the global commodity chain.

Understanding that their efforts include a wide range of programs is imperative. Buscones can be divided along twin axes: size of programs (big and little) and completeness of program (full service and partial service). In these spectrums, one end contains the smallest and most diffuse programs. These buscones resemble the so-called bird dogs of decades ago more than modern large operations, but they manage to wear the entire array of hats. The smallest Dominican player developers might persuade one or two very young players to train with them, but they know that at a certain point they will have to pass their finds to someone with a more complete facility. Still, before that day arrives, these small buscones must nevertheless identify the players and convince their parents of their capacity to develop them; then they must train the children, feed them, occasionally house them, and, most important, give them hope. The buscones' compensation will come in the form of a small share of the signing bonus if a player succeeds. At the other end of the spectrum are the most advanced buscones: the ones whose programs control all aspects of the players' lives and thus resemble the academies run by MLB (see below).

There are eight hundred to perhaps two thousand buscones in the Dominican Republic, depending on whom you ask. According to Ismael Cruz, former international scouting director for the New York Mets, everyone in the country is a buscón. "The teacher, the nun," he said, "everybody has a player for you."[27] When it comes to the most successful buscones, however, many claim there are fewer than two dozen. They have the biggest, most complete operations. Just below them are the middle ranks of player developers—they number about one hundred—who run full-service programs but on a smaller scale. Jesús Alou, the director of the Boston Red Sox academy, said that his directory held upward of eight hundred phone numbers of buscones.[28]

Depending on where on the spectrum they stand, buscones can be involved in feeding and housing players and taking them for physical therapy and medical treatment. The players are given equipment to play with, and their families often are provided for at a nominal level. If they prove to be talented, the prospects are taken to teams for tryouts and perhaps signed, and with a few exceptions (the very largest contracts), the negotiations are handled by the buscones. Thus, it bears repeating that buscones are much more than just "finders" of talent; they are also more than "independent trainers," as they prefer to be called. They are at times counselors, surrogate fathers, boarding-school owners, and agents. In sum, the Dominican player developer can become the most important person, after his mother, in a hopeful young ballplayer's life and deserves not to be trivialized or vilified. Below I present a series of case studies reflecting the range of player developers one is likely to find.

Aborted Career: Enrique Soto

Easily the most enigmatic figure in the Dominican player commodity chain, Enrique Soto has come to define the buscón in the American imagination. "Discovering" Miguel Tejada solidified Soto's reputation as an effective trainer who could get his players signed by professional teams, and in 2000, he played a key role in negotiating $1.4 million for Willy Aybar, further linking his name with large signing bonuses. He then came under fire when the press (primarily Steve Fainaru) accused him of stealing Aybar's bonus and later headed up the buscones' resistance to MLB's efforts to control them. Most recently, he has faced charges of sexual abuse. Through it all, he has remained defiant—and successful. "I am General Motors," he has said. "If not for us [buscones], these kids could turn into bad people. Getting rid of the system we have here would create more people like Osama bin Laden."[29]

Marcos Bretón and José Luis Villegas provide brief but pithy insights into Soto's background in *Away Games: The Life and Times of a Latin Ball Player*.[30] As early as 1990, Soto had already developed a training program for the most talented young players, marking him as one of the first modern buscones. To achieve his goal to become a full-time player developer, he combined his youth training program with his part-time job as a talent scout for the Oakland Athletics. He trained thirty to fifty boys a day, reserving the most talented for further training in the hope of getting them professional contracts. Tejada was his initial pride and joy. By the time Tejada signed with the As in 1994, one could describe Soto's relation to him only as paternal.

In time, Soto refined his program to include room and board and thereby became one of first to make the transition from training program to full-fledged, state-of-the-art player developer. His program is recognized for having some of the most sophisticated facilities (e.g., field condition, uniforms and equipment, and coaching staff). Even without a command of English, Soto has managed to get scores of players signed to professional contracts and has become rich and powerful in the process.

Soto shares a key trait with other pioneering figures in Dominican baseball: in his initial encounters with American life, he suffered humiliation and vowed to help others so they would not have the same experience.[31] Although he spent only one season (1980) playing minor league baseball in the United States, it was a lonely, alienating year for him. Like so many Latino players without language skills and cultural mentors, Soto was ill prepared to come to the United States and has only bitter memories of that time. "If [the San Francisco Giants] were interested in me, they didn't show it," he has said. "I was like a servant or a shoeshine boy. A common Latino. It's like I wasn't there. In reality, the only opportunity they gave me was to go back home."[32]

A sense of personal and cultural humiliation and of American disdain for Latinos not only rankled Soto, as it did so many others who experienced it, but also fueled nationalistic resentment. "Every time they sign a Dominican, they tell him, 'We're giving you an opportunity.' Like they're giving them this big chance," according to Soto. "They never tell the kid how talented he is or how good he's going to be. They always talk to him in a way to make the boy beholden to them."[33] Soto's resentment of Americans did not abate as his stature rose: "I like the United States. It's a great country and baseball gives our youth a lot of opportunities. But Americans get a lot out of it too. . . . They take and take and take and still want more. That's what I don't like. We are a country also. We're underdeveloped, we have a lot of problems but there are good people here. They don't deserve to be treated like common trash."[34]

Soto's early gamble—personally developing young players he might funnel to major league teams—paid off as his list of signed players grew, with quite a few signing large contracts. Soto also emerged as one of the first modern buscones in almost perfect parallel with the rise of the modern academy system. In time, Soto drew other elite buscones around him, and they developed a cohort that sought to control the flow of the best players. They contested MLB policy they felt were restrictive not only by protesting but also by constructing alternatives. In 2010, they started the Dominican Prospect League, which has its own season and plays a schedule just for MLB scouts.

Controversy remains a constant in Soto's life. In February 2011, the news broke that he had been accused of sexually assaulting two of his players some ten years earlier.[35] Within the month, it was reported that Soto was being "detained" in jail in connection that offense. No formal charges were brought against him, and—as expected—Soto has proclaimed his innocence to the Dominican press.[36] He has even claimed to be writing a book that proves the charges were driven by efforts to extort money from him.[37] Soto's friends were quick to point out that he had never been officially charged or brought to trial for the claims and that the entire affair stemmed from an attempt by certain well-connected people to shake him down: "They [judges and the legal establishment] know he has the money, and they expect to be paid off. That's the way it is here. But he won't pay, because then he would be admitting to something he didn't do. They have no evidence. The boys who made the claim don't even know when it occurred. It was the mothers of those boys who made the charge, not the boys. He's not gonna pay them a peso. Enrique's got big balls and will stay in jail forever if he has to."[38]

By February 2013, however, Soto had been convicted of the charges and sentenced to ten years in prison—although, as Astín Jacobo noted, "Soto is not in custody and has not yet reported to prison."[39] Many people would bet that he never will, insisting that this is a case of Soto's hubris in not paying off powerful interests who are determined to get access to his wealth.

In some ways it is easy to see how Soto has come to be portrayed as the ultimate street hustler. He projects a degree of arrogance, aggressiveness, and entitlement. His remarkable success may have added only to his feelings of invulnerability and to others' desire to level him and get some of his money. His detractors can be found at all levels. North Americans are not fond of him, but many give him grudging respect: "He produced a lotta baseball players and still does. . . . [N]o matter what's going on with him, he tells it like it is."[40]

Major League Baseball and the North American media see Soto as an impediment and a con man, respectively. But it is the people of his hometown, Baní, who are most divided about him. Soto's wealth makes him a magnet for those who envision escaping from poverty via baseball and a potential mark for others. He is also one of the most outspoken defenders of nationalist interests in the Dominican Republic, and he represents a major beachhead in the battle against MLB's hegemony. "Enrique Soto is a guy a lot of us working in Dominican baseball have to say thank you to," said Astín Jacobo, one of Soto's allies. "He put his job on the line with [Miguel] Tejada and said, 'If he doesn't do what I say he can do, you can fire me.' . . . He took six or seven guys to the majors. Sure, he gets a lot of money, but he spends a lot of money [on his programs]. He protects Dominicans."[41] The issue is not whether Soto is a saint or sinner. He is probably both. The issue is how long he can hold the latter role at bay without paying for it.

Former Major Leaguers: Ramon Martínez

After announcing his retirement from baseball, Ramon Martínez returned to his hometown, Manoguayabo, a northern suburb of Santo Domingo. His accomplishments in the major leagues included a twenty-win season and a no-hitter. He retired a wealthy man after a reasonably long MLB career. Although he did not need to, Martínez opened a new economic venture in 2002: his own baseball academy. He leases the field built in his town from Juan Guzman, a former pitchers with the Toronto Blue Jays, and brings two full teams of prospects there each day to play each other (or others). His program has about fifty players, who wear clean, new uniforms with "Ramon Martínez Baseball Academy" emblazoned (in English) across the front. One team has red script, hats, and socks, while the other sports blue. Martínez had just finished building a dorm to house eighteen players; the rest came each day in cabs paid for by the academy.

Scouts for the Anaheim Angels were looking at his players the day I observed Martínez's operation. His coaches had organized a game between the program's two teams to showcase their players. Pitchers were clocked on the radar gun; runners were clocked with stopwatches; and game performances were assessed. When I complimented him about how well the academy presented itself, Nelson Gerónimo, the head coach, responded, "Hey, man—thanks. We've only been open three months, and in those three months, we've had four players sign. A few more will probably go this month."[42] As early as 2000, I had been told that former players were running their own programs. Nelson Liriano, who had played for the Blue Jays, informed me that about ten former major leaguers had small programs.[43]

Martínez had the name and the resources to succeed immediately. Others have had to build their programs more slowly. The point is that former major league players have the credibility needed to draw young prospects to their programs. Yet they may also be more likely to tire of running player development programs and move on, primarily because they do have other options, whereas for other, smaller buscones, producing players is their best opportunity for prosperity.

Baseball Outsiders: Samuel Herrera

With a shaved head and hawkish nose, Samuel Herrera looks like a street hustler. He is anything but. His roots lie in academe. "I used to teach calculus at the university, but the money is better in training players," Herrera said, describing his transition from teaching in a classroom to teaching on the field.[44] His career trajectory may be unconventional, but his program is fairly typical of those of midsize to small player developers. When I visited his program, he had ten players and boarded six of them.

What is typical of Herrera's operation is that he has had limited but steady success—just enough to keep the lure of riches alive. He had succeeded in getting one of his players signed to a significant $400,000 contract, for which his commission was $100,000. Six others were signed in his first five years in the business. Still, running a player development program is nerve-racking: Herrera likened it to spending all of one's money to win the lottery.

Buscones follow a similar template that differs mainly in the completeness and luxuriance of their facilities and the quality of the training they provide. Herrera's program was serviceable. We initially met at a ramshackle field whose baseball diamonds had no grass and were marked by cracks, holes, and stones that guaranteed bruised shins from ricocheting balls. Garbage burned in several spots around the perimeter. Playing fields like these are typical at this level. (One such field in San Pedro de Macorís is nicknamed "Arizona" for its conspicuous lack of vegetation.) Herrera leases the field. In describing his program, he spoke proudly about the good food and clean surroundings he provided for his six charges, who lived at a nearby *pensión*. As we climbed the stairs to the *pensión*'s third floor, the woman Herrera pays to clean and cook the meals passed us and greeted him.

Herrera's *pensión* would not pass muster in the United States but is regarded in the Dominican Republic as perfectly adequate for housing young players. The walls were painted blue but streaked with large, faded splotches. The tiny kitchen contained a small refrigerator, a stove, a table, and plastic lawn chairs. The lights were nothing more than exposed light bulbs at the end of wires. Each small bedroom barely had room for the bunk beds in which the boys slept. Everything worked, however. The kitchen yielded three nutritious and tasty meals a day. The beds had clean sheets. There was even a small TV. Most important, the boys liked it. Food and shelter were not something they took for granted, and Herrera was doing a good job by providing all of this.

Several days later, while we were driving, I asked Herrera whether he felt that buscones were justified in taking a 25 percent commission (the fee he charges). He reached into the back seat and grabbed a handful of nutritional supplement packets and dropped them in my lap. "Do you know what these cost me?" he asked defensively. "I get these from Miami. They cost me $5 each, and my boys get them every day."[45]

"But 25 percent?" I answered. "Really?"

"You came to my *pensión*," he said. "You saw that they had beds, a TV, a refrigerator full of food. I hire a woman to cook for them. Look, I know that Major League Baseball is against us, but they don't know anything about what we do to get these boys ready. I talk to their parents and make them a promise that [the boys] will stay away from drugs. No rum. Only hard work. Some of these boys I train for a long time. The program costs me around $1,000 a month to run." I noted that rules eventually might be passed that limit the buscones' commissions. "That would crush me financially," Herrera said, "but that's why I have my other business."

He grabbed a manila envelope from the back seat and proceeded to show me a report on Cleveland Indians letterhead that included ratings for their facilities. "Beds . . . 15." "Mattress. . . . 15." "Sheets. . . . 15." "Excellent," he said pointing to each rating. "Excellent. Excellent." "You have a linen supply business?" I asked. "Yes," he said, "because being a buscón is like playing the lottery: You never know when you're going to hit, so you have to be prepared to play all the time."[46]

At the low end of the buscón spectrum, one has to have many irons in the fire. Herrera is a great example of how elastic and enterprising one has to be to deal with the vagaries of the business. Buscones with operations even smaller than Herrera's contacted him with leads or to seek arrangements for players they were developing—always for a share of the signing bonus if the prospect succeeded. Herrera may not be in the same league as the most successful buscones, but he is earning a living and is doing better than many others in this line of work.

Non-baseball Buscones: Edgar Mercedes

In 2008, sixteen-year-old Michel Ynoa signed a $4.25 million contract with the usually light-spending Oakland A's. It was, at the time, the biggest contract ever signed by an amateur Latin American ballplayer. His buscón, Edgar Mercedes, earned a seven-figure commission that also set a record. Mercedes had worked with Ynoa since he was thirteen (beginning in 2005), and Ynoa must have been impressive: even as a sixteen-year-old, he threw effortlessly in the mid-90s.

Mercedes is a new and different kind of buscón. He came to the enterprise not from the ranks of baseball but as an affluent Dominican entrepreneur, conducting all phases of the Dominican player production operation at a comparatively advanced economic level. For instance, the tryouts he holds at his Born to Play Academy in Haina, just east of the capital, are meticulously planned and lavish. Scouts who attend are provided with strong Dominican coffee and lunch, not to mention shade and water.[47] Mercedes's resources allow him to hire coaches, trainers, and even English teachers at higher salaries than his competitors can pay, making it safe to assume that the quality is higher, as well.

Being a buscón is a spin-off business for Mercedes, who also owns one of the country's largest bookmaking operations—Out 27—which has forty-five locations around the nation, including in some very large sports bars. The move into producing and signing players poses no legal challenge for Mercedes, because sports bookmaking is legal in the Dominican Republic. In the United States, however, this kind of link raises legal and ethical questions, especially for MLB, with its lengthy history of meting out punishment to anyone linked to gambling (e.g., Shoeless Joe Jackson and Pete Rose). In the DR, however, such operations are regulated by the government while the ranks of buscones are not—all of which allows Mercedes to operate unimpeded. Mercedes has tried to put American journalists and the MLB at ease by noting that "everyone here knows someone who owns a sports book. . . . [I]t's just normal for us here. . . . It's viewed more as it is in Europe [as opposed to the United States]."[48] Such arguments based on cultural relativity normally do not convince Americans or MLB. Mercedes also has claimed that if a conflict ever arose between his buscón business and his bookmaking businesses, he would seriously consider selling one, although he has not revealed which one.[49]

Mercedes differs most significantly from other player developers in the manner by which he goes about his business: he is distant. Just like any highly successful entrepreneur, Mercedes can afford to pay others to do the impor-

tant work. For instance, the intensive day-to-day search for and development of players bring many buscones into frequent contact with one another,
and they tend to develop networks of mutual dependence. Astín Jacobo, for
instance, routinely enters into arrangements to, among other things, take
over part of a player's training or organize a joint tryout. They chat, dine,
and commiserate, whereas Mercedes just showers people with cash: "A lot
of trainers don't have the money, they prefer to make a profit immediately.
. . . Poor trainers, instead of losing their kids to other trainers, would prefer
to sell them to me."[50] His model for Dominican player development involves
looking for the most talented baseball players, then outspending his competitors to get them. According to Jacobo, for example, Mercedes might find "a
guy with a Little League and . . . offer him $3,000 [now] and 5 percent [if the
player signs]. The guy . . . keeps on training the boy until Mercedes sells him.
The trainer is never really sure he would have been able to get that kind of
money for his kid [on his own]."[51]

By using money to build relations and speak for him, Mercedes is quite
modern in a world of baseball peasants. He considers himself a force to be
reckoned with, a Dominican Scott Boras (the most successful U.S. sports
agent). "All I want is to have the best 30 players in the Dominican [Repub-
lic]," Mercedes has said. "They [all of the other buscones] can have the rest."[52]
The cash nexus that rules over Mercedes's world of social relations is perhaps
a harbinger of things to come. By insisting on keeping the murky world of
social relations at a distance, Mercedes's model is certainly more in keeping
than that of other buscones in the DR with how MLB prefers to conduct its
Dominican dealings.

Non-Dominican Buscones

Question: When is a buscón not a buscón? Answer: When he's American.
Soto's barb, "If the teams invest, they're organized. . . . If the buscones invest,
we're thieves," is fitting here. Americans have been entering the buscón business since about 2008. And they are bringing the same arrogance to the
Dominican system that the Spanish colonizers showed five hundred years
ago—namely, they view themselves as saviors. Instead of pressing a Catholic god on hapless natives, the Americans have come bearing education and
smaller commissions. One of the more conspicuous examples of ethnocentrism in the relationship between MLB and Dominicans is the assumption
that American economic and social presumptions are intrinsically more
worthy and, hence, forcing others to adopt them is justified.

Take, for example, the Arias and Goodman Baseball Academy, opened in

San Pedro de Macorís in 2009 by Gary Goodman, a real estate lawyer based in New Jersey, and Alfredo Arias, a former minor league baseball player who runs the operation and provides its Dominican face. "Make no mistake about it," Goodman said when the program was announced. "We are in the business of preparing young Dominicans for careers in baseball; to help talented young men achieve their dreams. But there is also a social side that must be addressed. Reality is that most of these kids will not succeed in baseball and we owe it to them to make sure they are prepared for life after baseball."[53] Whether such a "lofty" aim is reasonable within the context of the Dominican economy and baseball is discussed elsewhere (see Chapter 2), but this is the peg on which Arias and Goodman have decided to hang their hats.

Offering a loosely defined notion of education has helped Goodman to justify his primary goal: to sell players for profit. Goodman, it turns out, was in the DR in 2008 looking for investment opportunities when he and Arias were approached by another buscón—José Canó, who once pitched for the Houston Astros and whose son Robinson Canó plays for the New York Yankees—to make a loan to the family of one of his prospects in exchange for repayment plus 7 percent. The money was lent, and the player eventually signed for $790,000. Goodman got his loan back, plus $50,000.[54] One can assume only that this gave him a very clear idea about where to invest his money for the best return. By June 2011, Goodman and Arias had added the educational component to their operation, clearly to gain the moral high ground, while sports reformers and other interested parties in the United States and Canada applauded their efforts.

The International Academy of Professional Baseball (known as La Academia), started by Steve Swindall, Abel Guerra, and Hans Hertell in 2009, looks like a much smaller version of the Mets Dominican Baseball Academy, which it abuts. Swindall is a former general partner of the Yankees, and Guerra was a vice-president of international relations for the team. Hertell was the U.S. ambassador to the Dominican Republic during the presidency of Hipólito Mejía (2001–2007). La Academia is leased and has all of the amenities that a facility built by Junior Noboa should have. It is "the nicest academy of any agent," Rafael Pérez, MLB's director of Dominican operations, gushed.[55] To distance themselves from the ranks of buscones, Swindall, Guerra, and Hertell claim to educate prospective players by sending them to school at night and on weekends. "Some of these students have never gone to schools, or they dropped out at the third- or fourth-grade level," Guerra says. "We try to give them some life skills."[56] Of course, some Dominican trainers, such as Astín Jacobo, also send their players to school, but this does not seem to help legitimate them for Americans.

A second trope Americans use to avoid being labeled "buscones" is that they take less in commissions than the Dominican player developers do. La Academia has made this claim, as has California Sports Management of Sacramento, which runs a program in Don Gregorio, Dominican Republic.[57] California Sports Management opened its operation in 2007 and is owned by Greg Maroni, a dentist who also operates fast-food franchises, and his son, who is a sports agent.

Conclusion

With so many buscones operating at so many levels, it was only a matter of time before a kind of natural order evolved among them. Most programs remained small in scale, like the ones that characterized the early days of the buscones. Some, however, morphed into larger and more complex, financially successful operations. Buscones exist in a hierarchy from small and insignificant to large and successful. However, they also engage each other in socially informal ways.

In the most significant of such relationships, small buscones turn players over to larger buscones in exchange for a percentage of the signing bonus (if there is one) or, now, for a straightforward, one-time cash buyout. In the Dominican Republic, this is called "giving someone a little taste," a metaphor for sharing strategies that distribute resources or gains optimally through a network or community. The social relationships that develop among buscones can pave the way for later exchanges that involve sending players from small to large programs. "Sometimes, another trainer will come to me because we played games against him and he likes my program," Astín Jacobo said, "or a guy in a Little League has a kid, and he thinks I'll be the best guy to develop him."[58]

During a visit to his academy in San Pedro de Macorís, I saw a number of players going through various actions as if they were in a tryout, but they were not. Jacobo was conferring with other buscones about the boys as they went through their paces. "This guy who is showing me [a] kid, he wants me to give him money," he said. "Some of these guys can develop the kids; some can't. Some can only develop them so far; then they need someone to finish him up. I'm talking to [this guy] about why he should leave his kid here. I'll give him a percentage if the kid signs, but it's gonna cost me money to get him to that point. That's what we're talking about."[59] The smaller buscón concurs. "Felipe [a pseudonym] is my player," he said, "but he needs someone like Astín to get him signed. I would like to get some money now and a percentage later when he signs. This boy is good, no question about it, and he'll get a good signing bonus."[60]

This funneling of players is based on economic separation between large and small buscones, but it is played out on the basis of social relations that have grown up among buscones who know one another. In this sense, it is an organic system that meaningfully ties together social beings and their economic needs. That organic quality is now in danger of being jettisoned by ties based more fully on economic transactions. Edgar Mercedes and others like him are having a serious impact on these relations. As Jacobo commented, "Mercedes . . . goes from program to program and offers money to trainers—maybe as much as a million pesos to develop a kid. The trainers are never sure they can get that kind of money for the kid if they negotiate, so they sell the kid before he's even close to trying out with an organization. . . . [*Laughs.*] Yup, that's what the Yankees do."[61]

These changes could end up marginalizing the smallest buscones in the chain. At the same time, the largest buscones may get richer, and some may be able to segue into the ranks of agents. Although the biggest buscones have the resources to develop the best players' baseball skills, they are often impeded at the contract negotiation level and need to bring agents into the mix. "These certified agents like Rob Plummer or even bigger guys, like Scott Boras, . . . can get your player the most money," Jacobo said, "and they get a 5 percent cut of the 30 percent I might make."[62] The commodity chain model as applied to buscones thus is taking on the characteristics of fractals in that each piece of the whole is starting to have the same characteristics and makeup as the whole itself. The smallest are doing what the largest do, only scaled back to a minimal level—providing only some meals, for example, or an occasional place to sleep to the players they are developing. What irks MLB the most about buscones is that, like broncos, they are not domesticated—or, in this case, they are not regulated. "The buscones are the most important tool in this business, and they shouldn't disappear," a Dominican lawyer and agent who has worked to create regulations to govern the player developers has said. "But first, we need to teach them about levels of management."[63] Ronaldo Peralta echoed this opinion: "Buscones are a part of our industry, and a very important part. What we want is for the government to have some regulations to prevent cases like that of Enrique Soto."[64] Buscones, in short, have come to symbolize all that is "wrong" in the Dominican baseball scene. The more that has been written about them, and the more they have emerged as prime brokers of talent, the more MLB has wanted them dealt with.

4

Astín Jacobo and
the "New Dominicans"

A number of Dominicans are actively influencing the topography of their national sport. Of them, I have picked five to profile here on the basis of the sway they have in how Dominicans today are engaging MLB. A large portion of the chapter is devoted to Astín Jacobo because of where he sits in the player production chain and the unique way in which he functions.

Astín Jacobo Jr.

Astín Jacobo in many ways is the public face of those I call independent trainers, buscones, or player developers. As the "go to" guy for the American media, he has been featured on *Dan Rather Reports* and in the insightful documentary *Ballplayer: Pelotero*.[1] Not only is he is successful, pleasant, and bilingual, but he also runs an ethical operation, having produced more than eighty players to date who have signed with teams. Jacobo, in fact, is anything but the "typical" buscón. He is my focus here not only because he can talk as easily to those at the top of the chain (MLB) as to street-level Dominicans, but he is also one of the most outspoken critics of MLB's attempts to control the game in his country. Jacobo is not afraid to confront those who need confronting, and he is not the first or even the most impressive member of his family to do so.

Before he passed away in 2002, Jacobo's father, Astín Jacobo Sr., was a most humble and remarkable man who had a profound influence on his communities and on his son. One of the first things Astín Jacobo Jr. did upon meeting me in 2005 was to drive us to San Pedro de Macorís's *Estadio Astín Jacobo* (Astín Jacobo Stadium), named for his father. Even in mid-week and late in the morning, a game was in progress with a reasonably large audience. Jacobo Field is also a baseball park in the Bronx, named to honor Astín Jacobo Sr. for the decades of community organizing he carried out there. Few people have facilities named after them in two countries.

The Jacobo family's history embodies just about everything I have come to know about the Dominican Republic. Astín Jacobo Sr. was born at the Consuelo sugar refinery, just outside San Pedro de Macorís, in 1929. Many of the inhabitants of *bateys*, as the company towns surrounding the refineries are known, had been brought to the DR from the English-speaking Caribbean as a cheap labor force; the descendants of these people are called *cocolos*, and their English has a Jamaican-like lilt. English surnames are also quite common in this area—for example, those of the Dominican MLB players George Bell and Alfredo Griffin. "Austin Jacob" took on Hispanic coloration as "Astín Jacobo." Life at Ingenio Consuelo was arduous, of course, and baseball was the primary diversion during lulls in the labor cycle. The workers loved baseball as much as they hated cutting cane. In the 1930s and 1940s, Astín Jacobo Sr. told me:

> Things were very hard for us. . . . To survive, you cut cane, you hoed and weeded. But in Trujillo's time, when he bought the estates, he [changed] all that. He brought in germicides to kill the grass, so then life was really hard for us. The people just stayed there [there was no livelihood during the slack season]. We played ball. We sucked cane, and people would plant vegetables in the back yard. . . . Each town had a team. Ingenio Consuelo used to provide one team with uniforms, gloves, and so on. But that couldn't fill the [baseball] needs of the majority.[2]

The Catholic Church played a pivotal role in developing Jacobo's sense of social justice, which spilled over into his love of baseball. When Father Joseph Ainslie came to Consuelo in 1942, his impact was immediate: "He saw that the people liked sports, and he started to get us together. . . . He taught us that we shouldn't be slaves . . . that we should be on our own."[3] Father Ainslie got the community organized enough to pool what little money they could to buy cloth to make uniforms and provide opportunities to play baseball to the whole community. "From that time on," Astín Jacobo Sr. said, "we started to really play and go out to San Pedro de Macorís, Santa Fe, Angelina."[4]

It was in moving outside of sports that Astín Jacobo Sr. ran afoul of the prevailing political powers. The most brutal era of Dominican dictatorship passed when Rafael Trujillo was assassinated in 1961 with the assistance of the U.S. Central Intelligence Agency, but political repression and murder continued through the presidency of Joaquín Balaguer (1966–1978). Two years of occupation by the U.S. Marines in 1965–1966, which the United States deemed essential to its national security because of the perceived threat of growing communist influence in the Caribbean, promoted political turmoil in the country. Many activists and supporters of the democratically elected and U.S.-deposed government of President Juan Bosch disappeared, murdered by Balaguer's auxiliaries. Because he was working on behalf of various unions, Astín Jacobo Sr. came under Balaguer's scrutiny. As a result, he was targeted for "arrest" in 1971 and was supposed to be picked up upon returning from work. Fortunately, on the day this was to occur, Jacobo's friends discovered the plot and notified him at work just minutes before he was going to leave. He was whisked away and, with the help of his church, fled first to Canada and then to the Bronx in New York City.

Jacobo found employment as a janitor at the church in the Crotona neighborhood of the Bronx, an area that is heavily populated by Dominicans and Puerto Ricans. People there called him "Jacob," and he picked up where he had left off in San Pedro de Macorís, organizing the community around housing and stemming drug abuse in the neighborhood. He founded and served as the president of the Crotona Community Coalition for the next twenty-five years, marshaling grassroots support and cultivating powerful political allies—for example, New York City's Mayor Ed Koch and New York State Governor Mario Cuomo—to save the neighborhood: "When drug addicts and urban scavengers threatened to strip pipes from half-burned buildings, he got local youths from his teams to stand watch. When the streets were ruled by gun-crazy crack dealers, he talked politicians into putting lights on a neighborhood field, luring parents and friends back outside for night games."[5] Baseball was never far from Jacobo's mind, though: "There was something we did in the Dominican Republic that we want to see here [in the Bronx]," he told David Gonzalez of the *New York Times*. "When we played baseball, our parents used to come to the park on the weekends and play dominoes, cards, have a barbecue and everybody stayed in one place minding each other. That is the future we are thinking of seeing."[6]

When he died in 2002, this humble man had had an impact on people in two countries. His admirers came from all walks of life, but Jacobo's primary constituents were the people who needed him the most: *los pobres* (the poor). His son lives in a less threatening world but shares his father's guiding vision.

Complejo Astín Jacobo

You will not find Astín Jacobo Jr.'s baseball complex unless you are familiar with the Kasbah-like nature of San Pedro's poor neighborhoods. They are a world made of rusted-out and badly bent corrugated fencing. Mottled chickens and mangy but smart mongrels prowl the sidewalks. Faded one-room cement shacks in various states of disrepair, whose tiny front yards are littered with five-gallon plastic cans, garbage bags, and other utilitarian items, rely on pirated electricity and communal water spigots. Flies, fetid odors, and four-legged creatures abound. Crumbling sidewalks and paved sections of road break up the mosaic of potholes so old that their ridges are polished smooth.

All of this, far from the sanitized world of MLB baseball academies, frames the thirteen-acre Complejo Astín Jacobo. A large, heavy metal gate that looks like a prop from the dystopian film *Road Warrior* slides open as one enters the complex, revealing a baseball field, concrete stands, and dugouts. They were painted blue long ago and need another coat but otherwise are quite functional. The field is cavernous and attended to. An office building made of concrete cinderblocks sits next to the third base dugout.

Jacobo's office is cluttered. One wall is covered with photographs of players he developed who have signed with MLB teams. Another is covered with photographs of his father. His desk reflects the mind of a man who operates his business out of his head. It is deep in written requests, printouts, letters, bills, and news clippings, punctuated with batting gloves and rolls of tape. I am certain he knows just where everything is. In the corner, one might find a box of baseballs or used baseball gloves, and the ringing of Jacobo's cell phone threatens to end almost every conversation. A group of his players or another buscón renting his facility for a tryout might be poised deferentially at his door asking him questions, so there is always a hum of activity.

Like his father, Astín Jacobo Jr. was born in Consuelo, in 1955. He was a fairly typical kid except in being the son of the local baseball swag, and he grew up in the raucous world of refinery baseball. "The first big-time game I went to was in Consuelo," he said. "It was late evening, and it was raining a little bit. This scout . . . took me, and it was against Angelina [a neighboring refinery]. There was so many people there that I had to sit on someone's shoulders to see, and the emotion in that game was unbelievable. The whole *batey* was there, and we got so into it. We even had a fight with George Bell's father because of a bad call."[7]

By the 1950s, the area around San Pedro de Macorís had become known as the hotbed of Dominican baseball, and nowhere more so than Consuelo. Games were occasions for everyone to gather and celebrate their identities as members of their communities, vying not only for bragging rights but also for the rewards of a win, which could include being given time off from work at the sugar refinery or some other remuneration. Astín Jacobo Sr. organized and managed Consuelo's team, and his son held a special place in that world. "I remember my dad gave me this yellow Spalding bat," he said. "It was the best gift I ever had as a kid in Consuelo. Everyone here played baseball— many in the United States—and they all played for my father. Rafael Batista [who played for the Atlanta Braves in the 1970s used to come by a lot, and he used to take me to the stadium in San Pedro. I always used to be around him and Rico Carty [who also played for the Braves]. I was Astín Jacobo's son."[8]

Astín Jacobo Sr. finally brought his family to the United States in 1975, and for his son, that meant the shock of adjusting to American schools and culture. "My first day at high school I remember going into the lunch room," he said. "I saw some of the guys I had met during the summer. They were all on the side where the Dominicans hung out and they played cards. They had this Dominican flag painted on the wall. Two of them were playing cards, and they got into an argument, and one of the kids pulled out a gun. A gun! In the middle of a lunchroom. And I'm thinking, 'Where the hell am I?'"[9]

The Jacobo family carried their intense commitment to baseball into the Bronx, where "Jacob," as Astín Jacobo Sr. came to be known, was instrumental in building and promoting sporting facilities. Local boys were beginning to get signed and play professionally. Young Manny Ramírez, for instance, emerged as a high-school baseball star in the nearby Washington Heights section of Manhattan. Indeed, by the 1990s entire varsity baseball squads at George Washington High School were often Dominican.[10] Games were almost pretexts for cultural celebrations; wherever a game was played, merengue music would be coming from someone's boom box, and Dominican food vendors seemed to materialize out of nowhere.

As a ballplayer, Jacobo was not a standout, but he had already begun forming his unique link to the game—one that would reverse his migration and send him back to San Pedro. The link between baseball in the United States and the game in the DR, it must be remembered, tends to be seamless for Dominicans, who move often and easily between the two countries. Issues in one context are felt in the other. "I remember we were talking about these reports on WFAN [in New York City about the problems with Dominican players in the United States," Jacobo said when I interviewed him in 2008. "To us, this was an embarrassment, and we felt shame. We would hear about kids [Dominican players] who would get into trouble. My dad was sick then [around 2000], and I told him that I wanted to go back [to the Dominican Republic] and work in baseball. . . . I wanted to deal with these problems. I read an article in [the Santo Domingo newspaper] *El Nacional* that Hipólito Hassim was building a place in San Francisco de Macorís, and he said that it was a great place for investing in the game."[11]

Jacobo's plan was to carve out a career in baseball by developing young men who played baseball better than he did and who could navigate the cultural problems they would face in the United States. He intended to build his own facility, for which he needed a great deal of land, preferably in San Pedro de Macorís. What he could afford was literally a garbage dump. "I built this place from the ground up," he said about Complejo Astín Jacobo. "There were mountains of garbage piled up, and I had to have three hundred truckfuls of garbage hauled out. Then I brought in the bulldozers."[12]

By 2002, he had finished the first phase of the complex, an enclosed facility of about thirteen and a half acres containing a playing field with a noticeably spacious outfield. "I don't want them to develop swings that go for the fences," he said. "They need to learn swings that hit the gaps."[13] In addition to the field and stands, the complex contains acres of undeveloped land for which he has detailed plans. By the spring of 2012, he had built a living complex that accommodates twenty players. The large, two-story building, which cost close to $250,000, includes a kitchen and dining room, bathrooms, bedrooms, a weight room, and a common room. When Jacobo began the project, the idea of buscones running such sophisticated operations was unfathomable. Now it is the standard one must meet to be considered among the top tier of Dominican player developers.

Jacobo as a Buscón

Being the son of Astín Jacobo Sr. may have made negotiating with families in and around San Pedro de Macorís a bit easier for Jacobo, but to build a reputation, he had to deliver a successful program. According to the contracts, Jacobo handles the players' expenses for room and board, health care, sports equipment, and training. In return, players who are signed to MLB contracts turn 30 percent of the bonus over to him. Thirty percent is an informal standard among trainers in the DR. It rankles Americans, who erroneously equate it with American agents' 5 percent signing commission. Most Dominican trainers are able to articulate the difference between what they do and what a U.S. sports agent does. For instance, they cite the fact that independent trainers develop a boy for years, while a U.S. agent handles only the last part of the process—the contract signing. It is the details of the day-to-day care and attention that player developers provide that makes the 30–35 percent commission comprehensible, as Jacobo described:

> I feed most of these guys every day. Some of them are gonna find a meal when they go home at night, but many are not. The ones who come from farther away, I provide them with food and a place to stay. Some of the guys from La Romana or Consuelo, if I don't have room for them in my *pensión*, I gotta pay for them [to go] back and forth. You gotta go deep in your pocket. I'm working on a budget right now of about 2 million pesos [$67,000] a year, and that's just for the kids.
>
> Six days, a week we have games. I have a vehicle that takes guys to them. Say that a kid spends three years with me and needs equipment. That's a lotta shoes, gloves, bats, and balls. I gotta buy bound bats. You can pay $300 for them. How many bats do I buy a kid over three years? Baseballs cost $9 [each], and sometimes I gotta buy a thousand at a time. And God help us that [a kid] doesn't have a problem with his mother or father. They become like my family, and a lotta times I gotta send something to them. It's Christmas, and the kid's gotta go home, and he doesn't have anything to bring. Here's 3,000 pesos to take home. Even the guys who bring you the players, if something happens, they're looking for you to help them. So when I have a [kid] for three years, and let's say I'm charging him 30 percent, I'm spending maybe 200,000 pesos per month to keep him and the other ones going. Let's say he signs for $30,000. I don't make a penny.
>
> If I have to handle construction on the field, that's extra. Last month, I went out twenty-two times to take kids to tryouts—that's gas, food. I have four guys working directly with the kids. I have a night watchman, a guy who maintains the place. I have a maid who takes care of the *pensión* where [the players] sleep and a cook who prepares three-and-a-half meals a day 'cause I got between sixteen and twenty kids who are burning a lotta calories.[14]

Other buscones may not spend as much on these individual items or tasks, but they will spend time and money just the same. There is no simple counterpart to this in the U.S. player development system. There, organized programs in the schools, as well as Little League and Babe Ruth League, develop young players, and high school and Amateur Athletic Union (AAU) coaches train the kids as they get older. Parents house, feed, and care for the health of their children/players. They drive them to tryouts and practices and tend to their injuries and ailments. College recruiters then find them and get them into scholarship programs; universities house them, and coaches further train them. Agents represent them at the time of draft. In the DR, by contrast, men like Jacobo do it all. They are the system.[15]

Jacobo does not always spot talent himself. He mostly is alerted to it, or talented young players are brought to him:

> You never know who's gonna get the best guy and how. It could be your next-door neighbor who spots him. It could be your compadre or your uncle or the guy working in the Little League. They usually come to me because I can develop their player and they can't. . . . I had a kid . . . I recently signed. He's from Manhattan, but his parents are from La Romana [a town in the eastern Dominican Republic]. They sent him back there to play in a league. The guy running the league told me he didn't have a place [room and board] for him.[16]

Because players come from so many different sources, a player developer like Jacobo has to be able to relate to many different kinds of people. At times, he really has to work the network. For instance, when he finds a player who might be courted by a rival, Jacobo might take the boy and his family to his complex to try to impress them. The family is key, because the boys are minors and thus cannot legally make the decision. These days, top-of-the-line buscones typically have strong bonds with players and their families. Those relationships are built on mutual trust and hope. "A lot of times, I don't have to talk them into it," he said. "They're already looking for a guy like me." He cited the example of Juan (a pseudonym), whose father died when he was eight. "His mom was left with nine kids, working as a maid and making about 1,500 pesos [less than $100] a month," he said. "Can you imagine what kind of situation that is? His mom was so eager to have me take him. When I [first] saw Juan, he weighed only 100 pounds. I signed him a little later, when he was sixteen and 150 pounds, and the Dodgers gave him $400,000 to sign."[17]

Sometimes parents do have to be convinced that letting go of their boy is the best thing to do. The mother of another player provides an example. "She said she was only gonna leave [her son] here for a few months," Jacobo said, because "she couldn't [bear to] have her baby son away. I told her, 'What will happen in the future if he asks [you] why [you] didn't let him really try to be a ballplayer?' I remember that she put her head down, . . . thought deep, and said, 'You know what? What you just told me hit me in the heart. I know he's gotta be his own man soon. . . . I'm gonna leave him here with you.'"

Although this player did not end up signing for a lot of money, Jacobo continued to believe in him because he was tough and smart.[18]

Jacobo thus knows how to get to parents by selling the dream that their sons will become ballplayers, but he is not selling snake oil. He is well respected and is known as a man who truly can develop the boys' talent and get them contracts. Further, the families he deals with are surrounded by examples of young men who have had varying degrees of success. They do not need for their sons to make it to the major leagues; what they are really after is the signing bonus. Any subsequent success is considered gravy. With a reasonable signing bonus, a family can get better housing, or start a small business, or simply buy better clothes and food for their children. When they go with Jacobo, however, they have a good chance to move up the ranks of professional ball.

Structurally, not a lot separates Jacobo's program from those of the MLB academies. The latter are, of course, more opulent and better funded, but even though they look better, they do not do anything differently. For years, Jacobo boarded players in the house he grew up in in San Pedro de Macorís. He hired a cook and a cleaning woman to take care of the facility; the boys trained at his playing field and returned to the *pensión* for meals and at the end of the day. Since he finished building the complex's new dormitory-clubhouse in late 2012, all of his operations have been consolidated, giving Complejo Astín Jacobo's an even greater resemblance to those of the MLB academies. His reason for centralizing his operations is the same as the academies': to optimize the environment for baseball playing and eliminate negative influences.

Jacobo's players spend their days practicing many of the same drills—bunting, double plays, and so on—that rookies at major league complexes are put through. In a departure from the programs run by most buscones, however, Jacobo's boys play as many as six games a week. This belies the criticism that many in MLB circles have leveled against Dominican players—that is, that they have little game experience. Jacobo transports his players to games a bus that once belonged to the Los Angeles Dodger but has seen better days, which again illustrates how closely his program parallels the major league operations.

Much of what Jacobo does establishes routine and executes the drudgery of baseball work, and fourteen- and fifteen-year-old boys take to it no better than do eighteen-year-olds at the MLB academies. Resocialization is as necessary for boys at this level as it is later. (Academy directors should, in fact, thank the better Dominican trainers for making their work easier.) Many young players encounter order for the first time when they enter Jacobo's program, and the potential for conflict between the boys and those who enforce the program's rules is rife. "I never had a problem with disobedience, at least to my face," Jacobo said,

> but there are guys who could be problems. We got a guy right now who is not a major leaguer because of that. His mom was a great athlete and got killed. Her brother got into a fight, and they lived in a bad neighborhood. When she tried to stop it, she got shot. When the boy's grandma died—she was his support—I told him, "I know you get into fights, but I'm gonna trust you. I'm gonna take you to my *pensión*, and you're gonna be with my other players, but I need you to respect me and them. Anything that happens between you and them, think that you're doing it to me." We never had a problem with him and the others. The problem was when he went back to his neighborhood. I remember we worked hard with him and got him to throw 92–93 miles per hour. Then he went back to the barrio and spent two days there and came back to try out with the Yankees. . . . He was in bad shape and was throwing [only] 84–85 miles per hour. [The] boy had a lotta potential but couldn't help himself when he went back to his home.[19]

Most people consider such street-tough boys (or *tigres*, as they are known in the DR) difficult to deal with because they are dangerous to others—that is, they are combative—but as Jacobo's example reveals, they can be equally dangerous to themselves. Jacobo often is able to use his close relationships with players to counteract their negative aggressive tendencies. Although he has designed his program to mirror the MLB academies, in certain key ways—particularly in the "father-son" relationship he develops with his players—it is very different. The best buscones foster these kinds of relationships. Jacobo's relationship with Julio (a pseudonym) is illustrative. One day, he took Julio to try out for the Texas Rangers. Jacobo and the other trainers were told to take seats in remote corners of the field. "It's a cat-and-mouse game [the MLB scouts] play," he said. "They don't want me too close, because he looks for me, and we communicate with our eyes and hands. . . . I'm gonna pull him early. The Rangers have seen him enough, and he's a little stiff. These teams don't care about my boy, so it's up to me to watch over him."[20] Jacobo's concern went far beyond that of a businessman protecting an investment: He cared about Julio and his entire family. "I got [another] kid who has been with me since he turned thirteen," Jacobo told me. "I pay a private school that will accommodate his baseball schedule. His father just had a car accident, and I helped pay for most of the repairs. Sometimes they don't have money to pay the rent, and I help out there, too. And I'll do this till he's sixteen and we find out if he'll get signed."[21]

Jacobo is well aware that of the risk he is taking; few, in fact, understand as well as he does that most of these relationships end without an MLB contract. Once a team makes an offer, negotiations begin. Attached to this is the verification of the player's identity and age, a process that is fraught with twists and turns and, frequently, surprises. Finding and training a genuinely talented player is sometimes the easiest part of what a player developer does, as Jacobo explained, citing another of his players as an example:

[This player's mother] left him at his grandmother's house and didn't come back for seven or eight years. I got a call from a guy from Consuelo who wanted me to look at him, and he was good—I mean, really good.

When he went to my *pensión*, . . . [w]e gave him his own bed, and I told him to go sleep in it 'cause he was gonna be cold. He told me that when he was little, his uncle would lock the door at 8:00 P.M., and if he was one minute late, he'd sleep on the streets. So he grew up sleeping on the street, and he was comfortable on the floor.

Eventually I got [an MLB team] interested in signing him. We needed his birth certificate, but we couldn't find his mother. I went out looking for her for two months. I [put the player on] a TV show [where] he said he was looking for his mother and that he had to sign a baseball contract. Being a minor, he needed his mother to sign with him. A neighbor was watching the program and got hold of her. A few days later, the mother showed up with some papers, but . . . they weren't filled out properly. [This player was] ranked twenty-sixth in the minor leagues. . . . [T]hat's how good he is. He won the Triple Crown here in the [Dominican Summer League], and it's only now [eighteen months later] that he has a birth certificate in the way that MLB wants it.[22]

Yet his identity check ultimately failed, and the player tragically spent four years trying to rectify the situation. Four years of lost development time is incalculable in the brief life of an athlete.

Jacobo had yet another case that went bad. In 2009, many people considered Jean Carlos Batista one of the brightest prospects of the year's upcoming July 2 period. (Signing players who have reached age sixteen and a half by July 2 is a high-stakes contest in which MLB teams engage each year.) Batista had convinced Jacobo that he was ready for what he hoped would become a bidding war for his services, and Jacobo talked openly about the likelihood that Batista would receive an offer in excess of $1 million from some team. They had a very close relationship. "I don't have a father, so you're my father," Batista was quoted as saying about Jacobo. "I get scared at tryouts. . . that I won't do well. [But] Astín has confidence in me. He says, 'I believe in you because you're the best.' When you have confidence, you can feel it, and I don't get scared anymore."[23]

As the July 2 signing day neared, anticipation soared. That morning, Batista paced at Jacobo's complex, but his mentor was nowhere to be seen. Finally, he arrived. The only offer they had received was $450,000 from the Houston Astros—not an insignificant sum, but far less than they had expected. They declined it. In September, questions suddenly surfaced about Batista's age. Jacobo learned, to his surprise, that Batista was a year older. A close look at Batista's school records revealed that he was listed as being nine years old through third grade and nine again in fourth grade. "My reputation went down the drain," Jacobo said. "I was out there pushing my player, working with my guy, telling everybody about all the wonderful things he could do as a baseball player . . . but he was lying."[24] Batista blamed his long-dead father for the error, but Jacobo wanted no part of that. After a one-year suspension, Batista wound up signing with the Astros for the much lower figure of $200,000. The lie cost him dearly, but Jacobo suffered a blow to his sense of self that hurt far more than the financial loss. His program did not suffer, however, and he continues to expand it in a climate of increasingly cut-throat competition.

Rafael Pérez

Rafael Pérez and Astín Jacobo got off to a rocky start when they dealt with each other for the first time in 2000. Pérez had just been appointed to head the MLB Commissioner's Office in Santo Domingo, and Jacobo was just beginning his career as a buscón. Their initial encounters were like putting a mongoose and a cobra in the same room. Since then, they have found a way to carve out a respectful relationship, although they probably will not be going out to dinner together anytime soon.

In their initial encounters, Pérez confronted Jacobo as the face of all unregulated buscones. The idea at the time was to start reining in Dominican player developers by incorporating them into the official MLB structure. Jacobo remembered those early encounters:

I had this discussion with Pérez. [MLB] wanted to create an organization called Scouts Independientes because "buscón" was a bad word.
I'm not sure, but I think Pérez gave us that name. I've never been
too happy with it, and we discussed it. I said to Pérez, "You know,
Rafi, you went to college in the States, and so did I. What do you
think Americans will think about us when something comes out in
the paper about buscones? How are you gonna describe that?" And he
said, "Well, like a pimp or a hustler." And I said, "Do you think that
describes what we do?" You know, I think his answer was the MLB
line, not so much his personal view.[25]

Pérez and Jacobo followed very different routes through Dominican
baseball. Pérez was a middle-class Dominican who earned a baseball scholarship to the University of Southern Alabama. Although Jacobo also attended
college in the United States, the two men seem—on the surface, at least—very
different from each other. Jacobo is gritty, for instance, while Pérez is smooth
and polished.

Pérez was groomed for his role in the MLB hierarchy. Following a brief
two years in the Pittsburgh Pirates system, he returned to the University of
Southern Alabama to complete his degree in business. He then worked for
a firm in Florida before returning to baseball when he entered Don Odermann's Latin Athlete Education Foundation, a program that trains bright,
young Dominicans to take on administrative roles in MLB. Pérez quickly
came under the tutelage of Lou Melendez, MLB's vice-president of international operations, and by 2000 had been named to head the organization's
new Dominican office.

To appreciate the role Pérez has played in Dominican baseball, one has to
understand that by opening the office in Santo Domingo, MLB was making a
commitment to take control of how major league teams were operating in the
DR. After some five decades in which oversight was absent, practices that had
become accepted suddenly were being questioned, and many were now recast
as unacceptable. Pérez oversaw the significant upgrading of all MLB teams'
Dominican academies; he also created and enforced strict new guidelines for
how those teams sign and pay Dominican rookies. Being Dominican and
a former player helped Pérez very little when it came to mollifying scouts,
academy directors, independent trainers, and government agencies. (The
Dominican Commissioner of Professional Baseball was also miffed because
MLB and the government agencies were bypassing him.) Pérez resigned himself to the initial dislike he experienced. "I think at first I was not very well

received," he said, "because we [MLB] basically said to them, 'Look, you've been doing this for so many years, but now you can't because you're breaking the rules.'"[26]

Pérez's job included governing the practices of Dominican player developers, who viewed him as an interloper who threatened to ruin established practices with unwelcome regulations. Success in this potential minefield required knowing when to tread lightly and when to draw lines in the sand. Pérez was savvy in this regard, but he may also have paved the way by focusing both the teams and the Dominican government on a common enemy: the buscón.

As much as he championed MLB's positions, Pérez was also keenly aware of the culturally relative position of many of the views held by North American interests. From his position as the head of the Dominican office, he routinely lectured MLB clubs about the need to consider Dominican facilities in the same way they would their U.S. facilities. And while he promulgated MLB policy to combat identity fraud among Dominican players, Pérez was outspoken about the dire conditions that led to those attempts to alter age and identity. "I'm not allowed to talk specifically about MLB positions, but I'll tell you this," he said. "From my position, as low as it is, I have a responsibility to communicate what MLB needs to know to better operate. That means teaching [MLB] about different cultures, understanding that [in the Dominican Republic] you have to be flexible to be successful. . . . When I got to this job, I felt it was important to tell Lou [Melendez, a senior executive with MLB that I had never lowered my age because I never had to [Pérez was signed after playing college baseball in the United States], *but if I had to, I would.*"[27]

Whatever may separate Jacobo and Pérez, they do share an understanding that Americans do not know enough about their country to make informed and sympathetic decisions about their conditions or practices. When Pérez said, "When Americans think of Dominican baseball, they cannot think like Americans. Things are very different down here. It's a cultural thing,"[28] I could just as easily have been listening to Jacobo.

In 2005, Pérez was lured away from the MLB Commissioner's Office to take a position as director of international player development with the New York Mets. Omar Minaya, who had become the Mets' general manager, specifically sought Pérez because of his experience in Latin American baseball and because he is sensitive to cultural issues that Dominicans and other Latinos face. Minaya amassed a group of bright, young Dominican administrators—including his friend and former major leaguer Rafael Bornugal—which made the offer very attractive to Pérez. In his new role, he was charged with overseeing players in Venezuela, Panama, and other Latin American countries as they attempted to move through the Mets organization. He described his scope of responsibilities as "everything that has to do with the academies in the Dominican Republic and Venezuela. Plus, I oversee [the Mets'] agreement with Mexican teams and, on top of that, [I] coordinat[e] players for the winter leagues in Latin America."[29]

Pérez was also asked to deal with international player migration, a role in which cultural brokering was key. Almost no one in baseball is better suited to do this. "It took a while for [organized] baseball to understand what having something like 40 percent of professional baseball players being international really means," he said, "and 90 percent of these international players are Latin American. Now you will be seeing Latin people in positions of authority. I am Dominican, but I went to school in the States and played in the States, and I consider myself completely bilingual and bicultural."[30] Ideas and feelings he had had for a long time were finally going to be recognized and implemented. "This is all a great laboratory for me," he said.[31]

Fostering conditions that would ease the cultural transitions that had plagued Dominicans and others included both little and big efforts. Ensuring that Latin American cuisine and bilingual coaches were available to players in their first year made the shift to the United States less psychologically disruptive for them. Pérez also instituted a "reverse migration" program that took Mets minor leaguers to the Dominican Republic to see where their Latin teammates came from in the hope that this would encourage more empathy among the American players.

The push to promote seamlessness between Latin America and the United States was so strong that Pérez was beginning to think like a sports marketer. One of the last times I saw him, he was talking about having Dominican Winter League teams play an exhibition game at the Mets' stadium in New York City. Nothing seemed too far-fetched to be considered.

When Minaya was fired in 2009, the "Los Mets" experiment ended, but Pérez was quickly called on to return to his job as head of the MLB Commissioner's Office in Santo Domingo. While the job was much the same as when he left it in 2005, new issues had surfaced that demanded a crackdown on identity fraud. The increased pressure MLB is exerting in the DR has made Pérez's job much more difficult, and he has become more guarded and careful with his words and actions. Yet it did not take long for Pérez to find the cultural middle ground where he is at his best. "There is so much to do in this country," he said in the first half-hour of our first meeting after he returned to Santo Domingo. Pérez was spinning an elaborate justification for promoting MLB's educational initiatives: "If we push education, and if it only succeeds a little bit, we're doing the right thing."[32]

Felipe Alou

Felipe Alou is one of the most impressive figures in Dominican baseball history. However, he earned his place in this chapter by his lifelong commitment to speaking out forcefully and articulately on issues that are important to Latino baseball players. His pioneering role as the second Dominican, after Ozzie Virgil, to play in the major leagues and the first to play as a starter is well known, as is his role as the first Dominican manager of an MLB team. But his capacity to act as the Dominican conscience over the course of his career has been more significant. Unlike most Dominicans, who speak openly against prejudice only after they have gained a measure of respectability and financial security, Alou began confronting racism and anti-Latino behavior he encountered early in his career. In 1963, for instance, his article "Latin-American Ballplayers Need a Bill of Rights" was published in *Sport* magazine.[33] It made public declarations and demands on behalf of Latinos in a world that could not have cared less, and although it had little (if any) immediate impact, it is striking that it came from a foreign player who was still learning to negotiate both baseball and U.S. culture.

Although his family was not affluent, Alou was able to attend the university, where he attempted to pursue a career in medicine. He also was not a typical Dominican ballplayer in demographic terms: his father was black, and his mother was white. This biracial heritage enabled him to relate to race in a nuanced way. Although he is vigilant, he is not quick to judge and is able to confront racial issues in ways that most Dominican players cannot grasp.

Alou has never been perceived as a "hot-headed Latin" or a "loose cannon." His is a quiet, smoldering defiance. The Hall of Fame pitcher Juan Marichal has recounted an incident in the San Francisco Giants' clubhouse in which the team's manager, Alvin Dark (who was well known as a racist), upended a table of food intended for the players following a loss. The players stopped in their tracks, with the exception of Alou. "I remember Felipe Alou bending over after Dark did this one night, picking up some of the food off of the floor, and eating it while looking Dark right in the eye," Marichal has said. "[Dark] couldn't understand that for us, even if you lose, you don't kick food on the floor. You just don't do that."[34]

This willingness to confront bigotry was seen again in 2005 during Alou's stint as manager of the Giants. Following a racist rant by a local radio talk show host (he criticized the team for having "brain-dead Caribbean hitters hacking at slop nightly"), Alou boldly declared that the one-week suspension the host received was a "slap on the hand" and was insulting to Latinos and progressive people everywhere. "It made me sad to know that 40, almost 50 years later, we have comments like that, especially in San Francisco," he said. "There are more countries [represented] in San Francisco now than when I was a player here and I never heard anything like that. I heard it in the South and in some other cities, but not here. A man like me and the Latin guys out there, we have to be aware now that [racism] is not over yet. It is coming back."[35] Felipe Alou is arguably the most important figure in Dominican baseball history, but his presence also hovers over much of the present.

Omar Minaya

He may have left the big market (New York Mets) a bit disgraced, following six years of heavy spending with no World Series appearance to show for it, but Omar Minaya's impact has to be measured beyond winning or losing sporting contests. In his capacity as general manager of the Mets, Minaya forged the first transnational sporting franchise, in the process creating a template for reconfiguring Dominican-MLB relations. His story is captivating as much for its rags-to-riches quality as for the way he changed the face of international baseball.

Background

Like the Jacobos, the Minaya family immigrated to the United States from the Dominican Republic to escape political repression during the tumultuous 1960s. Lolo Minaya, Omar's father, had openly opposed the despotic Trujillo regime, for which he spent two years in a prison. After he was released, in 1965, he opposed the right-wing junta that sought to overthrow the democratically elected President Juan Bosch. When the situation became personally dangerous, Lolo Minaya fled to the United States.[36]

The family settled in the Corona (and, later, the neighboring Elmhurst) section of Queens and thus entered the cultural mélange that is New York City. For most chroniclers of Omar Minaya's story, it was this cosmopolitan upbringing that fostered his fluency with other people and cultures. Among the many "Queens things" he did as a child was ride the number 7 subway train into Manhattan and back. That train became infamous in 1999, when John Rocker, then a pitcher for the Atlanta Braves and a southerner, ranted that he would "retire first" before ever playing for a team in New York City: "It's the most hectic, nerve-racking city. Imagine having to take the [number] 7 train to the ballpark, looking like you're [riding through] Beirut next to some kid with purple hair next to some queer with AIDS right next to some dude who just got out of jail for the fourth time right next to some 20-year-old mom with four kids. It's depressing." About New York City itself, he said: "The biggest thing I don't like about New York are the foreigners. I'm not a very big fan of foreigners. You can walk an entire block in Times Square and not hear anybody speaking English. [There are] Asians and Koreans and Vietnamese and Indians and Russians and Spanish people and everything up there. How the hell did they get in this country?"[37]

While Rocker represented the part of America that is fearful of cultural pluralism, Minaya was refreshed by it. The ability to revel in diversity, mixed with his outgoing demeanor, was responsible for his success after his brief stint as a minor leaguer. His two-year stint (1982–1983) playing in Italy illustrates this point. Not everyone who plays baseball abroad can derive as much from the experience as did Minaya.[38] It was a wonderful fit and a template for how Minaya would later help fashion a cultural experiment with the Mets.

With no college (he chose not to take a baseball scholarship offered by Mississippi State), Minaya entered baseball as a scout with the Texas Rangers. His employers wanted him to work in Latin America, which he did with enthusiasm. It was not long before he was noticed by the Mets staff and offered the position of assistant general manager in 1997. At this juncture, Minaya was considered a high-ranking Latino in the baseball world, but baseball had never had a Latino general manager. Felipe Alou, the first Latino (Dominican) manager of a major league team, was not hired until he was fifty-one. Most dismissed the possibility as remote, at best. A fellow scout, Ramon Peña, for instance, openly questioned him on this point, quipping, "Omar, c'mon, do you think any rich man would trust a *Dominican* with his money?"[39]

After several unsuccessful attempts to get a general manager position, Minaya landed with the Montreal Expos in 2002. The Expos were in receivership and being run by the league when Minaya took the organization's reins. The team was also understaffed and in disarray. The former owner, Jeffrey Loria, had cannibalized the Expos, taking most of its employees, computers, scouting reports, and so forth, leaving Minaya virtually nothing to work with. Undeterred, and through sheer personality, he infused a messianic fervor into the organization. As a former employee recounted, "He energized everyone. . . . You wanted to do it for Omar. You'd run through a wall for him."[40] He turned the team into a club that was in contention, even after making one of the worst trades in recent baseball history.[41] (Minaya's tragic inability to gauge the consequences of trades would haunt him as much as his enthusiasm and magnetism would help him.) Working with a small-market team that it was more forgiving of flaws and welcomed strengths suited Minaya. As a result of his success in Montreal, he was wooed to the Mets as general manager in 2004.

The First Transnational Major League Team

Becoming the first Latino general manager in MLB history was a pioneering move, but it was the way Minaya redefined the Mets that truly stood out. In the 2004 off-season, he got to work by signing that winter's two most prized free agents—Pedro Martínez and Carlos Beltrán—for significant sums. Sports circles in New York instantly registered the importance of the signings, which Jonathan Mahler of the *New York Times* called a "rebranding" of the Mets.[42] Martínez and Beltrán were followed in succeeding years by, among others, Sandy Alomar Jr., Ambiorix Burgos, Miguel Cairo, Luis Castillo, Ramón Castro, Carlos Delgado, Orlando Hernández, Endy Chávez, Kelvim Escobar, Julio Franco, Geremi González, Rubén Gotay, Jorge Julio, Ricky Ledée, José Lima, Eli Marrero, Guillermo Mota, José Offerman, Oliver Pérez, Duaner Sánchez, Jorge Sosa, and José Valentín. While these signings were not always wise, Minaya was clearly focused on international—especially Latin American—players. Rafael Pérez, the head of international player development for the Mets at the time, saw these moves as keeping with the times. "What [the Mets are] doing is no different from what IBM has done for years," he said. "It's part of the globalized marketplace."[43]

Minaya's vision for the Mets was nothing less than to craft the first transnational baseball franchise in history. Other teams, such as the Los Angeles Dodgers, had pioneered international relations long before Minaya, but they were not transnational.[44] The O'Malley family, who owned the Dodgers from the 1940s through the 1980s, had established impressive relations with Japan in the 1950s, for instance. And the Pirates and the Giants had developed relations with Cuba more than a half-century earlier. What Minaya did, however, was craft a social order *within* the Mets that seamlessly moved from the DR to Queens, New York. Latinos and Americans were able to function easily in each setting.

Beginning at the top, he asked Tony Bernazard (Puerto Rican) to leave his position with the MLB Players Association and take over as vice-president of player development for the Mets. Sandy Johnson (American), who had a great deal of experience in Latin America and spoke Spanish, was brought in as vice-president of scouting. Minaya also tapped players who had benefited from Odermann's Latin Athletes Education Fund in the 1980s and hired four of them. Rafael Bournigal, who had played baseball for Florida State University and then in the major leagues for seven years, became the Mets' chief international scout; Pérez, who had played at the University of South Alabama (where he earned a bachelor's degree in accounting) became the international director; Ismael Cruz, who had played for Eckerd College in St. Petersburg, Florida, became the director of international operations; and, finally, Juan Henderson, who had played at the University of Southern Mississippi, became the director of the Mets Dominican Baseball Academy. These hires were expected to translate information gained in one cultural setting into action or a decision in another cultural setting. This is analogous to arbitrage in finance—that is, the purchase of securities in one market to resell for profit in another on the basis of the difference in prices. Whenever I watched Pérez deal with the myriad situations that came up in the course of his day, I could not help thinking that his job involved cultural arbitrage and that it is just this kind of skill that globalized, twenty-first-century life demands of its leaders.

In recognition of the Latin-centric direction in which Minaya appeared to be taking the Mets, "the team started to be called *Los Mets*" by both detractors and supporters. Minaya was more than prepared to take flak. "In this day and age, this conversation is being held in 30 clubhouses," he said. "The game is becoming so diverse. . . . I feel as proud to be able to speak to the Spanish player as to be able to speak with an African-American player or to be able to speak with a kid from Atlanta, Georgia, or the Midwest. To me, that's very important as a general [manager]."[45] Minaya's transnational organization went way beyond hiring Latino players. He placed transnational people at every level, from the Mets Dominican Baseball Academy, through the minor leagues, into the parent organization itself.

Further, the Mets have pursued this kind of organizational engineering on every front—for example, by aggressively promoting Spanish broadcasting and marketing and building business relationships with Latino companies such as Banco Popular. This is the single most important development of Minaya's tenure as general manager because it has the potential to alter how MLB teams interact with Dominicans and their baseball establishment.

Junior Noboa

"I'm looking at a large, flat expanse of land that has been cleared of trees so that it resembles a lunar landscape. . . . Out in the middle of it are three men, specks really. As I near them, one speck turns out to be Junior Noboa, who is responsible for this empty canvas. Soon it will become a sleek, modern baseball academy that rivals any of MLB's Spring Training facilities."[46] I wrote these words in 2009 while conducting fieldwork in the Dominican Republic. At that time, I watched Noboa, cell phone to his ear, relay information to men standing beside him, the heads of the large Dominican construction firm that was carrying the project out with hundreds of workers and every conceivable kind of construction vehicle. On the other end of the phone was the architect, ensconced in his office in Santo Domingo. The $2 million to build the facility had been put together by Noboa, as well. In short, the project had Noboa's thumbprint all over it.

If anyone had told me when I began researching Dominican baseball twenty-five years ago that Dominicans would own and build the most modern baseball facilities in the hemisphere one day, I would have considered it science fiction. But here is a former player brokering and building facilities that will house major league teams with Noboa as landlord. Nothing in his life prepared Noboa for the role he has played in this change. He, like so many Dominican boys, grew up in a baseball-playing family, but unlike most, he succeeded in reaching the major leagues, where he debuted with the Cleveland Indians at nineteen. His well-traveled eight-year MLB career spanned the mid-1980s to the mid-1990s and included playing for six different teams. At his best, Noboa was a journeyman player who registered a .239 batting average and a total of 493 major league at bats. And like the many players who barely manage to cobble together a professional sporting career, Noboa had ample opportunity to think about his post-playing days. "I started [thinking about that] in 1991 when I got hurt and knew my career was in jeopardy," he said. "'What will I do when I retire?' One thing that I kept coming back to was that, except for the Dodgers and Epy Guerrero's Blue Jays, nobody had academies or a place where you could have twenty-five, thirty, forty players. I played a few more years, and finally, in 1995, I returned to thinking about this."[47]

The nomadism of Noboa's six-team playing career has been offset by his remarkable tenure with MLB's Arizona Diamondbacks. He became the team's first international administrative hire in 1995 and has been with the Diamondbacks since. He has scouted, signed, and overseen many of the organization's Latin American players since that time. In 2012, he was named vice-president of Latin American operations. That certainly involves traveling throughout baseball's Latin American world, but Noboa will continue also to direct the Diamondbacks Dominican Baseball Academy in the Boca Chica area.

The side of Noboa that is less well known, and the one that propels him into the ranks of the influential men profiled in this chapter, is his role as a broker in building the most sophisticated baseball academies in the world. As he said, this idea began to germinate even before his playing days ended. In the 1990s, as the academy system was beginning to mature, Noboa started approaching MLB organizations to sell them on the idea of building facilities in the DR:

Most teams just leased a field and a house and had twenty-five to thirty players in one house with one or two bathrooms. Really, the conditions were only so-so. We presented the possibility of having their players in a nice facility with a great field and nice living conditions. A lot of teams liked the idea that they could try it for three years and then, if they liked it, they could stay a little longer or they might buy the place.[48]

At first, his proposals were not seriously considered: "In the beginning I called a couple of players [with money]. I said, 'Listen, I have an idea about building these facilities for major league clubs. Let's get together and make a partnership to do this.' And they said, 'Oh no, that's never going to work.'"[49] Undeterred, Noboa reached out to the business community, which had close ties to the government of Dominican President Hipólito Mejía (2002–2004), and formed a partnership with the businessman Edmundo Gonzáles to assemble a team that included an architect and a general construction company. They went to Detroit to see Joe Klein, then the general manager of the Tigers. "In the beginning, we were only going to try to build for one club," Noboa said, "but [Klein] said, 'Why don't you build a place where you can have two teams together? The teams could share some things, and it could be cheaper, and they could play against each other more easily.' That's how we started Las Americas Baseball Academy."[50]

Las Americas was leased to two major league teams, marking the first time Dominicans engaged MLB at this level. Heartened by this, Noboa formed a partnership with another Dominican businessman, Manolín Dumé, to build an even larger project: Baseball City, with headquarters for four teams. Noboa was convinced that an academy built in the right spot could do several things at once. It could keep players focused on training and away from distractions—a vitally important consideration. It could be close enough to Santo Domingo to take advantage of its communications infrastructure, as well as close enough to other teams' facilities to increase playing options. "In the north, where the Dominican Summer League had a division, they would spend like an hour to get to a game," he said. "That's a waste. The more time [players] can spend on the field, the better."[51]

Perhaps most important, it needed to be near the airport to increase direct interaction between the United States and the Dominican Republic. When the Mets were contemplating building an academy in the Boca Chica area, Noboa noted that the team's front office personnel "could take a plane from New York, spend five hours on the ground, and go back the same day."[52]

Milton Jamail, a scholar and writer on Latin American baseball who now works for the Tampa Bay Rays, noted that being near the airport also works to "better integrate the Dominican academy into [U.S.] minor league operations."[53] In other words, the roving coaches who work in the Rays' minor leagues can now include the Dominican academy as a regularly scheduled stop. This is not only invaluable in building a transnational operation, but it also fosters a view among others in the organization that the Dominican academy is on par with U.S. minor league teams.

Some thought Noboa was crazy for building Las Americas Baseball Academy in Boca Chica. He recounted that when Peter O'Malley, former owner of the Dodgers and the force behind Campo Las Palmas (see Chapter 2), visited Las Americas in 1996, he said, "Junior, it's a beautiful complex but why did you build it in this place? There's nothing around here—not even electricity." (Las Americas relied on generators for six years.) "I said, 'Peter, the airport is only ten minutes from here. You got the hotels, the highway nearby. San Pedro [de Macorís] is only thirty minutes away. We're located near everything.' Five years later, he came back and saw . . . that about twenty teams had come [to this area]. He said, 'Junior, congrats. You've got great vision.'"[54]

Las Americas was leased by the Cleveland Indians and the Washington Nationals, and Noboa moved on to his next project: a mega-complex that would concentrate six major league teams. It was called Baseball City, and when it was completed in 2004, it contained ten full fields, two half-fields, a dorm, and an office building for each team. Noboa would go on to build the Yankees' academy and a complex for the nonprofit Rawlings Foundation, Mariano Rivera's church-based youth complex. The pace and scale of building these academies has escalated so quickly that some facilities, hailed as state-of-the-art just a few years ago, are now regarded as decidedly downscale. Even Noboa's projects are not immune. One MLB administrator recently referred to Baseball City as "a ghetto," Noboa himself has commented that his new projects exceed the grandeur of Baseball City. These rapidly rising standards are testimony to both the booming growth of MLB as an industry within the DR and the powerful presence of Noboa in making it happen: "This has become a serious and mature industry in the Dominican Republic. It's the Silicon Valley of baseball."[55] Noboa's role as an academy developer, MLB landlord, and academy broker cannot be understated. It is not only pioneering but also unique in that it forces both individual teams and the MLB Commissioner's Office to think about Dominicans on new and more equitable footing.

Conclusion

All of these men profiled in this chapter have found ways to defend Dominican interests in their relationship with Major League Baseball. Four of the five men have done so from within MLB. Felipe Alou was the first, and he has not stopped confronting the kinds of racism and intolerance he first encountered when he arrived in the United States as a young baseball player. Omar Minaya and Rafael Pérez have worked in a number of capacities for MLB teams and the Commissioner's Office, consistently taking up the cause of Dominican players and of Dominican baseball. Junior Noboa has had a somewhat less direct effect on MLB's relationship to the DR, even though he has held just about every position in Latin American player development with the Diamondbacks. It is, however, his business of building training facilities that has helped dismantle the notion that is secretly held by many people in the United States that Dominicans do not have the competence to take control of baseball's development infrastructure.

Of the five men, only Astín Jacobo has worked outside MLB's official circles. He has engaged in confrontations when necessary, yet also showed impressive restraint and tact when dealing with MLB operatives, who often treat him dismissively. These five men, as I have said, have defended their country—in baseball terms, and in a wide variety of ways.

5

Demonizing Dominicans

When Americans think of Dominican baseball,
they should not think like Americans.

—Rafael Pérez,
interview by the author, October 1, 2005

The compression of time and space associated with a globalizing world certainly intensifies contact between disparate peoples and cultures. This suggests some sort of homogenization, but it can just as easily fuel acrimonious juxtapositions of ideas, norms and rules for how affairs are to be conducted. The result can be toxic—a social cocktail made up of impasse, impairment, and intimidation—whether one is talking about joint Mexican-U.S. efforts to clean up the Rio Grande, Microsoft hammering out arrangements with one of its numerous outsourcers, or the NBA working on a licensing deal in Europe. The type of resolution Rob Manfred, MLB's vice-president of labor relations and human resources, strives for usually thinly hides a concerted effort to override the views or practices of other parties. His comment on the use of performance-enhancing drugs is illustrative: "We think it would be helpful if the legal framework in the Dominican Republic were similar to ours in terms of the regulation of performance-enhancing drugs."[1]

Being "helpful" is just MLB's way of saying that the Dominicans are not in compliance with MLB's policy, which, in turn, rests on a bed of ethnocentric hubris. North American norms and policies in this context are considered better than Dominican norms and policies, a kind of culture trumping that involves promoting the superiority of one system while dismissing the other. As Pierre Bourdieu (among others) pointed out, "Domination no longer needs to be exerted in a direct, personal way when it is entailed in possession of the means (economic or cultural capital) of appropriating the mechanisms of the field of production and the field of cultural production."[2] In this scheme, the cultural "other" must become a diminished other, an alien and subservient other. These fabricated subalterns might be depicted as comically inept, possibly without virtue, or just lawfully wrong. At its worst, cultural trumping can result in a sociocultural demonization of the other that leads to policies that are designed to cripple the subaltern. Dominican baseball offers an excellent example of that process.

Initially, I did not realize that, in looking to continue its domination of Dominican baseball, the North American baseball establishment (including the media) was resorting to *systematic* disparaging of Dominicans and their culture. I missed it because I incorrectly assumed that MLB's earlier arrogance had given way to a view that Dominicans constituted such an important part of the global baseball family that they deserved some measure of respect. After all, MLB and the media had regularly been portraying Dominicans as significant contributors to the playing of the game.[3] I heard off-color remarks, of course, but I had become inured to the lack of political correctness in sports and attributed them largely to the culture of sniping and backbiting typically found among competitors. A certain amount of personal venom also is spewed by people who bear serious grudges. Over time, however, I did begin to see that the attitudes and views of so many involved in the sport were patterned and derisive. In this chapter, I look at how MLB has attempted to frame Dominican baseball as the alien other. The motive for "demonizing Dominicans" is clearly rooted in maintaining MLB's domination in an era which its investment in the DR had grown substantially.

Since my book *Sugarball* was published in 1991, Dominicans have reconfigured their political and economic relations with MLB. To reproduce its domination and continue its control over the Dominican player commodity chain, MLB has had to co-opt locals when it can and bully them when it cannot. "Demonizing," or dismissing through negative characterization, is a tried-and-true culture-trumping technique in which the dominant group reinterprets its subordinates as embodying attributes that it devalues or disdains. In anthropological circles, this is often referred to as the anthropology of difference.

What follows is an examination of a range of issues that have become stumbling blocks in the relations between Dominican baseball and North American baseball interests. Each side sees these issues differently, but the conflicts go well beyond "agreeing to disagree." By labeling them corrupt or inept, MLB has been able to depict the actions and views of Dominicans as unworthy of consideration. This, in turn, has paved the way for MLB to use its considerable power to run roughshod over Dominican practices. For Dominicans, by contrast, the differences result from efforts to respond to MLB that, at best, are only partially successful and that can be understood only in relative terms. The difference is that Dominicans do not possess the cultural clout to make their views dominant, or even comprehensible.

The Buscón as Dickensian Villain: Enrique Soto

The first, and primary, targets of MLB in the DR are the buscones. Most news stories about Dominican baseball blame them for just about everything that is wrong in Dominican baseball. An extreme example comes from an article by Jorge Arangurá Jr. and Luke Cyphers for *ESPN Magazine*: "A decade of scandals has spawned a sequel, a horror movie beset with villains called buscones: middlemen in a festering, corrupt hellhole who lie about players' ages, keep them out of school, inject them with animal steroids, then take most of their signing bonuses, sometimes without their knowledge."[4] Many North American writers paint buscones with this broad brush, associating them with the unseemly and the crooked—and, most important, the unregulated.

As I discussed in Chapter 3, the incident that crystallized North American views of buscones involved the baseball player Willy Aybar and Enrique Soto, the man who developed him and, allegedly, took advantage of him by making off with almost half of his signing bonus. This case provided both a template for the future demonizing of buscones and justification for MLB's increased efforts to control baseball in the Dominican Republic.

Buscón Bashing

Willy Aybar, a sixteen-year-old Dominican from the town of Baní, signed with the Los Angeles Dodgers in 2000 for what was then the astounding sum of $1.4 million.[5] At the time, there had been only a few seven-figure signings in the Dominican Republic, so the news spread quickly through the country's baseball community, as well as through the offices of the major league teams.

The Dominican Republic's most successful buscón, Enrique Soto, had developed Aybar. For his efforts, he was to get 25–35 percent of the bonus. The Dodgers deducted 30 percent ($420,000) for U.S. income taxes, in accordance with MLB's guidelines, then wrote two checks ($490,000 each) to be given to Aybar. This is where the situation took a bad turn. Following MLB protocols, Luchy Guerra, an administrator with the Dodgers, called Aybar to ask him where to send the first check. Aybar has said that he told Guerra to send it to his American agent, Rob Plummer, who would forward it to Soto.

Then Soto would hold on to it until Aybar returned to the DR. (Aybar's parents were bypassed because they knew nothing about banks.) Guerra, however, claims that she sent the check directly to Aybar at the Dodgers' spring training complex in Florida and does not know how it got to Soto. However the $490,000 check reached Soto, it was subsequently deposited in his bank account. Although it did contain two endorsements—Aybar's and Soto's—Aybar has denied that he signed it, and Guerra has noted that Aybar's signature does not match the one on his contract, which he signed in front of the Dodgers' administrators, and both signatures on the check "appear to be the same handwriting."[6]

Aybar has said that he wanted Soto to oversee the money until he returned to the DR. Once the bonus was under his control, Soto gave Aybar's mother a lump sum of 100,000 pesos ($6,250) and a monthly allowance of just under $2,000. Plummer received a check for $35,000 for his role in overseeing the signing (plus repayment of a $10,000 loan he made to Soto). The rest—about $430,000—Soto is alleged to have kept. Aybar claims to have received nothing from the first check. Aybar confronted Soto that Christmas in the DR and claims he was told, "Money? I don't have any money."[7] The second check, also for $490,000, was given to—and kept by—Aybar.

Deconstructing the Case

Steve Fainaru broke the Aybar-Soto story in the *Washington Post* in 2001, and his article still includes its most thorough discussion.[8] Virtually everyone who discusses this case cites his examination. There is no doubt that Fainaru intended to write a conscientious piece that both defended a vulnerable young man who had been badly taken advantage of and lashed out at the culprit who appeared to have victimized him, and to some extent, he did. Yet the article has also given rise to a disturbing larger view of Dominicans that I term "progressive ethnocentrism."[9] This form of ethnocentrism emanates (ironically) from progressive political leanings but nevertheless results in ethnocentric error. It most likely reflects differences of class and culture. When he wrote the story, Fainaru was positioned to interpret the events as a middle-class, white American (not a poor, mulatto Dominican). Anthropologists make much of the notion of "place," which includes the social and cultural position of an author. One's social status can affect one's views and ability to interpret events on the ground, potentially clouding rather than clarifying. Fainaru was not wrong to fault Soto for what certainly looks like an instance of theft (or, at the very least, inappropriate handling of the money), but he erred in fusing his portrayal of Soto with that of all buscones and thereby inadvertently denigrating Dominicans in general.

Fainaru's sole attempt to provide a balanced view of buscones—and thereby isolate Soto's actions from those of others—begins positively and ends negatively: "In many cases, the buscones . . . are above-board coaches who spend considerable time and resources to support athletes, but their growth has been accompanied by reports of over-charging, extortion and outright theft."[10] Almost everything that precedes and follows this sentence maligns trainers and swamps the attempt to achieve balance. Treating buscones (via Soto) as brigands or street hustlers situated on the margins of mainstream Dominican life and baseball misplaces them. As Chapter 4 showed, player developers sit at the structural core, rather than at the margins, of contemporary Dominican baseball.

Fainaru's article takes the buscón-as-hustler theme as a launching point from which buscones can never be redeemed. He introduces Soto (and thus buscones in general) using the following words: "Enrique Soto *speculates* in infielders. He drives his big green pickup through the dust-coated streets, stopping near the vacant lots, near the playgrounds, near the dirt fields filled with kids playing baseball."[11] Note the menacing tones that evoke trolling cities and towns in search of kids—almost as if Fainaru is describing a pedophile rather than a serious developer of talented young Dominican ballplayers.

Like Fagin in Charles Dickens's *Oliver Twist*, Soto is shown to be extremely successful at finding boys who are young enough to mold into the kind of players to whom MLB will pay significant signing bonuses. "[Soto] said he looks for pliant boys who abstain from wearing jewelry 'because that's a sign they're not thinking the right way,'" Fainaru writes.[12] Fainaru also portrays Soto's efforts to mold players as somewhat callous and distant—not unlike those of a farmer raising a hog for market. For example, Fainaru describes "a tiny, reed-thin boy wearing red, white and blue shorts" who inspires Soto to say, "See this? . . . This is what Willy Aybar looked like when I got him. So you can see: To develop a kid so he can sign is a very big investment for me."[13]

Fainaru also paints Soto as a predatory Fagin rather than as a legitimate talent developer when he describes Aybar's signing with the Dodgers: "Soto had prepared for this moment. Knowing that Aybar couldn't write, he had given his player a pencil and notebook and taught him how to write his name. For weeks before the signing, Aybar hunched over his notebook, his fingers cramped around his shrinking pencil."[14] Fainaru's repeated decisions to go for drama instead of straightforward reportage not only detract from the power of the story but also end up painting with such a broad cultural brush that one can no longer see Soto as one kind of trainer, and the signing as one kind of event, among many.

Further clouding the Soto equals buscones (and Dominicans in general) equation is the disjuncture in how MLB's representatives perceived Soto and how Dominicans themselves have understood him. Dominicans are not naïve, and many no doubt believe that Soto played fast and loose with Aybar's bonus. That said, however, they have not shunned him as a thief or portrayed him as morally reprehensible. If anything, they admire his successes, and he has become even more desirable as a developer who can get significant signing bonuses for their sons. And in some cases, Dominicans have blamed Aybar, rather than Soto, for his lack of savvy in these dealings.

But what might the reader of Fainaru's article conclude about the cultural context for a man such as Soto? As skillfully written as it is, the piece can still be interpreted as portraying the DR as a banana republic—that is, as a struggling nation void of moral bearings, with an inept, corrupt government that looks the other way while its ignorant people become easy prey for those who want to take advantage of them. In short, it confirms the view that the Dominican Republic is in fact the "Wild West" that some have called it, and in need of U.S. intervention.[15]

Dominicans Overlook the "Thief"

As noted above, despite the Aybar case (or, perhaps, because of it), many hopeful Dominican players and their families see Soto not as a criminal but as someone who cares enough to train, board, and care for their sons for years in a world where simply eating three meals a day is problematic. Such long-term involvement often translates into surrogate father-son relationships between buscones and players, who often lack active fathers. Viewed from an American social and cultural distance, Soto's behavior may look more like pimping than genuine concern, as illustrated in Fainaru's conflation of Soto the man with Soto the manipulative buscón. Ironically, Fainaru's strategy of ostensibly attacking the culprit (i.e., Soto the buscón) and defending the victim is turned on its head in the Dominican context: In the DR, Soto the man may be suspect but Soto the buscón certainly is not shunned.

Soto's defenders are quick to point out that the Aybar case was a rush to judgment on the part of the American media. The first of Aybar's two checks, according to Soto's allies, represented no more than the commission to which he was entitled. "He was getting 35 percent," an informant told me. "Do the math: 35 percent of $1.4 million is $400,000." The informant also said that Soto had paid for surgery for Aybar's mother before the signing, "so he took his share, no more."[16] In other words, according to this informant, Soto was entitled to his cut before taxes and other repayments. One would also think Aybar would have hard feelings, but he and Soto reportedly have remained friends. "Not long ago, Enrique needed $30,000, and it was Aybar who gave it to him, no questions asked," the same informant told me. "That doesn't happen if you steal from a guy."[17]

In all of its turns and twists, the Aybar-Soto case reads like a soap opera, prompting one to ask whether Soto realizes that he is responsible for sullying not only his own reputation but, indirectly, that of most buscones—at least in the United States. It is possible that Soto does not really care what we, in the United States, think. In the final analysis, he will no doubt continue to succeed, regardless of the sideshow he tends to provide.

Identity Fraud as a Dominican "Problem"

Identity fraud in Dominican baseball generally consists of altering birthdates and identities in the official documents submitted to MLB teams by prospects they intend to sign. It is a long-standing practice spawned, as pointed out in the discussion of the informal economy, by lack of access to legitimacy and economic opportunity. A crackdown on Dominican players' falsifying their identities was triggered directly by the events of September 11, 2001, and the U.S. State Department's more stringent visa regulations. Between 2003 and 2008, the percentage of Dominicans who were caught in identity fraud ranged from a low of 25 percent to a high of 43 percent.[18] MLB responded quickly to heightened State Department demands and has now invested heavily in eradicating identity fraud, which it considers a "Dominican problem."

Although the identity fraud issue results, in part, from Dominican-U.S. relations, it is certainly not a "Dominican" problem so much as a problem with Americans' dissatisfaction with Dominicans. In other words, MLB does not believe that the Dominicans (in Rob Manfred's terms) are being "helpful" enough.

Steven Gregory's study of Dominicans working in the informal sector of the tourist industry goes a long way toward providing context for this issue. "It was not uncommon for persons' identities to be publicly in dispute, ambiguous and shot through with contradictions," he writes. "In a sociopolitical milieu where full citizenship rights were difficult to achieve, subject to recurrent verification and at risk of being diminished and even negated, much was at stake in whom people were believed to be."[19] In baseball, identity fraud is very specific. Although there are scattered instances of young players claiming they are older to meet the minimum signing age (sixteen and a half), almost all cases involve older players trying to pass as younger.

Altering one's documents; obtaining new, false documents; and taking over a younger person's birth certificate are all fairly easy to do in the Dominican Republic. Compounding the problem is an antiquated record-keeping system (only recently computerized) in which vital information often exists in only handwritten form. Many poor people, for instance, do not register births of children with the state until years after the fact, a phenomenon referred to as "late declaration." One scout informed me that he had a player who was disqualified when the late declaration his parents provided in 2009, just before he signed with a team, was found to be false.[20]

Rafael Pérez, heads of the MLB Commissioner's Office in Santo Domingo, described the ease with which birthdates can be altered:

> Before 1998, what you found was that a player who wanted to lower his age would go to a friend who worked in a government office [in the Dominican Republic] and say, "Hey, just don't put that I was born in [a certain year]." When they [MLB] implemented the first verification program in 1998, suddenly there was an increase in late declarations. They don't record the birth right away. They go to another city and come up with false supporting documents to be able to get a late declaration, two or three years later, so when you go to the books, everything seems to be in order.[21]

As MLB and the State Department ratcheted up their efforts to verify the identities of foreigners coming into the United States, Dominicans' documents came under more thorough scrutiny. MLB and the State Department "clamped down, and together we found that 90 percent of late declarations were false," Pérez said. "Then they started using their brothers' IDs. They're using their friends' birth certificates. We have cases of buscones going to New York graveyards looking for kids who died around the age they're looking for, and they get the birth certificate."[22] In one case, a young boy who was approached by a scout to begin arranging for tryouts said, "I can't sign because I've been released." The scout was incredulous. "What do you mean 'released'?" he said. "You're a kid [too young to have been signed and released]." The boy answered, "My mother lent my birth certificate to my cousin. He signed and then got released, so now I'm him, he's me, and I've been released."[23]

In the two years following the September 11 attacks, MLB found 550 cases of identity fraud, and 99 percent of them were Dominican.[24] In some cases, almost no care had been taken to avoid detection, as when it was discovered that the San Diego Padres had a twenty-four-year-old minor league player named Isabel Giron. His documentation turned out to belong to his sister. He was twenty-nine, wanted to sign as a younger player, and apparently figured that, when it came to gendered names, the gringos would not know the difference. He was right, at least for a time.[25]

Other attempts to commit identity fraud are more calculated—none more so than the Washington Nationals' signing in 2006 of sixteen-year-old Esmailyn Gonzalez with a $1.4 million bonus. Like too many others, that deal was flawed because Gonzalez was neither sixteen nor "Esmailyn." He was twenty-year-old Carlos Alvarez Lugo. What set this case of identity fraud apart was the elaborate nature of the scheme and how it affected the team. "There were a number of people involved in it," Stan Kasten, president of the Nationals, said. "Falsified hospital documents. Falsified school documents. Other family members changing their identities. Bribes were paid. Really elaborate stuff."[26]

Sixteen Is the New Eighteen

Despite the serious punishments handed out for identity fraud and the large number of Dominican players who have been caught since 2001, significant numbers of prospects are still willing to attempt it. Driving this is a combination of desperation, ignorance, and street-smart responses to MLB's decision to skew the market in favor of young talent. The desire to sign sixteen-year-olds rests on the socio-physiological theory that Latin Americans players take longer than their North American counterparts to "mature," and it has fueled MLB's willingness to pay more for younger players.

Although MLB believed this to be true early in the academy era, it took time for it to evolve into policy. For instance, early in his tenure as the Dodgers' point man in the Dominican Republic, Ralph Avila observed a need to bring Dominicans up to physical and cultural par with Americans:

In 1975, I sent Al Campanis [the Dodgers' general manager] a report on all of the problems that, in my opinion, Latin players were gonna face when they came to the United States. I was scouting international tournaments and saw strong Dominican teams. It was clear that they had great players. Then I saw that these players come to the United States and get released. I started taking notes and talking to players and decided that 99 percent of the time, Dominican players [were getting] released for lack of education and bad work habits.

They need time to be taught what they need to succeed in the United States and get on the same level as the Americans.[27]

In other words, Avila saw a need for the Dominican players to make cultural adjustments. Today his views are widely accepted as protocol for all teams. Juan Henderson, director of the Mets Dominican Baseball Academy, noted the impact remedial cultural education has had on Dominican rookies: "It makes them able to listen to coaches. They can focus on instructions longer; they get more disciplined, and that's something they didn't have much of coming in."[28] John Seibel, a consultant to MLB and a longtime resident of the Dominican Republic, similarly observed: "One of the biggest breakthroughs has been that the Dominican athlete matures at a much later age than his North American counterpart. Down here, the first professional socialization they get is at the academy with keeping schedules [and] obeying rules, and this has been approved all the way up."[29]

For the most part, when Dominican players think about being promoted to the rookie leagues in Florida, they are not concerned so much with cultural remediation as with playing baseball at a more competitive level. One rookie player flatly stated, "I know we're as good as the American guys, maybe even better, but we have to show the coaches."[30] Even if the players do not completely buy into the need for remediation, however, the academies and the minor leagues are built around it. So before they can accept remediation, however grudgingly, Dominicans players must face the daunting challenge of getting signed, and that is the market driven by sixteen-year-olds.

It strains credulity to believe that an eighteen-year-old baseball player is losing value by the month. Yet few place the blame where it belongs: squarely on MLB's decision to put the highest value on the legally youngest Dominican players. The older a person is, the lower the individual's value in this market. Further, this policy does not even apply to all Latin American players. Cubans, for instance, can sign for enormous bonuses without being age straitjacketed. "The Cuban can come [to the DR] and be thirty years old, and they'll give him all the money in the world," Astín Jacobo said. "And our kids? Once he's past eighteen, they don't wanna give him a penny. . . . [W]hen a Dominican's nineteen, he's old."[31] Joel Peralta, a pitcher with the Tampa Bay Rays, claimed he was sixteen and a half when he signed, though he was actually twenty. "I wish I never had to do that, but if I didn't do it I wouldn't be here," he says. "We don't have the chance after [we] turn 18, 19 years old to become a professional ballplayer. . . . [H]ere in the United States, [players] can be drafted when they're 22, they get a chance to play pro ball.

We don't have that. The only chance when you're 20, like I was, to sign was to lie about your age."[32]

While MLB may not intentionally have skewed the market toward young players, a cultural view within the organization combined with particular conditions of competition and opportunity have fostered an environment in which sixteen-year-old Dominicans have a decided advantage. Identity fraud, from the Dominican perspective, is just one available strategy to respond to this market and find a place within it.

If the MLB Shoe Fits, Wear It

Whether it be falsifying documents by players or skirting strict governmental regulations on who can and cannot work with tourists, in Gregory's study many Dominicans willingly risk detection and punishment out of their need to survive in a climate that has excluded them. For MLB and others, however, identity fraud is proof of an inherent "problem" with Dominicans.

Major League Baseball, claiming to understand the "problem," has found fault with Dominicans both individually and collectively by characterizing identity falsification as a cultural shortcoming. It is common for North Americans to feel that the sixteen-year-olds they see playing baseball in the DR should be going to school or getting more practical training (see Chapter 2). That, after all, is what sixteen-year-olds do in the United States. At the same time, however, scouts for MLB teams are well aware that they benefit when education is not privileged over baseball in these Dominican youths' lives. Major league teams thus have pursued a public strategy of lamenting young Dominican players' lack of educational opportunity while privately enjoying the bounty that it creates and seeking a scapegoat for the problem.

Buscones, as discussed in Chapter 4, have taken the greatest share of the blame. Take, for example, Jose Ortiz's analysis in *USA Today*: "At the root of the problem are the largely unregulated buscones, . . . some of whom have been accused of regularly misrepresenting players' ages, furnishing them with steroids and scamming to extract large portions of their signing bonuses, sometimes in conjunction with major league team employees."[33] Jeff Passan put it in even stronger terms for the Yahoo! Sports website: "For years, hustlers and pimps have taken advantage of impoverished and undereducated children while Major League Baseball allowed the entire racket to continue. . . . [D]ozens of bad seeds litter Dominican ball fields, happy to change a boy's name or pump him with performance enhancing drugs to secure a larger signing bonus."[34] The press has also blamed Dominican parents blinded by the chance that their sons will save the family with baseball earnings and, more generally, the lack of emphasis on education as the route to economic opportunity in the DR. The point is that in almost all instances, the problems are being framed as shortcomings in the Dominican culture or character. As John Mirabelli, assistant general manager of scouting operations for the Cleveland Indians, summarized the situation: "Nothing really seems to have acted as a deterrent, because it keeps on happening—the false ages, the false identities. So I think that's going to be [the] biggest challenge, . . . changing a culture. It's hard to do anywhere."[35]

Dominicans and Steroids

On July 10, 2001, Lino Ortíz, a nineteen-year-old baseball prospect, prepared for a tryout by injecting himself with a veterinary steroid. He died three days later. Three months earlier, another prospect, William Felix, had also died after using veterinary substances for several months.[36] But a search for real meaning would take a turn that most reporters, at best, only partially grasp. As Fainaru reported for the *Washington Post*, American athletes' fascination with steroids appears to have spread to the Dominican Republic. Fainaru correctly identified the root of the problem as grinding poverty in the DR, writing, "The deaths seemed to underscore the desperation that is the context for baseball in the Dominican Republic."[37] However, he then turned almost immediately to the familiar straw men—buscones—to place the blame: "The system that produced [the buscones] is rife with corruption and exploitation, according to baseball officials and scouts. . . . Because many prospects are malnourished, street agents often provide supplements. . . . [T]he growing use of veterinary substances is an extension of this practice, according to scouts and coaches."[38]

Fainaru certainly is not alone in this belief, as seen in Geoff Baker's account, published two years later in the *Toronto Star*: "[Veterinary] substances are legal [in the DR], sold over the counter in pharmacies and pet stores and given to players as young as 13 by parents and gurus alike, freelance street agents—known as buscones."[39] Without doubt, some buscones do encourage their charges to use steroid-like products. But there is no evidence to support the idea that players gain access to performance-enhancing substances overwhelmingly, or even predominantly, through buscones. Nor does Fainaru provide any evidence to show that Dominicans are taking steroids or steroid-like substances in great numbers. Instead, he relies on anecdotes and guesses. "Put down 99.9999 percent," he quotes an unnamed player as saying.[40]

Since Fainaru's article was published, MLB has released information showing that Dominican players are testing positive for banned substances at a higher rate than U.S. players. In 2008, for instance, 22 out of 1,000 Dominicans (.02 percent) playing in the Dominican Summer League tested positive, compared with 7 out of 4,000 (.002 percent) in the U.S. minor leagues.[41] While acknowledging that steroids are used more widely by Dominican prospects and players, I also want to note that 988 of 1,000 (98.8 percent) of the Dominican rookies tested refrained from using steroids—a figure that, by my reckoning, falls short of an "epidemic," not to mention the unnamed insider's claim of "99.999 percent" using performance-enhancing drugs. Still, determining why steroids are used as much as they are may lead to figuring out who is really promoting them, which, in turn, may lead to new insights into the issue.

Rather than viewing steroid use as a "Dominican problem," it might be more enlightening to place it within a Dominican context that normalizes it. Although most accounts of Dominican baseball mention the poverty that the overwhelming majority of players experience, they do so in the context of trying to explain why those players violate MLB rules and even U.S. State Department regulations.[42] They generally fall well short of portraying the conditions in a way that evokes real understanding or empathy—that is, that leads readers to ask themselves what they might do in similar circumstances.[43]

Dominicans could not help but notice the irony of the 2008 hearings held in Washington, D.C., to look into the use of performance-enhancing drugs by MLB players. The director of a major league academy in the DR commented, "I laughed! Here they are going after [the Cuban] Rafael Palmero for taking performance-enhancing drugs, and I'll bet that most of those old senators take Viagra."[44] This raises a very interesting point: Performance enhancement is situationally, not to mention culturally, relative. What makes prescribing performance-enhancing substances acceptable in one context and illegal in another? Is health really the primary concern behind legislating such substances' use? To my knowledge, no scientific study has linked the ability to maintain erections to longevity in men. Even in the medical context of hormone replacement therapy for men, what is the difference between aging men's and athletes' use of testosterone? Are there reasons that go beyond "enhanced performance"? Health risks certainly are associated with testosterone use for both aging men and young athletes, yet older men are free to ask their physicians to prescribe steroids to enhance their sexual performance and address other such "quality-of-life" issues.

Further, the U.S. and Latin America take different institutional approaches to prescription versus over-the-counter drugs. For example, a much wider range of medication can be purchased over the counter in Latin America than in the United States, and a range of veterinary steroids are legally available at pet stores. When the journalist Tom Farrey said "anabolic" during a visit to a pharmacy in Santo Domingo, a young clerk held up a bottle of Anotesten (based on a steroid precursor) saying, "This is what our baseball players buy." She also sold concoctions that mask the presence of these steroids.[45] From the Dominican perspective, U.S. law restricting access to so much medicine must seem not only unnecessary and but also frightening.

Latin America's more permissive culture regarding access to medicine socializes young people to regard some drugs that are strictly controlled in the United States as fine for normal consumption. Further, given their low level of education, most Dominican ballplayers are not willing to wade through MLB's lists of and pronouncements about "banned substances. Many Dominican players who have tested positive for performance-enhancing substances have declared that they did not knowingly take anything. I believe they are telling the truth. The recent rounds of testing have also caught players who were well aware of MLB's policies and who eschewed drugs.[46] One example is David Ortiz of the Red Sox. He was incensed in 2007 when a Boston newspaper printed a defamatory headline saying he had tested positive for a banned substance in 2003. Two years later, in the wake of the BALCO Investigation—the federal probe into steroid use by the MLB player Barry Bonds that netted the names of more than one hundred players who had tested positive for banned substances—the names from MLB's survey testing in 2003 were leaked to the press, and Ortiz found out that he had in fact tested positive.

Ortiz emphatically denied any wrongdoing but acknowledged that in his homeland, the Dominican Republic, the regulations concerning illegal and legal (over-the-counter) medications are different from those in the United States. Ever forthright, Ortiz somberly acknowledged, "You've got to be careful. I used to buy a protein shake in my country. I don't do that anymore because they don't have the approval for that here. . . . I don't know if I drank something in my youth [without] knowing it."[47] Michael Weiner, general counsel to the MLB Players Association, has noted that in the 2003 tests, "legally available nutritional supplements could trigger an initial 'positive' [reading]."[48] For this reason, the Dominican government refused to punish players who tested positive for substances that were legal in their country—not only a clear-cut refusal to comply with MLB but also a declaration of cultural difference and sovereignty.

Thus, the use of banned substances is a contested issue. But MLB has the transnational authority to trump Dominican culture and practice. When Dominicans refuse to comply with North American mores and practices, they are further demonized.

How Scandals Become "Dominican"

"It always seems like it's something in the Dominican [Republic]. Every year there is a new story, new problem or new controversy."[49] No single issue creates the impression for the American public that Dominican baseball and the Dominican people are tainted. Rather, a mosaic of interpretations of constructed "infractions" lead people to draw that conclusion. "The revelations [of yet another scandal] underscore the Dominican baseball scene's reputation as a lawless Wild West landscape with little oversight."[50] How Dominicans become equated with "illicitness" is made very clear in three additional depictions of the anthropology of difference: cases of fraudulent marriages; a misunderstanding based in U.S. Little League; and kickback scandals involving MLB.

Fraudulent Marriages

In March 2005, ten Dominican minor leaguers were caught participating in what turned out to be a fraudulent marriage scheme. In a post-9/11 world, this kind of machination can and did invoke the ire of U.S. immigration officials, who permanently banned the players from receiving that lifeline of foreign players: a U.S. visa.[51] Twenty more players were under investigation for a scheme that alleged they had been paid $5,000–$7,000 to marry Dominican women. The women would then receive visas as players' wives, which would allow them to immigrate, then file for divorce once they reached the United States. The players wanted the money; the women wanted entry into the United States or, possibly, the chance to resell their visas on the black market.

While these violations outraged U.S. officials, the Dominicans involved saw them only as another means to a desired end. "Every Dominican has a tail that can be stepped on" is an old adage meaning that Dominicans routinely violate rules.[52] This difference in interpreting the law reveals the gulf between the two cultures. For Americans, law breaking is part and parcel of understanding Dominicans as problematic. "Another year, another Dominican visa scandal," in fact, is how John Manuel and Chris Kline led their article about the fake marriage scheme.[53] Dominicans, by contrast, view such incidents as legitimate strategies used to thread one's way through a legal system that prevents people from entering in a straightforward fashion. The buscón Amaurys Nina told me a story that illustrates how most Dominicans feel about skirting the law by interpreting it in ways that allows them to gain entry and thus survive: "During [a] World Series, [a friend who scouts for a major league team] got free tickets from the [team]. He sold them for $2,000, and when the team found out, they fired him. He did something illegal. He said to me, 'What am I gonna do? I could feed my family for three months with that money.'"[54] "What am I gonna do?" is, of course, a rhetorical question whose answer is never in doubt.

Nina interpreted his friend's action within the context of the moral economy: "Pay people enough to live on, and they will not have to do wrong things."[55] Here is another way to think about this: Is the law being broken intentionally for private gain based not on need or social considerations? Or is it being broken inadvertently or on the basis of what the person perceives as a higher, more ethical need or social outcome?

A Little (League) Misunderstanding

Danny Almonte has become a footnote in Little League baseball history. As a twelve-year-old pitcher, he threw the first no-hitter in forty years of Little League World Series history for his 2001 Bronx team. He followed the no-hitter with two more victories, allowing a total of three hits in three games. The public fell in love with the Dominican-born wonder. All that public scrutiny, however, opened the door for others who were not so positively disposed to raise questions about Almonte's age. In short order, the truth was revealed: Almonte was not twelve but fourteen. His team was stripped of its victories, and the public soured on him, ruining him as a youth icon. Rolando Paulino, the founder of the predominantly Dominican Little League in the Bronx in which Almonte played, and Almonte's father, Felipe, were banned from the league for life.

Why would a child engage in such deception—and in Little League, of all places? The media and other parties quickly determined that Almonte had been victimized. "Clearly," wrote Robert McFadden in the *New York Times*, "adults have used Danny Almonte in a most contemptible and despicable way."[56] Even President George W. Bush felt obligated to weigh in, commenting, "I'm disappointed that adults would fudge the boy's age. I wasn't disappointed in his fastball and slider. The guy is awesome."[57]

For a time, Almonte considered going back to the Dominican Republic, but he opted instead to stay with Paulino in the Bronx. His father, however, did return to the DR, partly because charges were pending against him there that required his presence. The Little League incident has become a cultural Rorschach test of sorts, and most of the U.S. media has rushed to interpret it as a tawdry affair that besmirches the reputations of all Dominicans. A notable exception is Paul Dougherty, who, with some cultural sensitivity, has pointed out that the Almontes are not monsters. "The Almontes are not from some leafy suburb where the ice cream truck makes regular stops and every kid has a clean uniform for every game," he wrote. "There isn't a chemistry book beneath their pillows, if they have pillows, which sometimes they don't."[58]

Americans saw the Almonte case as a scandal. Dominicans in both the United States and the Dominican Republic, however, interpreted it quite differently. Many were quietly uneasy about the bad press that was generated, fearing that it fueled anti-Dominican sentiment. Peeved about how easily and quickly Almonte was judged deviant, the Dominican superstar Pedro Martínez stated, "If he was from America, that kid would probably be . . . getting a little medal from George Bush. Now all of a sudden because the kid's from the Dominican [Republic], he's not legal."[59] While Dominicans understood that Almonte's age had been deliberately altered, they also accepted the circumstances that framed his case and viewed Paulino as having done only what other institutions all over the United States and the Dominican Republic do: work the system to win.

When Almonte's Little League team returned to the Bronx after being roundly criticized by the media, the players were greeted by thousands of supporters chanting "Danny! Danny!" One carried a sign that defiantly proclaimed, "12 or 14—So What?"[60] In the Dominican town of Moca, where Almonte's mother lived, people chanted, "Doce! Doce!" (Twelve! Twelve!), and his mother continued to insist that her son was twelve.[61] The records, however, showed conclusively that Almonte was fourteen. Why would people persist in lying publicly? Dominican nationalism may have played a role: Danny Almonte was one of them, and that may have mattered far more to Dominicans than how old he was. As one teenage boy boldly declared, "I don't care whether Danny changed his age. He's still my hero. I would do it, too, if it [got] me to the major leagues."[62]

Once again, an explanation can be found in the lure of a professional baseball career, which is so strong and so grounded in ordinary Dominicans' experience with want that it constitutes not simply a lifeline but, for the very poor, the only real chance for economic survival. The potential payoff is so large that it both defies comprehension and justifies any risk. Chanting a lie, in such cases, is akin to waving one's flag in the face of an enemy.

When the press disclosed that Almonte was not enrolled in school until almost a year after he arrived in the Bronx, some Americans felt that his father should be charged with negligence. Asked what his son was doing during school hours, the father matter-of-factly declared, "He has been eating. . . . and he's been playing ball."[63] The comment outraged many Americans, yet in the DR that response would have earned him kudos as a great parent.

But because Danny Almonte transgressed in the United States rather than in the Dominican Republic, and because he did so within one of baseball's iconic venues—Little League baseball—the temptation to externalize the blame to Dominicans simply proved too strong.

Kickback Scandals

In 2009, the Chicago White Sox executive Dave Wilder was arrested at Chicago O'Hare International Airport with $40,000 in cash that he had failed to declare when he entered the United States from the Dominican Republic. This touched off yet another scandal related to Dominican baseball. The $40,000 turned out to be Wilder's share in a kickback scheme in which a Dominican prospect was told he was being signed for one figure (e.g., $50,000) while the team was given a higher number (e.g., $70,000). The team would then pay the higher amount, and Wilder and others in the scheme would pocket the difference.

Major League Baseball immediately launched an investigation that uncovered more infractions. Employees of two other teams—the New York Yankees and the Boston Red Sox—were found to have received money inappropriately from rookies' signing bonuses, and they, like Wilder, were fired. The most serious consequences, however, befell the Washington Nationals, where the issue of kickbacks was conflated with that of identity fraud in the form of the Esmailyn Gonzalez/Carlos Alvarez Lugo case discussed earlier in the chapter.

José Rijo, a special assistant to the Nationals' general manager and the head of the team's Dominican academy, came under federal investigation for taking kickbacks. As it turned out, Rijo was also responsible for having signed Gonzalez. Rijo was not a low-level MLB functionary. As a player, he had been a star, helping the Cincinnati Reds win the World Series in 1990. He was also married to the daughter of Hall of Famer Juan Marichal. Although Rijo was never formally charged with committing a crime, the botched Gonzalez signing combined with innuendos about kickbacks made it easy for the Nationals to decide to dismiss him. General Manager Jim Bowden, who had strong ties to Rijo, also was not charged but chose to resign.

Although these kickback scandals, both proven and alleged, clearly are centered in MLB, the media has drawn cultural connections to the Dominican Republic. For instance, in the middle of reporting on the Nationals' problem, a *New York Times* article says, "At the heart of the issue are local talent brokers known as buscones, who have close ties to government and who sign players as young as 10 to contracts in the hopes of later cashing in."[64]

Another article states, "The recent escalation of bonuses that teams are paying in Latin America has made it easier and more profitable to skim money from players and teams. . . . Dominican scouts, known on the island as buscones, or 'searchers,' have been doing that for at least a decade."[65] In other words, Dominicans, not Americans, are the reason MLB employees violate their own organization's rules.

Wilder was caught red-handed in such an egregious case of rules violation that it could not be ignored, yet the reporting once again ended up in the realm of "Dominican corruption." The sports super-agent Scott Boras was embroiled in a similar case. In 2006, Boras entered an agreement to represent the fifteen-year-old Dominican baseball player Edward Salcedo and gave Salcedo's family $70,000 over the next three years. As one sports lawyer has pointed out, this kind of relationship can be dangerous because it "gives the agent leverage, and coerces the athlete to do what the agent wants because of fear of foreclosure."[66] The arrangement also violated the rules of the MLB Players Association, which, as Michael Schmidt reported in the *New York Times*, could "levy penalties [for such rules violations] ranging from a fine to revoking an agent's right to represent players."[67]

Interestingly, Boras himself interpreted the situation quite differently: He felt that he was simply helping someone in need. One of his affiliates characterized the transaction as nothing more "helping the kid out and retain[ing] him as a client."[68] This attitude is much closer to what one would hear from many Dominicans, who consider social relations and concern to be on par with the letter of the law. The difference is that when a successful American such as Boras uses this justification, he is viewed as concerned, whereas when a Dominican uses it, it tends only to confirm his culpability.

Conclusion

Today, many young people connect "Banana Republic" with a trendy clothing store. However, it originally applied to nations with mono-crop economies, unstable and undemocratic governments, and abundant foreign interference. The Dominican Republic has often been considered a classic example of the banana republic, largely because of the long and brutal reign of the dictator Rafael Leonidas Trujillo Molina (1930–1961). As a trope, "banana republic" has also continued to be associated with Dominican baseball.

The top of any hierarchy—whether it is a corporation, a government, or MLB—sets norms, conventions, and laws in the expectation that those with which it engages (citizens, employees, and so on) will comply. Noncompliance is viewed as a violation of those norms or laws, and for Americans, this is often further interpreted as proof of legal and moral turpitude. The view from the bottom (in this case, the Dominican Republic) is quite different: There, laws must be viewed as rough guidelines that are open to negotiation, and violating these laws marks effective avenues of engagement with (in this instance) American practices and policies.

Identity fraud, marriage schemes, steroid use, and other so-called Dominican baseball scandals thus are better understood when viewed as rational responses by Dominicans (as subalterns) than as instances of willful cheating for personal gain. The Scottish psychiatrist R. D. Laing famously characterized insanity as "a perfectly rational adjustment to an insane world."[69] In the same vein, Dominican baseball "problems" may just be perfectly rational adjustments to an irrational system.

6

"It Felt like the Marines All Over Again"

The Battle for Dominican Baseball

Astín Jacobo's comment "It felt like the Marines all over again" is an appropriate title for this chapter because it is how he (and others) chose to characterize the arrival of Sandy Alderson, point man for the MLB Commissioner's Office, in the Dominican Republic in April 2010. Alderson had been sent to rid the Dominican Republic of what U.S. baseball officials had come to perceive as a host of problems sullying the sport. Back in the US, at the same time, many Americans were growing weary of the ongoing wars in Afghanistan and Iraq and disenchanted with invading other countries. Yet in a policy and institutional way, MLB was invading the DR without a hint of public outrage. In place of "weapons of mass destruction" as a rationale for the invasion, MLB was using the host of problems that seem to be rampant in the DR.

This chapter examines some of the attempts by MLB to rationalize Dominican baseball to make it a more workable part of the global commodity chain. It also highlights instructive attempts, by Dominicans and others, to resist and thereby change the dynamics of the commodity chain.

The MLB Invasion: Threats and Public Posturing

As I mentioned in the Introduction, U.S. Marines invaded and occupied the Dominican Republic twice in the twentieth century: the first time for eight years (1916–1924), and the second time for one year (1965–1966). Both were invasions in the fullest sense of the word, and most Dominicans I have spoken with—regardless of where they stand on the reasons behind the invasions—felt that the Marines were an unwelcome occupying force. In both instances, there was considerable Dominican resistance to the foreigners. The historian Bruce Calder's *The Impact of Intervention*, which chronicles the U.S. occupation of the Dominican Republic in 1916, offers a compelling portrait of an entrenched guerrilla war in the eastern half of the country.[1] The 1965 occupation, in which resistance was more diffuse, still piled up thousands of Dominican casualties.

The invasions illustrate both U.S. presumption (i.e., that it has a right to intrude in sovereign Dominican space) and the Dominican will to resist. The former is predicated on the entrenched and dominant U.S. economic presence in the DR, backed by foreign policy; the latter speaks to the range of ways Dominicans respond. The past quarter-century has seen simultaneous deepening of U.S. (MLB) control over Dominican baseball and increased ability of Dominicans to find ways to assert their will in what has been a one-sided relationship.

The "Marine" Lands: Sandy Alderson

By 2009, MLB Commissioner Bud Selig had grown contemptuous of how Dominicans were conducting their baseball affairs. He tapped Sandy Alderson to deal with the problems that he felt were hindering the development of baseball in the DR and embarrassing MLB. At first glance, Alderson, one of the game's most respected figures, seemed like a sound choice. He is a former Marine infantry officer who did a tour of duty in Vietnam, went on to Harvard Law School, and then entered baseball, where he served as a general manager and, later, as Selig's executive vice-president for baseball operations. Together with several other top-level baseball administrators, Alderson studied the issue for a year. Although he was well versed in international baseball issues from his years in the front office of the Oakland Athletics and was one of MLB's most powerful figures, working on the ground in the DR requires more than experience, intellect, and fortitude. It also requires a sense of awareness, subtlety, and patience worthy of the best U.S. State Department personnel. And most important, it requires guarding against exhibiting hubris (however unintentional).

Alderson tends to live in a clearly demarcated world of black and white; he favors incisiveness over nuance, a trait others have noted. Billy Beane, who worked for Alderson when Alderson ran the As in the 1990s, has characterized him as follows: "[Alderson has] always had a moral compass which guides all his decisions. There's a right way to go about your business and a right, ethical way to do things, and it guides all the decisions he makes, even when they're private."[2] Such a sense of absolutism might be considered commendable in U.S. culture, but it can pose difficulties in other cultural settings, where situations might be different or more subtle. Most important, Alderson's entry into the world of Dominican baseball would be scrutinized by everyone in that country involved with baseball—which is to say, everybody. Remembering the adage "You never get a second chance to make a first impression" would be vitally important in this assignment. Publicly, Alderson said all the right things—for instance, "We always have to be mindful that we're dealing in a different country, with a sovereign government, and all of that has to be approached on a collaborative basis."[3] But how his internal sense of absolute right and wrong would square with such publicly traded comments about cultural and political sovereignty remained to be seen.

Performing Consensus

On April 15, 2010, the Dominican baseball summit was held at the Hotel Embajador in Santo Domingo (ironically, the same hotel that housed the Marines during the occupation of 1965–1966). The attendees included the U.S. ambassador; the Dominican baseball commissioner, Porfirio Veras; the Dominican sports minister, Felipe Payano; MLB scouts; and other members of the official baseball community. They assembled in one of the hotel's meeting rooms to hear about what Alderson had come to do and, perhaps, gain insight into how his investigation would affect them. In an indirect way, the attendees had also come to pay homage. Alderson laid out the issues and his plans succinctly and tersely. His opening comments were tactful: "What we want to do is to strengthen baseball in the Dominican Republic, maintaining the country as an attractive venue to sign players and try to eradicate the problems that have affected signings on the island."[4]

In short order, however, the proverbial stick (threat) was presented, and it was the crux of his presentation: "If the problems that currently exist don't get resolved, there are many people in the United States who understand that the Draft would be the best option. But that's not why we're here."[5] By "many people," Alderson meant the MLB Commissioner's Office. He quickly reiterated the threat, warning again that if the abuses were not cleaned up, "There's a very strong likelihood there will be a draft."[6] "Abuses" meant practices that MLB had identified as problems—notably, altering players' ages and identities and the use of banned substances. He also tacked on issues that made MLB appear more generally concerned about the welfare of players—for example, education and ensuring fair treatment by buscones.

The summit's attendees were already well acquainted with the issues being discussed, and officially they agreed with the declared goals. Privately, however, their responses ranged from uncritical support to vague wait-and-see positions. Only one person questioned the proceedings, and he was "admonished by Alderson and chose to leave the gathering."[7] Dominican Baseball Commissioner Veras openly and warmly supported Alderson, which is not surprising: Dominican baseball institutions have been rubber stamping MLB policies since the relationship began in the 1950s.

As a cultural performance, the meeting was a textbook example of neo-colonialism in globalization garb. Its veneer was unanimity between the sovereign U.S. and Dominican nation, but its essence—that is, its message—promoted subservience. The Dominicans took their traditional position of listening as North Americans told them what was wrong with them, their docility evident in their nodding heads and eagerness to shake MLB officials' hands. For all of Alderson's attempts to appear collegial, he wound up erecting boundaries, reproducing hierarchy, and foisting it all on those in attendance. Alderson's self-presentation as clipped, precise, and hypercompetent came off as officious.[8] His professionalism, combined with a sense of personal distance, gave his address a slightly menacing tone.

The media outlets covering the summit were divided in portraying Alderson as either someone the DR badly needed or a cause for concern. The North American media predictably reported on the visit as justified and long overdue.[9] The response from the Dominican press was mixed. Some commentators fixated on Alderson's outsider status (e.g., "Baseball's Sheriff in High Noon Showdown with Dominican Desperados"), but editorials also appeared lauding him as badly needed to address the problems.

The baseball summit officially opened a new phase in Dominican-MLB relations, but the weeks that led up to it were filled with rumblings in the US press about MLB's need to deal with Dominican problems. The Dominican press began picking up on the threats that MLB was making, some of which were subtle, and some were not. For example, one media outlet reported that if identity fraud was not addressed, major league teams "could *reduce their investment in the country* and withdraw from [the Dominican Republic]."[10] Threatening to transfer investments elsewhere is hardly subtle, but it is a neo-liberal tactic that is widely used, usually successfully, to foster compliance in the Third World. Alderson also repeatedly mentioned the possibility of imposing the draft during his presentation. The meeting thus was also the opening move in MLB's effort to step up its presence in the DR, and Alderson was the embodiment of foreign entry into the country.

Performing Third World Baseball Nationalism

The baseball summit bore no trace of the trepidation that gripped many at the fringes of the Dominican baseball community. What followed is best described as a series of skirmishes in which the DR's independent trainers, or buscones, attempted to openly confront MLB. While MLB was choreographing the events inside the Embajador Hotel, a hastily organized demonstration against Alderson's visit was under way outside. To the best of my knowledge, the demonstration was the first organized baseball protest against MLB in Dominican history—and possibly anywhere in the world.

It makes sense that the protest originated with the buscones. Alderson had made no effort to bring them into the meeting at the hotel, and rather than passively accepting it, they decided to make a bold statement. The most powerful buscones, led by Enrique Soto, Astín Jacobo, and Victor Baez, gathered their players and converged on Santo Domingo to march outside the hotel. Somewhere in the vicinity of a thousand boys wearing their baseball uniforms marched as their trainers chanted, "No Draft! No Draft!" Once word got out that the buscones would protest Alderson's meeting, Jacobo began receiving threats: "I remember I had a phone call that morning from a guy [who] said, 'You gotta be careful because you and Enrique [Soto] are going to jail today.'"[11] Like his father, who had faced threats forty years earlier, Jacobo was undeterred. He set off for the capital with his players. He recalled:

> There were people from a lot of places.... [I]f it [hadn't been] a school day, we could have put thousands more kids out there.
>
> When we got there and got all the guys together, we started to march, and I was leading it. . . . We had to keep the kids in line. We didn't want anything to happen, and they were getting impatient. Before we got to the Embajador, an anti-riot squad was set up to stop us from getting any closer. Very scary guys! We call those cops Black Helmets. A line of them were blocking our way, and we stood confronting each other. A lieutenant came up to me and said, "*Moreno* [brown-skinned guy], I can't let you go by." And I said to him, "Listen, think like this is 1965, and what we're doing here is defending our nation, our people. That's what I'm doing here. Do you have a son or nephew who plays baseball? You know that if [MLB] gets away with what they're trying to do in that hotel, your son will have lots of trouble [becoming] a ballplayer." He waved us through, and said, "Go by. No one's gonna mess with you."

We kept everyone in line, although when the ambassador was leaving the hotel, we had to stop the kids from going after him. "Don't anyone touch that car!" we ordered. And I know the government is aware of all this 'cause we heard comments that they didn't wanna deal with us because we make things rough for them. There were speeches and lots of TV. We wanted to get in the meeting, but they didn't want us there.[12]

By invoking a nationalistic stance—equating MLB with the U.S. Marine invasion of 1965—Jacobo drew on a view that is fairly widespread. Most politically astute Dominican observers quickly make the connection between baseball and national pride. In discussing the Dominican government's inability to enact and enforce legislation to regulate the industry, Ronaldo Peralta, former director of the MLB Commissioner's Dominican office, commented:

Remember, baseball here goes with nationalism, and it's very important for Dominicans. If you try to regulate and affect [the buscones'] economic interests, they will go to the press and say you are against those who want to develop the Sammy Sosas and Albert Pujolses, that you are forbidding a kid from becoming the next Dominican star. . . . [I]t would be devastating for [a public official's] career. . . . Baseball is the one thing that makes this country great. We have failed in everything we have tried. The one thing that makes us great is to have ninety-one Dominicans in [the] major leagues. Who wants to go against that?[13]

Another march leader boasted, "We could have had a half-million [people] there because baseball is a Dominican passion. If we show the people that what Alderson is doing is hurting our game, there will be so many people in the streets that we could even cause the president to lose an election.[14] The Marine invasion trope has even more resonance, given Alderson's military past. At least one other person at the march made a similar comment: "He comes into a room . . . like he's an army general."[15]

The protest leaders very much doubted the truth of Alderson's claims that he was not in the DR to impose the draft. "These people want to introduce the draft at all costs," one trainer declared at the march.[16] Soto, who was perhaps the most outspoken of the march leaders, dismissed Alderson's denial: "Alderson has to prove [that his presence in the DR] is not to impose the draft. As we see it, they [MLB] often say one thing and do another."[17] Fear and outrage sometimes gave way to conspiracy theories. Some people worried that the major league teams' academies would disappear; others thought the Dominican Summer League would become a victim; and most felt that the buscones were being targeted. Some even believed that Alderson's visit and the baseball summit were an effort by MLB to create a quota system in the DR and in Latin America generally.[18]

Alderson sought to dismiss the march outside. He joked about buying the protesters lunch (echoing "Let them eat cake," the comment commonly attributed to Marie Antoinette) and suggesting they were nothing more than a bunch of kids being manipulated by greedy buscones. "There were about 1,000 kids. But nobody tells them why they're coming here," he said about the march. It was the buscones who "were against the draft. Well, these are 13 and 14-year-old kids. They don't have a clue."[19] Jacobo refuted Alderson's claim, noting that the marching players ranged in age. Some were as old as eighteen and had a clear sense of how Alderson could affect their future. The march was a one-time event, but it served to set up a semi-adversarial relationship between MLB and the Dominican player developers.

Jacobo characterized the march as standing up to a playground bully: "They showed up like rough kids on the block, and we pushed them back a little here. They weren't expecting that."[20] The trainers continued to press for a meeting with Alderson. "He did not give us the slightest courtesy, to meet with us. We tried to speak [with him], and he has been quite blunt and arrogant, not returning phone calls or anything," recalled Baez.[21] The march did, however, grab the attention of Sports Minister Payano, who, in turn, helped broker a later meeting between Alderson and the leading buscones. "When we finally met with Alderson and the Dominican sports minister, one of the first things I said was, 'I feel like we're being invaded all over again,'" Jacobo said.[22] He felt that the meeting with Alderson was only marginally successful:

We came up with a proposal, and [Alderson is] only applying things that are convenient for him—like if you don't want people to mess with your money, make them sign an agreement with a lawyer that if there's any wrongdoing, they'll have to give back the money. Now he's taking credit for that. But he's not taking into consideration some of our other points, like the investigation and release of the player being signed should take place [be limited to] between forty-five and ninety days. That hasn't happened.[23]

MLB's Big Gun: Dictating Legitimacy

The meeting between Alderson and the buscones may not have gone the way the buscones had hoped, but it did serve notice that Dominicans were ready to confront MLB. Alderson had arrived in the DR determined to make fundamental changes—to "govern the chain"—while choosing words to forestall fear. "[My presentation is] trying to convince people of what the mission here is and that my goal is really a constructive one," he said. "I'm here to preserve what baseball and the Dominican Republic have while, at the same time, eliminating those problems that cast baseball, and the Dominican Republic itself, in a negative way. Baseball is the international identity of the Dominican Republic. It's important for them, and I think they agree with this, that their reputation is as positive as possible."[24] What MLB was not prepared for was a confrontation with the buscones, and to achieve its goals, MLB would have to figure out other ways to govern.

Major League Baseball's most potent weapon in demanding compliance is its monopoly on legal regulations. Instituting identity verification requirements, punishing people for giving and taking kickbacks, and performing drug tests are all matters that MLB considered within its jurisdiction, but until recently the Commissioner's Office in New York had not sought to extend its oversight abroad. Despite the obvious potential for conflicting cross-national cultural understandings of the law, MLB felt little compunction about pushing into the sovereign Dominican nation. The post-9/11 preoccupation with securing American borders aided its efforts—or, perhaps, fueled them.

First, MLB revamped its Commissioner's Office in Santo Domingo and set up an investigation unit to deal with the signing of players. The stepped-up scrutiny of identity documents netted hundreds of cases of fraud in the period immediately following the attacks in New York City and Washington, D.C. This was touted as a success in the United States, but in the DR it resulted in an atmosphere of intimidation as the paperwork for teams looking to establish identity tripled.[25]

Major League Baseball had its own investigations unit to aggressively launch inquiries. These investigations had the overall effect of slowing down the vetting process. Questions have arisen about how effective these investigations are and how ethically they are conducted. "The investigators are not always that professional," said Astín Jacobo, by a player developer who had represented a player signed by the Tampa Bay Rays. "The player's birth certificate said he was born on April 1 of a particular year, but that date was slightly off. He was actually born on April 9 [of the same year]. When the investigator was at [the player's] house, he was there with a young lady and

. . . had been drinking a little bit. He decided that because he was looking for the April 1 date and didn't find it, my guy was a liar, a fake." Ultimately, Jacobo said, the investigator was found to be inept, and MLB was able to verify the player's age. In another case, he said he saw an investigator "slam his gun on the kitchen table as he was talking with the parents of [a] kid" and swearing at them. "They're using former military guys to do this," Jacobo said.[26]

The overall effect of the investigations has been to slow down the signing process. Given the time-sensitivity of that process, in which sixteen-year-olds who will be seventeen by the next Dominican Summer League season ideally are signed on July 2, this has cost teams and prospects both time and money. Further, by holding back confirmations, the verification process has reduced the size of signing bonuses. "[MLB is] manipulating the investigations so the guys get less money," said Jacobo. "I need to have a player okayed by MLB, but they make it difficult to get their service. We have a case like Miguel Sano [who signed with the Texas Rangers]: His papers were no good when they offered him $5 million, but he was good when he signed with those same papers at $3 million." Jacobo also mentioned Juan Saltero, who signed with the Atlanta Braves. "When he was offered $2.9 million by the [Cleveland] Indians, his paperwork was no good, but then, with the same papers, he signed for $1.6 million [with the Braves]. You don't have to be Albert Einstein to realize that something's going on."[27]

Fingerprinting July 2 Prospects

A foreign power's belief that it is entitled to legislate in another sovereign country is sheer hubris, but that is precisely what MLB did when it instituted a fingerprinting program in the Dominican Republic in 2011. Alderson and MLB want to fingerprint aspiring Dominican players as young as eleven or twelve to identify them and control who enters the system. The legality of the procedure in the DR is in question, however, so MLB retreated to a less controversial position of fingerprinting players who had already been signed but were still at major league teams' Dominican academies.

The procedure still raises hackles. I knew that the trainers and agents were not happy, and I wondered how the players would respond. Confining the fingerprinting to signed players who had already received their bonuses dampened much of the outrage, I found. The player developers fumed, but the players themselves appeared to take it in stride.

I witnessed the fingerprinting program being carried out in the summer of 2011. A group of players were brought together in a classroom at their academy to await the MLB representative. They had won a game earlier in the day and were rambunctious as the representative entered carrying a computer, a camera, and a digital fingerprinting machine. To keep the teenagers under some control, coaches were also in the room. After setting up the equipment, the representative signaled to the boys that it was time to settle down—a message that was lost on them. He began to call their names from a roster. Each rookie took a seat directly across the table from the representative, answered a few questions to confirm his identity, and placed his forefinger over the machine's small opening to have his fingerprint scanned. Afterward, each player's photo was taken, and the data were entered into his record. The entire process took less than five minutes per player.

My preconception, based on an Orwellian reading of such procedures, was that this intrusion by MLB into their lives would cause resentment among the players. I could not have been more wrong. The players viewed the fingerprinting session as an extension of their victory celebration, joking and teasing as the MLB representative tried to get through the process. As the first player sat down, other players taunted him about his dark complexion, yelling, "Get him some [white] cream for his face!" and "Use a flash on him!" During another player's turn, the catcalls continued: "With a head like that, you know he has Down's [Down syndrome]!"[28] No one was spared.

So how can one reconcile the levity that filled in the room with the Foucauldian sense of disciplining and infringement of individual rights that fingerprinting seemingly represents? The answer may be embedded in the very structure of Dominican baseball. From the time young ballplayers enter a relationship with an independent trainer, and continuing through their time at the major league academies, their actions are directed, and their behavior is scrutinized and evaluated. Thus, the fingerprinting session might not strike them as unusual or out of line. Willingness to submit to such practices marks their habitus—the relationship between their bodily practices and successful integration into the larger society to which they seek entry and full recognition (see Chapter 3).

Politically, MLB's fingerprinting of Dominican prospects is less about individual rights than a power move to legislate legitimacy. It is not the players but the buscones who are being trumped, because they are made extraneous to this process and, consequently, to subsequent ones.

The "Goals and Challenges" Symposium

Major League Baseball continued the offensive by organizing a symposium, "Goals and Challenges of MLB in the Dominican Republic" in Santo Domingo on March 14–15, 2011. Commissioner Selig sent some of his most respected administrators to the summit, again to impress on the Dominican audience how seriously MLB takes what it considers to be Dominican problems. Alderson gave the keynote address, titled, "What Is Needed to Guarantee the Long-Term Economic Sustainability of MLB in the Dominican Republic?" Reiterating his message of the previous year, he emphasized that the mining of Dominican talent needed to continue. According to some attendees, Alderson seemed to be trying to make a better impression than he had a year earlier, when his arrival in the country resulted in demonstrations and widespread fear.[29] For instance, he admitted that some of the investigators MLB had hired to conduct identity verifications had been less than fully professional and that MLB would have to do a better job.[30] This resonated with the nearly three hundred people who packed the ballroom. Still, for all of Alderson's expressed concern about the well-being of Dominican baseball, the fact is that MLB was in Santo Domingo to change it—that is, to make it more rational and "law-abiding."

The underlying message of the conference was the same as that of the summit a year earlier: If the DR wanted to continue to reap the benefits of substantial MLB investment, it would have to address several problems—the very same problems with which everyone in the room was already quite familiar. Specific "problems" on which sessions focused included independent trainers/buscones, age and identity fraud, education, and drug use. Attendees and panelists included notable Americans and Dominicans, such as the New York Mets' former general manager Omar Minaya, as well as the former major leaguer and local legend Winston Llenas and Dominican Sports Minister Felipe Payano. Rob Manfred, executive vice-president of labor relations and human resources for MLB, and John McHale, executive vice-president of administration and chief information officer, flanked Alderson. Most teams had representatives in the audience, and former players filled the room. This time, buscones were invited.

Excellent reports by knowledgeable people, such as John Seibel, highlighted the substantial and varied economic impact of MLB in the Dominican Republic. In fact, the pride and power of MLB were on display everywhere. On the surface, it is tempting to interpret the symposium as a microcosm of the symbiosis that exists between MLB and Dominican baseball. It is true enough that each side receives something vital: Dominicans get jobs, remittances, and opportunities to play professional baseball, and MLB gets unprecedented access to highly talented athletes. But examined at a deeper level, MLB is gaining substantially from the exchange while the DR is only nominally better off for it. Thus, the power is really on MLB's side, Astín Jacobo pointed out:

[Alderson] said that MLB was bringing about $40 million to $50 million into the country and all these jobs, and I said, "Thank you for that, but you're making $7 billion, and we're the principal guys helping to make that for you." I've been telling [MLB] that we're baseball's best partners, and they look kind of surprised. So I said, "Why do you look surprised? For the past twenty years, the minor leagues have existed because of Dominicans. You survive because of the cheap labor you get from us. And on top of that, the best major leaguers have been Dominicans, breaking every record you have. So we have been your best partners."[31]

Thus, as Jacobo reminds, even if the U.S. organization does not factor this into its public depiction of the relationship with the DR, "cheap" Dominican labor, at the minor and major league levels plays a significant role in generating billions of dollars in annual revenue for MLB. By comparison, what the DR gets in return is dwarfed. This is vital to understanding what informs MLB's power-based notion of "sustainability." For all of its efforts to appear sensitive to local culture and politics, MLB held the symposium in the DR largely to make clear that it regards the challenges it is identifying in the MLB-Dominican relations as Dominicans' problems to solve, not MLB's. So while most of the attendees came away with a sense that they were part of the establishment's tidal wave of reform, they were also being served notice that there were Dominican issues that they needed to address.

Organizing the Opposition

The baseball saber rattling that has been going on since 2010 continues as Alderson and the MLB Commissioner's Office repeat the mantra about cleaning up problems in the DR while respecting Dominican sovereignty. The most vocal resistance has continued to come from the ranks of the player developers. "We feel strongly that MLB doesn't want us in the business," said Astín Jacobo. "We have become a problem for them because we have become so good at training players and selling them."[32] Amaurys Nina expressed even stronger feelings: "Alderson lies. He says he doesn't want the draft but holds it behind his back the whole time."[33]

Dominican Prospect League

In 2009, Astín Jacobo Jr., Enrique Soto, Amaurys Nina, and Christian Batista laid plans to form the Dominican Prospect League (DPL) in an attempt to prevent what they felt was yet another attempt either to put them out of business or bring them under control (i.e., back into the chain). The goal of the league, which was created in conjunction with the Pa'lante Management and Consulting Group,[34] is to build a league of the top prospects, most of whom were already in the buscones' programs. They also intended to streamline signing by centralizing the process, providing a single venue to attract scouts and providing background checks for its players.

Initially, the DPL consisted of four teams, one in each of the Dominican Republic's key regions. Soto managed the team from the south, which was based in Baní; Jacobo managed the team from the east, based in San Pedro de Macorís; Herrera managed the team from the north, based in Santo Domingo; and Nina headed the team from the west, based in San Cristóbal. Each Dominican player developer was permitted to carry as many as seven players from his own program, filling the rest of the rosters with the best players in the region. The DPL played one game a week—on Wednesdays—at various major league teams' academies. This offered the scouts an easily accessible and familiar location. "We thought of everything," Jacobo said. "We know that major league scouts have a tight schedule and that Wednesdays are usually an off-day for them. So that's the day we hold all of our games."[35] The league was supported financially by sponsorships and via a 2 percent tax on each player's signing bonus. It was understood that holding their games in a single venue rather than having each buscón work independently would keep costs down and allow the prospects to be showcased to a much larger array of scouts. As Jacobo pointed out, "If your player goes four for four, he's [now] doing that in front of thirty scouts, not one."[36]

Predictably, MLB tried to obstruct the DPL from forming—for example, by making phone calls to the San Francisco Giants Dominican Baseball Academy to prevent the DPL from playing its all-star game there in 2010. Such efforts riled the DPL's organizers, who retaliated during the league's first all-star event:

> When we had [the DPL's] first all-star game at the Tampa [Bay Rays'] academy, MLB called its Scouting Bureau to look at it. We didn't know what the bureau was doing there. There was a lot of commotion, so we asked them [the scouts] to leave. We weren't gonna play in front of them, and they wanted to fine Tampa Bay. The next day, we went to play at the Giants' complex, and [the MLB scouts] showed up again. We said we wouldn't play in front of them. They didn't ask us; they just showed up. So Alderson called the Giants and told them not to let us play.[37]

At their first meeting with Alderson, Soto and his colleagues mentioned the lack of respect Alderson had shown them. Jacobo was the most adversarial, in large part because he was bilingual and had grown up in the United States, with its culture of confrontation:

> I said to him, "You came to our country, our game, in front of Dominican parents, over a hundred players and thirty scouts, and you just sent the bureau there without contacting us? And because we wouldn't let them in, you took it out on us? What's that about?" He tried to deny that he was pushy. That's how our relationship started out—very rough. [Alderson] said to me, "Well, you knew that we were here, and you knew that previously you kicked us out [of the] Tampa Bay complex." I responded, "Well, you knew that we gave you a letter two months before this happened to sit and talk with you and find out your plan."[38]

Some people feared that the buscones' face-to-face meeting with Alderson signaled collaboration with the oppressors that would usher in the draft. Jacobo, however, countered by saying that, when it comes to the MLB making changes to Dominican baseball, "It's not 'if'; it's 'when.' The status quo is not gonna hold, so we gotta do something. Otherwise they're gonna come down here and do it to us Dominicans. On the radio I said, 'I think we're still a sovereign nation. [MLB is] coming here to steal our prize jewels, our players. We should decide how and when we sell our jewels."[39] Soto, Jacobo, and others feel that instead of facilitating the draft, they are being proactive and showing a form of Dominican independence: "What we're trying to do in this league is let 'them' know that we are capable of managing ourselves."[40]

Major League Baseball responded to the buscones' effort to organize by instituting "El Torneo Supremo" (The Supreme Tournament), its own version of elite player tryouts. The "tournament," it claimed in a press release issued in March 2011, seeks to "maximize the ability of Major League Baseball organizations to scout in the Dominican Republic and provide unsigned prospects both with resources to enhance their game skills and a venue to showcase their talents."[41] As a high-profile maneuver to offset the fact that it was so far behind the buscones, MLB brought in Moisés Alou—a former superstar major leaguer in his own right who, as the son of Felipe and the nephew of Jesús and Matty, is also a member of the Dominican baseball-playing Alou dynasty—to head up the effort. Alou had the MLB line down as he declared, "'El Torneo Supremo' has the potential to help many young Dominican players. I care about the image of the Dominican player, and I want to help improve it. In addition to the 15 and 16-year-old prospects, I want to help older players get the opportunity to showcase their talents."[42]

Major League Baseball has tried to claim that team owners were the ones who wanted the tournament started, but Dominicans find that difficult to believe. "One of the guys tried to tell us that the owners asked them to make the league," Jacobo said. "I said, 'You know what? You lie! The owners don't even know the names of the players they got down here.'"[43] Ironically, despite MLB's economic and political clout, El Torneo Supremo is fairly disorganized, with major league academies being asked to provide everything from fields to sandwiches for the games at the last minute.[44]

When the DPL refused to buckle under to El Torneo Supremo, MLB used its administrative muscle to coerce the buscones into bringing their players into the fold. In a move reminiscent of the U.S. government's use of the Internal Revenue Service to audit—and thereby harass—its enemies, MLB had its investigative agency pay visits (or threaten to do so) to those unwilling to send players. "We started [the DPL], and it started to look so good," Jacobo said, "[that MLB's] view of us as undisciplined and unorganized was ruined, so they came in with their 'supreme league.' They're trying to force guys to go into their league, and the [guys are] not going voluntarily. So Juan De Jesus [a special assistant to Alderson charged with recruiting international players] calls twenty times [asking us] to send him [our] players. If he can't get [us] to give him [a] player, then [Nelson] Tejada, the head of investigations for MLB, might come and investigate [us]. Our players are the best in the nation, and we're not sending our players there."[45]

MLB Apes the Buscones?

In January 2013, MLB seemed to be borrowing a page from the buscones' playbook when they held a showcase (their mutated version of the DPL's showcase) outside Santo Domingo. They featured twenty-five Dominican and twenty-five Venezuelan players who would be at eligible for the July 2 signing. More than two hundred scouts, a range of MLB officials (including Senior Vice-President Joe Torre) and Dominicans of note (including Rafael Pérez and Omar Minaya) showed up to watch sixteen-year-olds run a sixty-yard dash with stop watches at the ready. In the initial offering of this showcase, MLB had been stymied by the refusal of the nation's top player developers to allow their players to appear, but by 2013, that situation had been ameliorated. Some players from the International Prospect League (Astín Jacobo's newly reconstituted group) were there—although Jacobo did not choose to participate—as were players from other elite player developers' programs.

For those present, the showcase was orchestrated mayhem, a massive baseball fair in which all were simultaneously hawking their wares. One day a tryout took place in which top players wore wearing uniforms with "MLB" emblazoned on them; the next day, the same players wore uniforms emblazoned with "IPL," for International Prospect League tryouts. Adding to the confusion, some groups chose to hold tryouts at a different location, forcing scouts to move around the country in small herds. Outliers who did not run programs but were connected to a promising player might hand out fliers advertising off-site showcases. The event harked back to the trope of the Dominican Republic as the Wild West, except that this was taking place under the aegis of MLB, the entity that professed to be concerned about eliminating Dominican "chaos."

Even more telling, a mini-showcase was held for players age fourteen and fifteen, who would not even be considered for signing until July 2, 2014. They stayed at a different location but clearly were part of the proceedings. How can we make sense of this? Has MLB coopted the buscones, or are the buscones now in the lead? The only thing that is clear in this swirling field of competing interests is that all of the parties involved are clashing over who will control players and their development. In short, they care clashing over who governs the chain.

Conclusion

Rectifying problems associated with Dominican baseball is a key battleground on which MLB is attempting to coerce Dominicans into compliance while the Dominicans seek to accommodate only so much, stopping short of undoing the advantages it has already won. The most serious difficulty in the MLB-Dominican baseball relationship is that the two sides cannot even really agree on what constitutes a problem. From MLB's perspective, Dominicans will not adhere to norms and practices laid out by the major league teams' owners and the commissioner. From the Dominican perspective, MLB does not really want to understand their culture and country, and that "compliance" would cripple Dominican baseball. Confrontations of the sort that brought Sandy Alderson to the DR arise only when the MLB Commissioner's Office deems that violations require official intervention. The "problems" that irked Commissioner Selig in 2010 actually were practices that had been ingrained in Dominican baseball for decades.

Who gets to define the issues, and who has to resolve them? MLB's rules have existed more or less in place for a long time, but the North American baseball establishment had little interest in how those rules operate in other countries. In the Dominican Republic, practices emerged that blended the major league teams' desire for talent with opportunity for local brokers and trainers to develop the players. Although there was ample room for disjuncture between the two sides, little concern was expressed about it so long as the talent continued to flow. Only when the scale of business became significant—when major league teams' investments in the DR became large, competition grew fierce, and the cost of signing players escalated—did MLB determine that the Dominican Republic was rife with problems.

Eradicating the "'problems" identified by Alderson would, in the Dominicans' view, jeopardize their rising position and gains. Preserving Dominican baseball, to which Alderson repeatedly has claimed he is committed, seems to be more about preserving Dominican-U.S. relations as they used to be than as they are evolving. Take, for instance, age and identity fraud. Major League Baseball is dealing with the issue by nullifying the contracts of those who provide fraudulent information and placing the guilty parties' future in doubt, yet Dominican prospects continue to falsify their ages and identities. It may seem irrational to jeopardize what could be one's sole chance to escape poverty by presenting falsified documents, but it is actually a rational response to a market that has been foisted on these young players.

Living in accordance with a market that is being dictated to them by MLB teams leaves a very narrow range of opportunities for Dominicans. If it is intentional, this fabrication of an artificial market niche for younger players while denigrating older ones is truly sinister and fits neatly into neoliberal market strategies of obtaining cheap labor abroad. It is more likely, however, that the causal chain that entraps Dominicans into violating MLB regulations, which, in turn, provokes even more regulations, is one of the many unintended outcomes of such transnational commodity chains. Viewed from the top, the process only further justifies the need for governance and more regulation. Those who are the objects of governance, though, see only additional obstacles that they must be creative enough to circumvent.

Conclusion

iven all of the tumult discussed in this study, it would be easy to think of contemporary Dominican baseball in one of two ways. One could see the events as chaotic, random, and resembling a baseball version of a "failed state." Or one could see the heavy scripted imprint of MLB reproducing the "natural" hegemonic order of things. Neither of these views would accurately characterize the Dominican system that has evolved, because much of it was unanticipated.

Robert Merton brought the concept of *unintended consequences* into modern usage in the social sciences as a way to speak about seemingly capricious results that emerge within social systems.[1] Merton's five sources of unanticipated consequences were ignorance, error, immediacy of interest, values (e.g., the Protestant ethic), and self-defeating prophecy or prediction (public understanding or prediction that proves wrong). All of these are at work in terms of incorrectly anticipating a desired effect in complex systems. While Merton was concerned with "purposive action" in talking about unintended consequences, the term has come to be generally understood as an acknowledgment of anything unforeseen. And although it is intriguing, it does not really advance our understanding—certainly, at least, of the Dominican baseball system. However, thinking of unintended consequences as informed by the push and pull of systemic power relations might yield some insight.

The "consequences" part of the concept rests on the assumption that the will and ways of those in power are always successfully imposed on subordinates (hegemony); hence, for that group, a certainty about the outcome exists. "Unintended" happens when something goes awry. Whether because of hubris or ignorance on the part of those in power, they fail to fully sense that even the most successful systems destabilize over time. In other words, the processes that worked smoothly early on can fray or lose their efficacy later. In addition, they fail to fully appreciate the impact of resistance from below in changing conditions around them. If all of this is unanticipated, the change they ultimately confront must come as a challenging surprise. Maybe it is just human to assume that a good thing will go on forever.

As I have pointed out, MLB has been in complete control of its relationship with Dominican baseball since that relationship was formally established in the 1950s. The air of social arrogance on the part of MLB operatives in the Dominican Republic, which over time has turned into a cultural standard operating procedure, has always troubled me. I began to spend time in the DR in 1987, often in the company of Ralph Avila, vice-president of Latin American operations for the Los Angeles Dodgers. I remember a visit to Campo Las Palmas back then by Tommy Lasorda, the Dodgers' high-profile former manager. The academy had recently opened, and many people in the baseball world marveled at its grandeur and the success of the franchise in the DR. Members of the rookie cohort training at Campo Las Palmas were excited that someone of Lasorda's stature would visit them and watch them play.

Arriving in the midst of their practice, Lasorda made his way to the field. Rather than observe the talent (as most everyone does), he sat down, peeled off his shirt, and turned his back to the players. Tilting his chair to get more sun, Lasorda yelled to Avila, "Ralph! We got anybody good here?" Lasorda's indifference did not go unnoticed. The rookies closest to me had the sheepish, hurt look of those long accustomed to being invisible. That scene of disregard for others, which is so typical of Americans in developing nations, would be repeated, and in even worse ways, over the years. For me, it has come to be emblematic of MLB-Dominican relations. Although baseball scouts and others now ogle Dominican players instead of ignoring them, the patronizing continues in less obvious areas.

The conflict-riddled nature of contemporary Dominican baseball revolves around MLB's attempt to retain control of player development even as it grants Dominicans respect. The heightened regard is most immediately visible in MLB's increased spending to sign players, build lavish facilities in the DR, and more generally protect its investments. Rising admiration for Dominicans in the game also results in, among other things, a more culturally sensitive environment and more support for players in the farm system.

Major league teams no longer treat language acquisition purely as an after-thought; instead, they hire bilingual staff at all levels. Back in the DR, how-ever, acrimony has grown over the issue of who should control key aspects of player development. Most of this controversy concerns the position of Dominican player developers, but it sometimes spills into areas of policy and, more generally, business practice. In all cases, the conflict affects how the commodity chain is run.

The production of players is social in nature in that humans are pro-ducing humans (see Chapter 1), which makes for a very unstable chain. The methods used to produce the players, how players respond to being pro-duced, and the impact of other parties on the chain all have the capacity to alter the outcome. For Dominican players, the first links in the chain—from MLB's Dominican baseball academies to the Rookie leagues in Florida—are the most difficult to navigate, and it is there that I have focused my atten-tion. For other Dominicans in professional baseball, from MLB administra-tors to player developers, these early links also represent areas where they feel they can have some effect on the outcome. Figures such as Felipe Alou and, more recently, Rafael Pérez are working from inside MLB and pushing its agenda, but they are also giving voice to Dominicans' concerns and needs: When they find themselves at odds with MLB, they too can use their stature and positions to articulate these concerns in ways that can effectively counter MLB and its teams. The buscones, by contrast, are outsiders. But when they work together, they can form a counterweight to MLB.

The volatility of baseball's global commodity chain is particularly evi-dent in the unintended consequences that the chain seems regularly to pro-duce. Thus, I use this concept to examine the emergence of four practices/institutions that can be explained (and possibly predicted) only when one uses an analysis informed by power and agency.

Unintended Consequence 1: Rise of the Buscones

The modern academy system was designed to grow and harvest Dominican players more efficiently for MLB. Little thought was given to the system's longer-term effects, which are creating startling new challenges for MLB and its system of development and governance. In Chapter 2, I briefly discussed the withering of amateur baseball in the DR that has occurred alongside the rise of the academy system. Here I examine it more fully to highlight how its weakening inevitably gave rise to the buscones.

Much has been made of the impressive numbers of major league play-ers who have come out of the small, economically hard-pressed Dominican

Republic. We marvel at their prowess, often shaking our heads in sadness or disbelief at the difficult conditions so many have had to overcome to get to the majors, but we pay scant attention to the rich and varied environment that honed their playing skills. I am referring to those fertile amateur fields that yield so many excellent athletes, which include everything from the ubiquitous feral sandlots and organized Little League knockoffs to the ranks of amateur and semiprofessional players.

Sandlot and Amateur Adult Baseball

While many anecdotes have been told about sandlot baseball being played in the DR, no systematic studies of it exist. This kind of baseball played casually by children serves as a backdrop to more organized amateur leagues in which players are discovered and developed in the DR. Pedro Martínez and others have told stories about using dolls' heads or taped stones as baseballs when they played in the yard. In the streets, boys play *trapaga*, a game in which bottle caps from five-gallon water jugs serve as balls.[2] When the opportunity presents itself, these kids migrate to nearby fields to continue their games with more players. And most important, they play the game morning, noon, and night and in every nook and cranny of the DR some version of baseball serves as a springboard for Dominican boys to dream about a better life.

Players occasionally have been discovered during these informal games: Jesús Alou, for instance, is fond of declaring that he was signed right out of the sandlots.[3] But that is rare. More often, young sandlot players move up to amateur teams, and if they are good enough, they eventually catch the eye of a buscón. So while the sandlot tradition is the oldest form of baseball in the DR, and is still widespread, it has declined in importance as a venue in which young players are sought.

Prior to the emergence of the modern academy, most discussions of amateur Dominican baseball concentrated on accomplished adult (or young adult) play in Santo Domingo, San Pedro de Macorís, and Santiago. This is semiprofessional baseball rather than children's leagues. For decades the Bermúdez rum company sponsored teams in the Santiago region, while in the San Pedro area baseball was organized both in the city and at the sugar refineries. These company teams were the original font from which generations of major league talent flowed. Juan Marichal, the only Dominican (thus far) in MLB's Hall of Fame, was discovered while playing for the Bermúdez team Las Floras.[4] Tony Peña and Winston Llenas also played for amateur company-run teams in the Santiago area.

The sugar refineries around San Pedro de Macorís have come in for the lion's share of attention in discussing amateur play. Arrayed around the port city were sugar refineries such as Consuelo, Angelina, Porvenir, Colón, and Santa Fe. Each eventually fielded competitive teams that played a form of amateur baseball referred to as "Wild Ball."[5] "These games [between refineries] were bigger than the World Series to us," said Astín Jacobo Sr. "When you go to one of these *ingenios* [refineries], baseball was the only thing [diversion] you [were] gonna see. There were no movies. Everybody was on the field. So when you lose a game, everybody's crying or . . . fighting or something. If you go to Angelina and they win, they fight you. And if they lose, they fight. It was because they were so excited, you know?"[6]

The government also created highly competitive semi-amateur teams. The dictator Rafael Trujillo, for instance, encouraged the cultural hegemony of the capital when, beginning in the 1930s, he essentially conscripted the best players in the country (supplemented with highly paid players from the U.S. Negro Leagues) for his Escogido. Marichal has recalled playing for the Dominican Air Force's Aviación team in 1955 under the personal watch of Trujillo's son Ramfis: Immediately after beating Aviación while pitching for another team, he was "selected" by the Air Force via an induction notice.[7] Playing for Aviación usually led to playing in the Dominican professional leagues, but that trajectory was aborted when Marichal signed to play professionally for the San Francisco Giants.

The most talented Dominican players eventually were spotted by bird dogs, who alerted major league teams with which they had connections (see Chapter 2). Elite Dominican players also made it to the Dominican professional leagues, which have existed, in one form or another, for most of the twentieth century.

The Academies' Impact on Amateur Ball

Dominican amateur baseball continues today, but it does so in abbreviated form. Where traditionally amateur baseball funneled players to the top Dominican professional teams or, in smaller numbers, to U.S. major league teams, today amateur baseball is completely geared toward getting players into North American professional baseball. It was MLB's rising interest in Dominican talent and the need for a place to refine the players that they signed that spawned the emergence of baseball academies.

In short order, this parallel structure morphed into a predatory one. The more established academies began to hold regular tryouts for unsigned youth (i.e., amateurs). In turn, young Dominicans began to direct their energy toward trying out for major league teams at the academies. This lessened their reliance on Dominican amateur baseball as a venue for being seen by scouts. I witnessed many such tryouts at Campo Las Palmas in the late 1980s and saw the number of hopefuls swell.[8] This outcome was neither intended nor expected, but it was undeniable. As I wrote at that time, "The physical and organizational presence of baseball academies run by major league franchises in the Dominican Republic has fundamentally undermined the long-standing sovereignty of Dominican baseball. First, the academies have undercut the traditional role of professional Dominican teams in locating talent. . . . [And] academies contribute to the cannibalization of the Dominican amateur leagues."[9]

An internal factor also worked to weaken the amateur leagues, including those dedicated to the very youngest players. Big Dominican firms that historically had sponsored teams as a form of advertising came to understand that their budgets were better served buying television time. Avila noted this development:

Twenty years ago [in 1968] television was zero in this country. The best way to get publicity every Monday morning was to have an amateur team. . . . Now all the big companies don't spend a penny on amateur baseball because to receive good publicity now you have to have a good ball club. In the past they don't care whether it was positive or negative. Now players don't have the chance to play in AA 'cause [sponsors] want experienced amateur players to win and receive good publicity. Thousands of kids coming from the class A program don't have any place to play. They got three choices: come to the academy, go to another sport, or go to the Malecón and sell drugs.[10]

Major league academies ended up drawing young unsigned Dominicans who sought more direct access to those teams, changing the impact of the academy from replicating and distantly competing with the amateur leagues to directly usurping their players. Combined with the loss of sponsorship by local firms, the amateur leagues withered while no one in MLB's corporate offices noticed.

Where would the next generation of Dominican baseball players come from? The major league teams operating in the DR could not train—or, for that matter, have any kind of legitimate contact—with players younger than sixteen and a half, creating a vacuum that was both a cause and an unanticipated effect. Vacuums offer opportunities, and the buscones made the most of the situation. No one saw their emergence and subsequent rise to prominence coming. It is imperative to understand that this powerful and adversarial sector originated in MLB's lack of insight as it promoted the academy system. Major League Baseball's vilification of player developers, built on depicting them as the source of so many problems, not only assigns the blame to the wrong parties but, in hindsight, may also be an attempt to deflect responsibility from the party that is truly at fault: MLB.

Unintended Consequence 2: Returning to the Chain

With all of the attention paid to players who are signed to MLB contracts, little has been said about those who get released (i.e., removed from baseball's global commodity chain). This is shortsighted, because it means that some of the most dynamic aspects of the chain are being overlooked. "Getting released" is a lovely, pastoral phrase that conjures up a sense of gaining freedom from confinement. This is especially telling, given that the released player is regarded as a casualty of the sports system—a flawed widget in the manufacturing process, so to speak.

What happens to athletes who are deemed "redundant" or "expired" at eighteen or twenty-two? In the United States, they might undergo a difficult readjustment period, then find their way back to school to pursue a degree in computer programming, physical education, or another field, or they might find a job at a car dealership or with the local Department of Public Works. Or they might join the ranks of players who end up with nothing after their years of effort. Failed athletes who come from disadvantaged communities are particularly prone to going down in flames when they are released.

In the aftermath of a game played at one of the DR's baseball stadiums, long after the fans had left, I watched small children and older folks search through the stands and in the dumpsters for plastic cups. They rinsed the cups out, stacked them, and threw them into heavily used plastic bags. They knew that a buyer would be found—a bodega owner, a street vendor, or even the stadium itself. The point is that in the United States, a wide variety of options—good and bad—are available to released athletes, but returning to the chain is only minimally likely. The same is not true of the Dominican Republic: Although opportunities outside the chain are limited, everything seems to get recycled. Nothing is thrown away after only one use.

In the Dominican player chain, the end may come at any point—from the academy all the way to the major leagues. No one is ready when it does come, but in the DR, former players often find their way back into the chain. Their stories tend to run along similar lines: Most return to the world from which they came, and if they were smart enough, their families benefited with new or better housing and, perhaps, a little money left over. With little education or skills, many will try to make it on the streets, working occasionally and informally, legally or illegally. MLB has recognized this situation and, to its credit, entered into an agreement with the Dominican government in 2012 to provide education and training for Dominican minor league players who were released after January 2009. Its Educational Initiative Program for Latin America has yet to be tested in any serious way, however, and whether Dominican players who have not been raised to value formal education will take advantage of it remains to be seen.

Quite a few released Dominican players who have made it to the United States simply refuse to return to their homeland, taking their chances with illegal immigration status and the opportunities available in U.S. cities that have large Dominican populations. I interviewed several who felt the risk was worth taking. "I knew I was never going back," one former player said. "I just left [my minor league team] at night and had some relatives pick me up. . . . They [found] me work, and I'm living with two [other former players]. Baseball was my life, but I got hurt and saw that others were doing better than me. I was pretty sad, but I felt that my injury was gonna end baseball for me soon anyway, so I took this chance. Now I got a life here [in the United States] and can send money back to my family."[11]

Many Dominicans find opportunities to return to the chain. Some, like Felipe Alou, who managed the Montreal Expos and the Giants, do it in the United States and at the highest levels. Many more do it back home in the DR, becoming scouts, coaches, or administrators for major league teams. Felipe Alou's younger brother Jesús ended his fifteen-year career as an MLB player in 1979, returning to the DR to enjoy his other passion, deep sea fishing. But by the mid-1980s, he had returned to the chain as a scout for the Expos. Easygoing and a favorite of all of the major league administrators he had played for, Alou was asked in 1994 to head the Miami Marlins' Dominican operations. In 2002, he became the director of the Red Sox Dominican Baseball Academy.

The Alous' command of the English language and fluency with U.S. culture, gained as minor leaguers in the United States, allowed them to reenter the chain directly. Many others do so indirectly by running small businesses, relying on their baseball experience to sell their services to the MLB academies. Occasionally, former players become wildly successful in these businesses. Junior Noboa, for example, worked his bicultural skills and business acumen to become the Dominican Republic's major developer of baseball facilities (see Chapter 5).

And a few released players reenter the chain as flawed, offering difficult lessons. Gilberto Reyes, who played in the major leagues during the

1980s, then coached in Mexico and at the New York Mets Dominican Baseball Academy in 2006, provides an interesting example of this trajectory.
Reyes debuted in the major leagues in 1983 at the tender age of nineteen.
He had been signed at sixteen, however, and shipped off almost immediately
to the United States. With no support, and with his lack of sophistication,
he endured culture shock that today's players probably could not imagine
(see Chapter 2). Sent over without remediation and coming from a sheltered
home ("I only had one girlfriend, and my mom watched closely over me"),[12]
Reyes was little more than a child. He suffered through those first months
without mentoring of any kind, and poorly prepared, he developed substance
abuse problems that no doubt harmed his career.

Oddly, perhaps because of these "worldly" experiences, Reyes was very
effective as the manager of the Mets' Dominican Summer League team. I
witnessed players listening to him with unusually rapt attention. The Mets,
then led by General Manager Omar Minaya, were nevertheless nervous about
having someone with such a checkered past influencing the players and
released Reyes. A year later (in 2007), he was arrested when a truck he was
driving from Mexico, loaded with furniture and 420 pounds of marijuana,
overturned on a New Mexico highway. He claimed he was innocent, refused
a plea bargain, and spent fifteen months in jail. But it is not safe to assume
Reyes will never return to the chain. As noted earlier, Dominicans recycle
everything.

Other released players become player developers, and they can affect the
chain in unexpected ways. Some who have traveled from the DR to the U.S.
minor league system can use what they learned to help their players. That
certainly is what the super-buscón Enrique Soto did. Although Soto spent
only one year in professional baseball, in the U.S. minor leagues, the experience scarred him deeply. He did not speak English and had no cultural
mentors. Like Reyes and most others of the time, Soto was young, alone, and
unable to communicate, which led him to conclude that Americans had little
respect for or interest in Latinos (see Chapter 3).

Many Dominicans share the view that MLB uses them to fill out minor
league rosters, with little real intent to promote them to major league play.
This conclusion, while tempting to draw, is belied in some way by the number of Latino players who carve out remarkable careers in baseball. Although
disappointment and resentment congealed for Soto into a "never again" attitude about playing major league ball, he nevertheless held on to his dream of
working with MLB. Soto became determined to create strategies that allow
his trainees to succeed where he failed, and he has built his training program around teaching discipline, which begins and ends with learning to

follow instructions. "Without discipline, the Americans will never give you a chance," he has been quoted as telling his young charges. "I can give that to you, and if you have the ability, you can become a star."[13] Men like Soto thus can return to the chain and work to alter it, as he has said, "by any means necessary."

These men have all entered the chain at various points, for varying amounts of time, and with varying degrees of success. Collectively, they constitute an unintended consequence because (1) they were jettisoned by MLB, which assumes they will not play any further role in professional U.S. baseball; and (2), because they figured out ways to take their MLB experience back to Dominican baseball, affecting the perceptions of the many young players who are waiting to sign or have signed and are part of the academy system. Listening to these men admonish young men about the perils that lie ahead serves not only to connect generations of Dominican players with MLB but also as a template of sorts for Dominican-MLB relations.

Unintended Consequence 3: Buscones' "Trans-Planetary" Response to Signing Caps

The effrontery of MLB in sending Sandy Alderson to the DR in 2010 to confront "problems" caused by Dominican baseball, which Dominican player developers boldly countered (see Chapter 6), has prompted a long, connected string of skirmishes. In November 2011, MLB settled its latest collective bargaining agreement (CBA) and escalated the war of words and policies regarding the DR to new heights. The agreement included new, stricter policies for drug testing, as well as for draft picks and compensation. But the component of the CBA that was most devastating for Dominican baseball was the strong effort to rein in clubs' spending to sign international players. A special section in the CBA applied specifically to dollar limits on the July 2 signings of international free agents in the DR and Venezuela. In the first year (2012), the maximum total allowed per team would be $2.9 million, across the board. Thereafter, the maximum would range depending on where a team had finished during the previous season. The total allowable signing limits per team would be between $1.7 million and $4.9 million.

For buscones and players, the gains made in recent years had brought Latin American signings closer to those of American players, and the parity that was beginning to emerge would be in jeopardy. MLB's rationale therefore was priceless: It declared the cap as an attempt to create parity. "Our overarching goal was to prevent teams with the largest amount of money from becoming absolutely dominant in the market for international players, and we think this levels the playing field," declared Rob Manfred, executive vice-president for labor relations and human resources.[14] It could also be a segue into a full-blown draft in the DR, as Andrew Keh reported in the *New York Times*: "More intriguing [than the signing cap], though, is the ground-work that was laid in the agreement for the introduction of an international draft, a measure officials have concluded is necessary to combat the problems of fraud and drug use that baseball has encountered in its signing of players overseas."[15] The signing cap and the promise of a draft was a powerful one-two punch thrown at the unregulated Dominican player, by far the most seri-ous threat yet to the power they had amassed.

According to the sportswriter Ben Badler, total spending on signing bonuses in the DR had jumped from $44 million in 2010 to $50 million in 2011—a 14 percent increase in just one year.[16] The buscones saw the larger bonuses as an indication that parity *was* an attainable goal, but to MLB, they were an indication that the days of signing Latin players cheaply were over. For MLB, returning to the "good old days" was more of a motivation for the caps than any sense of concern for small-market teams, many of which had come to value the open nature of the Dominican market, where good scout-ing could beat big money. Thus, to those teams that the cap ostensibly was created to protect, MLB's claims appeared disingenuous—that is, just another effort to keep costs down and enhance profits. And to Dominicans, it looked like an attempt to return to the era in which Latin players could be signed "on the cheap," a point that was not lost on Astín Jacobo:

> I put it to [an audience of Dominicans associated with baseball in 2011]: "Which is worse: the major league team that knows a kid is worth $1 million but pays $25,000 for him, or me, who knows [the kid is] worth $1 million, gets it, and the kid goes home with $650,000? Which is better for the kid, for me, and for the game here in the Dominican Republic? For the last forty years, [MLB has] been taking advantage of us. In the last ten years, we've evened things out a bit, and they don't like it.[17]

The answer to Jacobo's question, of course, depends on who you are asking. Clearly, MLB would prefer to pay $25,000 for a million-dollar player, whereas to the Dominicans, splitting the $1 million 65-35 between player and buscón would looks pretty good.

Dominican Response: Go Global. Jan Scholte uses the term "trans-plane-tary" to refer to spatial relations in a globalized world. It has a sci-fi ring to it that I like. Thinking about globalization through space is grounding and keeps us out of the airy-fairy world of cultural abstraction. Space, we are reminded, is "the where of social life,"[18] and in globalization, the where is everywhere and all at once—tangible and intangible. What once could have been considered actions in two distinct spaces (say, New York and Santo Domingo) is, in a globalized world, one space. It is also a sphere of action that is occurring in real time, often instantaneously. So conceiving of player development within a Dominican player commodity chain should force us to think in terms not of a one-way flow but of multiple development flows. For example, although the St. Louis Cardinals signed the pitcher Alex Reyes out of the Dominican Republic for $950,000 in 2012, Reyes was raised in Elizabeth, New Jersey, where he played high school baseball before he relocated to Palenque to train with a Dominican player developer. National boundaries and one-way player development are fading in the "trans-planetary" world we live in.

Dominican buscones have not stopped with player development. They have been taking a page out of the globalization literature in forging their responses to MLB's neoliberal ploy to reframe the free market by restricting the size of signing bonuses. Some player developers have begun to consider approaching other nations, such as Mexico and Japan, with their best players to break MLB's stranglehold on talent flows. In 2013, the International Prospect League (IPL) sent a number of its best prospects to play exhibition games in Puerto Rico before the World Baseball Classic. "Lots of scouts and other people saw our boys play there," said Jacobo, who is affiliated with the IPL. "Puerto Ricans even played against us. It was important for our program, because whatever else went on, [the international baseball community] saw this group of Dominicans playing out there next to all the other things going on, including Major League Baseball."[19] The World Baseball Classic is a venue for baseball that, although sanctioned by MLB, is not entirely controlled by it and can provide a window onto the world to outsiders such as the IPL. Thus, local responses can also operate out of a global mind set: By expanding their operations to include other nations, Dominican player developers are taking their informal market strategies into "trans-planetary" spaces.

Whether such tactics will succeed is less important than the willingness of certain sectors of the Dominican baseball community to attempt them. In the history of U.S.-Dominican relations, standing up to the Americans in almost any capacity is unheard of. This attempt by the buscones, therefore, is precedent setting and should be recorded in Dominican history as a shot heard 'round their world.

Unintended Consequence 4: Second Coming
of the Amateur Leagues

While events in the DR were hiving off in so many directions, MLB's desire to continue signing the youngest players possible seemed to increase. A point was reached at which some player developers, including Edgar Mercedes, started purchasing thirteen- and fourteen-year-old players from their league coordinators outright, without even meeting them. The players were then stockpiled in his facility, a practice that irritates other buscones. "Now, when there's a kid with real potential, everyone goes after him and tries to buy him [outright]," Jacobo said. "I hate to compete with that. Why am I gonna pay someone for a kid I don't really know anything about?"[20]

To combat the chaotic rush for young players, Jacobo came up with a creative solution: to form his own youth leagues. Since 2008 he had been idly musing about converting a portion of his training complex into Little League fields, as much to give boys living in his neighborhood a place to play as to identify young talent. The efforts by Mercedes and others to cull the Little Leagues gave Jacobo's plan a new urgency. "So, I'm creating my own Little League system where I can pick my own ballplayers based on things I value," he told me in 2012. "It takes some time to locate these kids, but once it's done, you got them inside, and you have a fuller sense of the prospects [who you've] got [i.e., their family background, personal makeup, and so on]. Tomorrow, I have my first 50 kids playing in my backyard." His little league fields had been cleared and roughly prepared for play. "I'm gonna make them [the fields] really, really nice down the road, but for now we're ready," he said.[21] Two months later, Jacobo's version of Little League had begun with more than a hundred boys age six to thirteen. They practice twice a week and play twice a week after school. Jacobo was particularly proud that he did not have to beat the bushes for players. "People around here know that we're a place that plays baseball [and] that we're a safe place to send kids," he said. "They play behind walls, and mothers don't have to worry. . . . This is just the beginning. The next time you come down, you won't believe how fast we'll grow."[22]

Jacobo's strategy could lead some of his influential and unregulated fellow buscones to imitate his experiment, restoring some measure of the amateur baseball leagues that were eviscerated when the modern baseball academies came into being. Thus, the buscones, the "culprits" so maligned in official baseball circles, could just wind up restoring amateur baseball, a vital part of the Dominican game, to health. What a fitting way to complete the circle. And if it does come to pass, will the buscones continue to be demonized by MLB? Will people in the DR publicly proclaim them heroes?

Either way, I sense that the struggle for the body and soul of Dominican baseball is far from over. Skirmishes will continue, but the antagonists now cannot exist independently of each other, and Dominican baseball as a system is at once unified and fractious. In the end, MLB and Dominican baseball will sink or swim together. Dominicans cannot go back to the earlier era in which baseball was their own; nor will MLB ever again be allowed to cherry pick players in the DR without concern for the people there. And MLB's continuing effort to foster its brand of inequality in the Dominican-MLB relationship looks even more ludicrous when one understands that the two sides now desperately need each other to fend off the most serious challenge: the possibility that baseball, whose global footprint is insignificant compared with that of soccer and basketball, may face its most serious challenge to survival in the twenty-first century.

Notes

PREFACE

1. "Major League Baseball Statement Regarding International Draft Discussions," press release, May 31, 2013, available at http://mlb.mlb.com/news/article.jsp?ymd=2013 0531&content_id=49190958&vkey=pr_mlb&c_id=mlb.

2. "MLB Players Association and Commissioner's Office End International Draft Discussions," press release, May 31, 2013, available at http://mlb.mlb.com/pa/news/article .jsp?ymd=20130730&content_id=55266084&vkey=mlbpa_news&fext=.jsp.

INTRODUCTION

1. Robert K. Merton, "The Unanticipated Consequences of Purposive Social Action," *American Sociological Review* 1, no. 6 (1936): 904.

2. I thank Milton Jamail for introducing me to this concept, which I went on to research. The phrase originated in the sixteenth century in Mexico, where viceroys increasingly came into conflict with decrees from Spain.

3. Steven Gregory, *The Devil behind the Mirror: Globalization and Politics in the Dominican Republic* (Berkeley: University of California Press, 2006), 15.

4. Quoted in Adam Kilgore, "The Nationals in the Dominican Republic: One Last Word," *Washington Post*, February 11, 2011.

5. Astín Jacobo, interview by the author, August 29, 2010.

6. Alan Klein, *Sugarball: The American Game, the Dominican Dream* (New Haven, CT: Yale University Press, 1991).

7. Peter Cary, "Where Ballplayers Are Born and Made," *U.S. News and World Report*, August 13, 2012, available at http://www.usnewsandworldreport.com.

8. I have encountered African American and Mexican American players in these buscón academies. Sources there claim that the buscón academies have dozens of such players.

9. Alan Klein, *Growing the Game: The Globalization of Major League Baseball* (New Haven, CT: Yale University Press, 2006).

10. Trevor Martin, Ross Finkel, and Jonathan Paly, dirs., *Ballplayer: Pelotero*, documentary, Guagua Productions, New York, 2012.

11. Jan Black, *The Dominican Republic: Politics and Development in an Unsovereign State* (Boston: Allen and Unwin, 1986).

12. See Quentin T. Wodon et al., "Poverty and Policy in Latin America and the Caribbean, Volume 1," World Bank technical paper no. 467, June 30, 2000, available at http://econ.worldbank.org/external/default/main?pagePK=64165259&theSitePK=46 9372&piPK=64165421&menuPK=64166093&entityID=000094946_00072905364127.

13. Astín Jacobo, interview by the author, August 12, 2010.

14. Quoted in Marcos Bretón and José Luis Villegas, *Away Games: The Life and Times of a Latin Ballplayer* (New York: Simon and Schuster, 1999).

15. Francisco Cordero, interview by the author, October 22, 2009.

16. Jim Salisbury, "Search for Dominican Talent No Longer a Hit-or-Miss Affair," *Philadelphia Inquirer*, July 23, 2002, C1, C6.

17. Field notes, June 1, 2009.

18. Quoted in Klein, *Sugarball*, 91.

19. Jeff Shugal, interview by the author, June 2, 2002; Dan Evans, interview by the author, September 3, 2003.

20. Albert G. Spalding, *America's National Game*, repr. ed. (Lincoln, NE: Bison Books, 1992 [1911]), 21.

21. James Sullivan to Secretary of State William Jennings Bryan, November 1, 1913, U.S. National Archives, Department of State Records 839.00/962.

22. Orlando Inoa and Héctor Cruz, *El béisbol en República Dominicana: Crónica de una pasión* (Santo Domingo: Verizon, 2004), 60. Unless noted otherwise, all translations are mine.

23. For the GCC's essential position, see Gary Gereffi and Miguel Korzeniewicz, eds., *Commodity Chains and Global Capitalism* (Westport, CT: Greenwood, 1994).

CHAPTER 1

1. V. Gordon Childe, *Man Makes Himself* (Oxford: Oxford University Press, 1939).

2. Karl Marx, *The Economic and Philosophical Manuscripts of 1844* (Moscow: Progress, 1970), 91.

3. Terence Hopkins and Immanuel Wallerstein, "Patterns of Development of the Modern World-System," *Review* 1, no. 2 (1977): 111–145.

4. Ibid., 128.

5. Gary Gereffi and Miguel Korzeniewicz, eds. *Commodity Chains and Global Capitalism* (Westport, CT: Greenwood, 1994). By 2000, the global commodity chain would become the global value chain to reflect value added.

6. Stefano Ponte and Peter Gibbon, "Quality Standards, Conventions and Governance of Global Value Chains," *Economy and Society* 34, no. 1 (2005): 1–31; John

Humphrey and Hubert Schmitz, "Chain Governance and Upgrading: Taking Stock," in *Local Enterprises in the Global Economy: Issues of Governance and Upgrading*, ed. Hubert Schmitz (Cheltenham, UK: Edward Elgar, 2003), 340–381.

7. Jennifer Bair, ed., *Frontiers of Commodity Chain Research* (Stanford, CA: Stanford University Press, 2009).

8. Timothy Sturgeon, "How Do We Define Value Chains and Production Networks?" *IDS Bulletin* 32, no. 3 (2001): 9–18.

9. Gary Gereffi, John Humphrey, and Timothy Sturgeon. "The Governance of Global Value Chains," *Review of International Political Economy* 12, no. 1 (2005): 78–104.

10. Philip Rakes, Frederick Jensen, and Stefano Ponte, "Global Commodity Chain Analysis and the French Filigree Approach: Comparison and Critique," *Economy and Society* 29, no. 3 (2000): 390–417.

11. Bair, *Frontiers of Commodity Chain Research*. See also Ian Cook and Phillip Crang, "The World on a Plate: Culinary Culture, Displacement and Geographical Knowledges," *Journal of Material Culture* 1, no. 1 (1996): 131–153; Jeffrey Henderson et al., "Global Production Networks and the Analysis of Economic Development," *Review of International Political Economy* 9, no. 3 (2002): 436–464.

12. Debra Leslie and Seymour Reimer, "Specializing Commodity Chains," *Progress in Human Geography* 23, no. 3 (1999): 401–420.

13. Stefanie Barrientos, Catherine Dolan, and Anne Tallontire, "A Gendered Value Chain Approach to Codes of Conduct in African Horticulture," *World Development* 31 no. 9 (2003): 1511–1526.

14. Jane Collins, "New Directions in Commodity Chain Analysis of Global Development Processes," *Research in Rural Sociology and Development* 11, no. 1 (2005): 1–15.

15. Marcus J. Kurtz and Andrew Schrank, "Growth and Governance: Models, Measures, and Mechanisms," *Journal of Politics* 69, no. 2 (2007): 538–554.

16. Neil M. Coe, Peter Dicken, and Martin Hess, "Global Production Networks: Realizing the Potential," *Journal of Economic Geography* 8 (2008): 271–295.

17. Ibid.

18. Robert Foster, "Tracking Globalization: Commodities and Value in Motion," in *Sage Handbook of Material Culture*, ed. Chris Tilley et al. (London: Sage, 2008), 285–302.

19. George Marcus, *Ethnography through Thick and Thin* (Princeton, NJ: Princeton University Press, 1998), 16.

20. Claude Meillasoux, *Maidens, Meal and Money: Capitalism and the Domestic Community* (Cambridge: Cambridge University Press, 1981); Immanuel Terray, *Marxism and Primitive Society* (New York: Monthly Review Press, 1972); Maurice Godelier, *Rationality and Irrationality in Economics* (New York: Monthly Review Press, 1972).

21. Alan Klein, "Adaptive Strategies and Process on the Plains" (Ph.D. diss., State University of New York, Buffalo, 1977). I looked at how the hide trade had subsumed large portions of the tribal mode of production into a capitalist mode of production. Using a model that focused on "points of articulation" between these different economic systems engaged in a transnational form of production (Meillasoux, *Maidens, Meal and Money*), I described how they morphed over time into a distinct mode of production. The Plains tribes that engaged in the hide trade became a specialized labor force, along with the white employees of the fur companies (e.g., the American Fur Company

of John Jacob Astor). Today, that articulation between modes of production could just as easily be nodes in a commodity chain.

22. Keith Hart, "Small-Scale Entrepreneurs in Ghana and Development Planning," *Journal of Development Studies* 6, no. 4 (1970): 104–126; Keith Hart, "Informal Income Opportunities and Urban Employment in Ghana," *Journal of Modern African Studies* 11, no. 1 (1972): 66–89.

23. Alejandro Portes, "By-passing the Rules: The Dialectics of Labour Standards and Informalization in Less Developed Countries," in *International Labor Standards and Economic Independence*, ed. W. Sensenberger and D. Campbell (Geneva: Institute for Labor Studies, 1994), 159–176.

24. José Itzigsohn, *Developing Poverty* (University Park: Pennsylvania State University Press, 2000).

25. Jan C. Breman, *"The Informal Sector" in Research: Theory and Practice*, Comparative Asian Studies Program series, vol. 3 (Rotterdam, Netherlands: Erasmus University, 1980), 121–145. See also Manuel Castells and Alejandro Portes, "World Underneath: The Origins, Dynamics and Effects of the Informal Economy," in *The Informal Economy: Studies in Advanced and Less Developed Countries*, ed. Alejandro Portes, Manuel Castells, and Lauren A. Benton (Baltimore: Johns Hopkins University Press, 1989), 11–41.

26. Steven Gregory, *The Devil behind the Mirror: Globalization and Politics in the Dominican Republic* (Berkeley: University of California Press, 2006).

27. Ibid., 35.

28. Friedrich Schneider, Andreas Buehn, and Claudio E. Montenegro, "Shadow Economies All over the World: New Estimates for 162 Countries from 1999 to 2007," World Bank, Policy Working Paper no. 5356, 2010.

29. Karl Polanyi, *The Great Transformation* (Boston: Beacon, 1944).

30. Gregory, *The Devil behind the Mirror*, 193.

31. Quoted in Ben Badler, "Teams Welcome Players at Instructional League," *Baseball America*, November 13, 2012, 38.

32. Gregory, *The Devil behind the Mirror*, 170.

33. Ibid., 36.

34. Quoted in "Cheers and Jeers: Gonzalez an Example of a Dirty Little Secret," *Washington Examiner*, February 20, 2009, available at http://washingtonexaminer.com.

CHAPTER 2

1. Alan Klein, *Sugarball: The American Game, the Dominican Dream* (New Haven, CT: Yale University Press, 1991), 42–44.

2. For instance, Michael Kryzanek, "The Power of Baseball Strikes Out Diplomatic Rift," *Patriot Ledger* (Quincy, MA), May 27, 2012. See Ruck's account for the fullest assessment of the history of the Dominican game: Rob Ruck, *The Tropic of Baseball: Baseball in the Dominican Republic* (Westport, CT: Meckler, 1991).

3. William H. Beezley, *Judas at the Jockey Club and Other Episodes of Porfirian Mexico* (Lincoln: University of Nebraska Press, 1978).

4. Louis A. Perez Jr., "Between Baseball and Bullfighting: The Quest for Nationality in Cuba, 1868–1898," *Journal of American History* 81, no. 2 (September 1994): 493–517.

5. Ruck, *The Tropic of Baseball*, 6.

6. Klein, *Sugarball*, 25–27.

7. Ruck, *The Tropic of Baseball*, 13.

8. Alan Klein, *Growing the Game: The Globalization of Major League Baseball* (New Haven, CT: Yale University Press, 2006), 33.

9. For a biography of Avila, see Klein, *Sugarball*, 95–103.

10. Ibid., 35–39.

11. Ibid.

12. Ralph Avila, interview by the author, January 5, 1988.

13. See Klein, *Sugarball*, 42–43, 62–63.

14. Edy Toledo, interview by the author, May 15, 2012.

15. Klein, *Sugarball*, 83.

16. Ralph Avila, interview by the author, August 22, 2011.

17. Gilberto Reyes, interview by the author, October 5, 2005. Reyes learned English in a total-immersion setting and spoke in favor of that method.

18. Ralph Avila, interview by the author, June 1, 2008.

19. Ibid., January 6, 1988.

20. Ibid.

21. Luis Silverio, interview by the author, February 6, 2002.

22. Ralph Avila, interview by the author, May 30, 2008.

23. Jesús Alou, interview by the author, May 23, 2008.

24. Louie Eljaua, interview by the author, June 11, 2002.

25. Jesús Alou, interview by the author, June 30, 2002.

26. Junior Noboa, interview by the author, October 1, 2009.

27. Field notes, November 22, 2009.

28. Jesús Alou, interview by the author, August 2, 2010.

29. Arnold van Gennep, *Rites of Passage* (Chicago: University of Chicago Press, 1960); Victor Turner, "Betwixt and Between: The Liminal Period in *Rites de Passage*," in *The Forest of Symbols: Aspects of Ndembu Ritual* (Ithaca, NY: Cornell University Press, 1967).

30. Paul Willis, *Learning to Labour: How Working Class Kids Get Working Class Jobs* (New York: Columbia University Press, 1977).

31. Jesse Sanchez, "Academy Directors Play Key Role: Heads Help Prospects Deal with the Pressures of Pro Ball," MLB.com, September 18, 2007, available at http://mlb.mlb.com/news/print.jsp?ymd=20070918&content_id=2215652&vkey=news_mlb&c_id=mlb&fext=.jsp.

32. Klein, *Sugarball*, 100–103.

33. Avila interview, January 6, 1988.

34. Jesús Alou, interview by the author, April 23, 2008.

35. Sanchez, "Academy Directors Play Key Role."

36. Juan Henderson, interview by the author, May 26, 2005.

37. Edy Toledo, interview by the author, May 14, 2012.

38. Carlos Alfonso, interview by the author, October 4, 2008.

39. Field notes, November 7, 2007, November 2, 2010.

40. Silverio interview, February 6, 2002.

41. Field notes, October 11, 2012.

42. Luis Silverio, interview by the author, June 26, 2002.

43. Field notes, November 14, 2008.

44. Luis Silverio, interview by the author, June 7, 2002.

45. Klein, *Sugarball*, 69.

46. Rafael Pérez, interview by the author, April 11, 2012.

47. Juan Henderson, interview by the author, May 25, 2008.

48. Jesús Alou, interview by the author, May 20, 2009.

49. Ibid.

50. Ibid.

51. Ibid.

52. Ralph Avila, interview by the author, June 2, 2008.

53. Pierre Bourdieu, *Outline of a Theory of Practice* (Cambridge: Cambridge University Press, 1977).

54. Juan Henderson, interview by the author, October 29, 2010.

55. Native American language, physical appearance, and bodily and cultural practices were all prohibited for several generations of Native American children and replaced with Anglo-Saxon content.

56. Field notes, May 13, 2012.

57. Ibid., December 29, 2010.

58. Klein, *Sugarball*, 73–74.

59. Interview, November 14, 2007.

60. Juan Henderson, interview by the author, May 25, 2005.

61. Silverio interview, June 7, 2002.

62. Henderson interview, May 26, 2005.

63. Interview, April 20, 2018.

64. Silverio interview, June 7, 2002.

65. Quoted in Tom Weir and Blane Bachelor, "Spanish-Speaking Players Get Lessons in American Life," *USA Today*, May 13, 2004, 1C.

66. Henderson interview, May 26, 2005.

67. Interview by the author, November 14, 2007.

68. Epy Guerrero, interview by the author, November 14, 2007.

69. Klein, *Sugarball*, 78.

70. Interview, November 14, 2007.

71. Field notes, August 24, 2009.

72. Raul Guerrero, interview by the author, November 15, 2007.

73. Rafael Pérez, interview by the author, January 30, 2010.

74. Ibid.

75. Kevin Baxter, "Teams Are Teaching Players More than Just English," ESPN.com, March 1, 2006, available at http://sports.espn.go.com.

76. Field notes, August 25, 2010.

77. Ibid.

78. Ibid., March 7, 2003.

79. Jesús Alou, interview by the author, May 24, 2008.

80. Arturo J. Marcano Guevara and David P. Fidler, *Stealing Lives: The Globalization of Baseball and the Tragic Story of Alexis Quiroz* (Bloomington: Indiana University Press, 2002).

81. The person most responsible for bringing this issue into the public eye is the

sociologist Harry Edwards. See Harry Edwards, "Crisis of Black Athletes on the Eve of the Twenty-First Century," *Society* 37, no. 3 (2000): 9–13.

82. Henry Louis Gates Jr., "Delusions of Grandeur: Young Blacks Must Be Taught That Sports Are Not the Only Avenues of Opportunity," *Sports Illustrated*, August 19, 1991, available at http://sportsillustrated.cnn.com/vault/article/magazine/MAG 1139954/index/index.htm.

83. It should be noted that this bellhop/lawyer had dark skin; hence, in class terms, he was less networked for success.

84. World Bank, Inter-American Bank, and Government of the Dominican Republic, "Dominican Republic Poverty Assessment: Achieving More Pro-Poor Growth," report no. 32422-DO, October 30, 2006, 126–127.

85. World Bank, International Bank for Reconstruction and Development and International Finance Corporation, "Country Assistance Strategy for the Dominican Republic," report no. 31627-DO, May 19, 2005.

86. World Bank, "Dominican Republic: Review of Trade and Labor Competitiveness," report no. 30542-DO, March 28, 2005.

87. Rafael Pérez, interview by the author, August 23, 2005.

88. Valoree Lebron, interview by the author, April 26, 2007.

89. Gilberto Reyes, interview by the author, August 20, 2006.

90. Field notes, August 18, 2006.

91. Jesús Alou, interview by the author, May 27, 2007.

CHAPTER 3

1. Bob Nightengale, "Baseball's Oldest Bird Dogs Refuse to Give Up the Hunt," *USA Today*, May 19, 2008, C1.

2. Ralph Avila, interview by the author, November 20, 2007.

3. Edy Toledo, interview by the author, June 19, 2009.

4. Alan Klein, *Sugarball: The American Game, the Dominican Dream* (New Haven, CT: Yale University Press, 1991), 46–47.

5. Jesús Alou, interview by the author, June 11, 2002.

6. Ibid., May 23, 2007.

7. Louie Eljaua, interview by the author, June 10, 2002.

8. Quoted in Jim Salisbury, "Phillies Are Left to Lament One Who Got Away," *Philadelphia Inquirer*, July 22, 2002, D1

9. J. Alou interview, May 23, 2007.

10. "Field of Broken Dreams," *Dan Rather Reports*, season 5, episode 33, originally broadcast October 19, 2010.

11. Bill Chastain, "Dominican Connections Benefit Rays," *Tampa Tribune*, January, 28, 1996.

12. Juan Forero, "Cultivating a Field of Dreams," *Newark Star-Ledger*, July 5, 1998, sec. 5, 1.

13. Steve Fainaru, "The Business of Building Ballplayers: In Dominican Republic, Scouts Find the Talent and Take the Money," *Washington Post*, June 17, 2001, A1.

14. Field notes, June 30, 2006.

15. Ibid.

16. Field notes, June 2, 2002

17. Luis Silverio, interview by the author, June 12, 2002.

18. Juan Henderson, interview by the author, June 1, 2011.

19. Alou interview, June 11, 2002.

20. José Rijo, quoted in Barry Svrluga, "Tapping Into an Economy of Sale," *Washington Post*, December 21, 2006, D1.

21. Ronaldo Peralta, interview by the author, November 28, 2005.

22. Louis Eljaua, interview by the author, August 30, 2002.

23. George Dohrmann, *Play Their Hearts Out: A Coach, His Star Recruit, and the Youth Basketball Machine* (New York: Ballantine Books, 2012).

24. Ibid., 166.

25. Ibid., 332–333.

26. Quoted in Fainaru, "The Business of Building Ballplayers."

27. Field notes, June 12, 2011.

28. Ibid., August 30, 2009.

29. Quoted in Tom Farrey, "Young Ballplayers Looking for a Way Out of the Dominican Don't Have to Look Far to Get It—If They're Willing to Pay for It," *ESPN Magazine*, July 10, 2012, available at http://sports.espn.go.com/espn/magazine/archives/news/story?page=magazine-20040510-article39&src=mobile.

30. Marcos Bretón and José Luis Villegas, *Away Games: The Life and Times of a Latin Ball Player* (New York: Simon and Schuster, 1999).

31. The poor treatment he and other Latino players endured so outraged Felipe Alou, for example, that he published the first manifesto for Latino ballplayers in the U.S. media: see Felipe Alou, "Latin Players Need a Bill of Rights," *Sport* (November 1963): 78–79.

32. Bretón and Villegas, *Away Games*, 28, 54.

33. Ibid., 47.

34. Ibid., 56.

35. Kelvin Polanco, "Prisión preventiva para entrenador de Baní Enrique Soto por abuso sexual" [Baní coach Enrique Soto taken into custody for sexual abuse], February 10, 2011, http://pizaraterro.net (URL no longer available). All major Dominican periodicals carried a version of this story.

36. José Castillo, "Enrique Soto: Alegó que es inocente" [Enrique Soto: He claims he is innocent], July 6, 2011, http://canafistol.net (URL no longer available).

37. Gavy Paredes, "Enrique Soto: Dá ultimos toques a libro de escribo desde carcel de Baní donde expone lo que considera su verdad" [Enrique Soto: Putting final touches on book he is writing from the Baní jail to expose what he considers the truth], June 10, 2011, http://canafistor.net (URL no longer available).

38. Field notes, May 31, 2011.

39. Astín Jacobo, interview by the author, June 3, 2008.

40. Ibid.

41. Ibid.

42. Nelson Gerónimo, interview by the author, November 13, 2002.

43. Nelson Liriano, interview by the author, February 2, 2002.

44. Field notes, November 10, 2002.

45. Ibid.

46. Ibid.

47. Jorge Aranguré Jr. and Luke Cyphers, "The Dominican: It's Not All Sun and Games," *ESPN Magazine*, March 13, 2009, available at http://sports.espn.go.com/espn mag/story?id=3974952.

48. Quoted in Melissa Segura, "Ties between Dominican Prospects and Bookie Raise Concerns for MLB," *Sports Illustrated*, July 23, 2008, available at http://sports illustrated.cnn.com/2008/baseball/mlb/07/22/segura.drcrisis/index.html.

49. Ibid.

50. Quoted in Aranguré and Cyphers, "The Dominican."

51. Astín Jacobo, interview by the author, August 8, 2010.

52. Quoted in Aranguré and Cyphers, "The Dominican."

53. "Arias and Goodman Launch Education Program for Baseball," press release, June 17, 2011, available at www.dominicantoday.com/dr/sports/2011/6/17.

54. Michael Schmidt, "New Exotic Investment: Latin Baseball Futures," *New York Times*, November 17, 2010.

55. Michael Schmidt, "Steve Swindel, Steinbrenner's Once Heir Apparent, Finds New Success," March 7, 2012, available at http://newyork.cbs local.com/2012/03/07.

56. Ibid.

57. Schmidt, "New Exotic Investment."

58. Astín Jacobo, interview by the author, April 1, 2008.

59. Ibid., October 31, 2009.

60. Field notes, October, 31, 2009.

61. Astín Jacobo, interview by the author, August 29, 2009.

62. Ibid.

63. Quoted in Geoff Baker, "Dominican 'Field of Dreams,'" *ZUMA Press*, May 15, 2005, available at http://www.zreportage.com/zrep_text.html?storypath=2010/zrep063.

64. Ronaldo Peralta, interview by the author, May 27, 2005.

CHAPTER 4

1. "Field of Broken Dreams," *Dan Rather Reports*, season 5, episode 33, originally broadcast October 19, 2010; Trevor Martin, Ross Finkel, and Jonathan Paly, dirs., *Ballplayer: Pelotero*, documentary, Guagua Productions, New York, 2012.

2. Astín Jacobo Sr., interview by the author, March 19, 1988; Alan Klein, *Sugarball: The American Game, the Dominican Dream* (New Haven, CT: Yale University Press, 1991), 25.

3. Quoted in Klein, *Sugarball*, 26.

4. Ibid.

5. David Gonzales, "Melancholy in Bronx, but Not because of Stadium," *New York Times*, September 19, 2008.

6. Quoted in David Gonzales, "An Immigrant's Field of Dreams Transforms a Dingy Patch of the Bronx," *New York Times*, November 12, 1991.

7. Astín Jacobo, interview by the author, October 31, 2009.

8. Ibid.

9. Ibid.

10. Sara Rimer, "Before Manny Became Manny," *New York Times*, April 25, 2011.

11. Astín Jacobo, interview by the author, June 6, 2008.

12. Ibid.

13. Ibid.

14. Ibid.

15. Jacobo has spoken frankly about this issue, not only to journalists, but also to baseball insiders. At a public forum to discuss problems in Dominican baseball held in Santo Domingo in 2010, independent trainers came under attack not only from predictable quarters such as MLB but also from the renowned professional player Pedro Martínez, who railed against trainers for impeding young players' education and for taking what he felt were excessive commissions. "The [people] who could solve this problem are sitting here with us," Jacobo recalled saying at the time. "The government has declared [that] 4 percent of [the gross national product] is supposed to go to education, but it's getting only 2.3 percent. That's the problem." Ibid., June 1, 2011. Jacobo's willingness to take on these issues publicly is commendable and courageous, especially given the reluctance of the Dominican government office responsible for overseeing baseball to confront how MLB operates in the country.

16. Ibid., June 4, 2008.

17. Ibid.

18. Ibid.

19. Ibid.

20. Field notes, April 29, 2009.

21. Astín Jacobo, interview by the author, May 15, 2012.

22. Ibid., June 3, 2008.

23. Quoted in Martin, Finkel, and Paly, *Ballplayer*.

24. Ibid.

25. Astín Jacobo, interview by the author, May 14, 2011.

26. Rafael Pérez, interview by the author, November 8, 2002.

27. Ibid.

28. Ibid.

29. Ibid., August 29, 2005.

30. Ibid.

31. Ibid.

32. Ibid., May 14, 2012.

33. Felipe Alou, "Latin Players Need a Bill of Rights," *Sport* (November 1963): 21.

34. Quoted in Rob Ruck, *The Tropic of Baseball: Baseball in the Dominican Republic* (Westport, CT: Meckler, 1991), 83.

35. Quoted in Dave Zirin, "Si Se Puede: Felipe Alou Stands Up to Bigotry," Edge of Sports (blog), August 8, 2005, available at http://www.edgeofsports.com/2005-08-08-147.

36. For a wonderfully crafted article that explains the social milieu in which Omar Minaya grew up, see Gary Smith, "The Story of O," *Sports Illustrated*, June 18, 2007, 66–79.

37. Quoted in Jeff Pearlman, "At Full Blast," *Sports Illustrated*, December 27, 1999, 22.

38. See Smith, "The Story of O."

39. Ibid., 72.

40. Ibid., 75.

41. Minaya traded Cliff Lee, Grady Sizemore, and Brandon Phillips for the pitcher Bartolo Colón. Lee, Sizemore, and Phillips became high-impact players, whereas Colón delivered next to nothing.

42. Jonathan Mahler, "Building the Beisbol Brand," *New York Times Magazine*, July 31, 2005.

43. Ibid., 51.

44. Alan Klein, *Growing the Game: The Globalization of Major League Baseball* (New Haven, CT: Yale University Press, 2006).

45. Quoted in Adam Rubin, "Minaya Objects to Los Mets Label," *New York Daily News*, March 7, 2005.

46. Field notes, August 29, 2009.

47. Junior Noboa, interview by the author, August 26, 2009.

48. Ibid.

49. Ibid.

50. Ibid.

51. Ibid.

52. Ibid.

53. Milton Jamail, interview by the author, June 23, 2011.

54. Junior Noboa, interview by the author, August 24, 2009.

55. David Goldblatt, "Caribbean's Baseball City Pitches to the U.S.," June 19, 2008, available at http:// http://news.bbc.co.uk/2/hi/business/7458557.stm.

CHAPTER 5

1. Quoted in Jonathan Katz and Dionisio Soldevila, "For Some Dominican Baseball Players, Taking Steroids Worth Risk," Associated Press, September 27, 2009, available at http://lubbuckonline.com/stories/092709.

2. Pierre Bourdieu, "Structures, Habitus, Power: Basis for a Theory of Symbolic Power," in *Outline of a Theory of Practice* (Cambridge: Cambridge University Press, 1977), 164. See also Karl Marx, *The German Ideology* (Moscow: Progress, 1966); Raymond Williams, *The Sociology of Culture* (New York: Schocken Books, 1982).

3. Most media acknowledge the number and quality of players coming from the DR. See, e.g., Jorge Aranguré Jr. and Luke Cyphers, "The Dominican: It's Not All Sun and Games," *ESPN Magazine*, March 13, 2009, available at http://sports.espn.go.com/espnmag/story?id=3974952.

4. Ibid.

5. Steve Fainaru's invaluable article "The Business of Building Ballplayers: In Dominican Republic, Scouts Find the Talent and Take the Money," *Washington Post*, June 17, 2001, A1, is the basis for this outline of the case and the source of all of the quotes.

6. Ibid.

7. Ibid.

8. Ibid.

9. Alan Klein, "Progressive Ethnocentrism: Ideology and Interpretation in Dominican Baseball," *Journal of Sport and Social Issues* 32, no. 2 (2008): 121–138. See also Alan

Klein, *Growing the Game: The Globalization of Major League Baseball* (New Haven, CT: Yale University Press, 2006).

10. Quoted in Fainaru, "The Business of Building Ballplayers."

11. Ibid.; emphasis added.

12. Ibid.

13. Ibid.

14. Ibid.

15. T. J. Quinn, "MLB Pushes into Dominican Republic," ESPN.com, October 10, 2011, available at http://espn.go.com/espn/otl/story/_/id/7067334/major-league-base ball-pushes-dominican-republic-not-drawing-some-concern.

16. Field notes, May 31, 2011.

17. Ibid.

18. Jorge Ortiz, "Exploitation, Steroids Hitting Home in Dominican Republic," *USA Today*, March 26, 2009.

19. Steven Gregory, *The Devil behind the Mirror: Globalization and Politics in the Dominican Republic* (Berkeley: University of California Press, 2009), 170.

20. Field notes, June 1, 2011.

21. Rafael Pérez, interview by the author, November 8, 2002.

22. Ibid.

23. Field notes, August 16, 2008.

24. Mike DiGiovanna, "INS Throws Curveball to Dominican Players," *Chicago Tribune*, February 1, 2003.

25. Ibid.

26. Quoted in Ben Badler, "Latin America Reacts to 'Smiley,'" Daily Dish (blog), March 5, 2009, available at http://www.baseballamerica.com/blog/prospects/category/daily-dish.

27. Ralph Avila, interview by the author, June, 1, 2008.

28. Juan Henderson, interview by the author, November 3, 2009.

29. John Seibel, interview by the author, August 20, 2005.

30. Field notes, August 18, 2011.

31. Astín Jacobo, interview by the author, August 18, 2010.

32. Quoted in Roger Mooney, "Dominican Players Willing to Lie to Achieve Baseball Dreams," *Tampa Bay Tribune Online*, February 21, 2013, available at http://www.draysbay.com/2013/2/21/4012622/the-rays-tank--domincan-age-identity-joel-peralta-fausto-carmona-hernandez-leo-nunez-oviedo.

33. Ortiz, "Exploitation, Steroids Hitting Home in Dominican Republic."

34. Jeff Passan, "Alderson Addresses Dominican Corruption," Yahoo! Sports, April 22, 2010, available at http://sports.yahoo.com/mlb/news?slug=jp-dominican042210.

35. Quoted in Michael S. Schmidt, "Baseball Emissary to Review Troubled Dominican Pipeline," *New York Times*, March 10, 2010.

36. Steve Fainaru, "Injecting Hope—and Risk: Dominican Prospects Turn to Supplements Designed for Animals," *Washington Post*, June 23, 2003, A1, A14.

37. Ibid.

38. Ibid.

39. Geoff Baker, "Life in Needle Park," *Toronto Star*, May 14, 2005, E1.

40. Ibid.

41. Michael S. Schmidt and Joshua Robinson, "Failed Drug Tests Are Down, with One Exception," *New York Times*, August 14, 2008, available at http://www.nytimes.com/2008/08/15/sports/baseball/15drugs.html.

42. See, e.g., Farrey, "Finder's Fee"; Kathleen O'Brian, "In the Dominican Republic, Is Baseball a Ticket to Paradise?" *Fort Worth Star-Telegram*, February 23, 2004; Andres Cala, "Poverty in the Dominican Republic Drives Some to Desperate Measures in Race to Play Ball," Associated Press, September 6, 2001.

43. Perhaps the most significant exception to this is the work of Marcos Bretón, who truly captures the lived reality of these boys and makes comprehensible the ease with which one might consider violating rules: see Marcos Bretón and José Luis Villegas, *Away Games: The Life and Times of a Latin Ballplayer* (New York: Simon and Schuster, 1999).

44. Field notes, August 26, 2010.

45. Tom Farrey, "Results: Dominicans Fail More Tests than U.S. Players," April 14, 2005, available at http://sports.espn.go.com/mlb/news/story?id=2033711.

46. Some players (e.g., Manny Ramírez) knowingly took steroids for what they promised to do. Most young players, however, know little about the market (i.e., what steoids do and how to buy and use them without detection).

47. Quoted in Jackie MacMullan, "Ortiz Tries to Right a Wrong," *Boston Globe*, May 12, 2007, D6.

48. "Ortiz Apologizes for 'Distraction,'" ESPN.com, August 9, 2009, available at http://sports.espn.go.com/mlb/news/story?id=4385699.

49. MLB administrator, quoted in John Manuel and Chris Kline, "New Visa Scandal Leaves Ten Dominicans Banned," *Baseball America*, March 28–April 10, 2005, 3.

50. T. J. Quinn and Mark Fainaru-Wada, "MLB Scouts Scandal: A Little off the Dominican Signing Bonus Top," ESPN.com, September 26, 2008, available at http://sports.espn.go.com/espn/otl/news/story?id=3609833.

51. John Manuel and Chris Kline, "Marriage Penalty: Visa Woes Plague Dominican," *Baseball America*, February 1, 2006, available at http://www.baseballamerica.com/international/marriage-penalty-visa-woes-plague-dominican-139.

52. Seibel interview, August 20, 2005.

53. Manuel and Kline, "Marriage Penalty."

54. Amaurys Nina, interview by the author, August 22, 2010.

55. Ibid.

56. Robert D. McFadden, "Star Is Fourteen, So Bronx Team Is Disqualified," *New York Times*, September 1, 2001.

57. Ibid.

58. Paul Daugherty, "Walk a Mile in Almonte's Shoes," *Cincinnati Enquirer*, September 1, 2001.

59. Quoted in Bob Hohler, "Martínez Weighs In," *Boston Globe*, August 30, 2001.

60. "Little League Scandal Mesmerizing Dominican Republic," August 30, 2001, available at http://sportsillustrated.cnn.com/more/news/2001/08/30/almonte_little league_ap.

61. McFadden, "Star Is Fourteen."

62. Quoted in Cala, "Poverty in the Dominican Republic Drives Some to Desperate Measures in the Race to Play Ball."

63. "Little League Scandal Mesmerizing Dominican Republic."

64. Joshua Robinson and Michael S. Schmidt, "Nationals GM Resigns as Scandal Deepens," *New York Times*, March 2, 2009.

65. Rob Warmoski, "*L[os] A[ngeles] T[imes]*'s Baxter MLB Dominican Kickback Scandal Afoot," Can't Stop the Bleeding (blog), July 10, 2008, available at http://www.cantstopthebleeding.com/lats-baxter-mlb-dominican-kickback-scandal-afoot.

66. Quoted in Michael S. Schmidt, "Sports Agent's Loans to Poor Players Pose Concerns," *New York Times*, November 22, 2010.

67. Ibid.

68. Ibid.

69. R. D. Laing, *The Politics of Experience* (London: Routledge and Kegan Paul, 1967).

CHAPTER 6

1. Bruce J. Calder, *The Impact of Intervention: The Dominican Republic during the U.S. Occupation of 1916–1924* (Austin: University of Texas Press, 1984).

2. Quoted in Anthony DiComo, "Alderson Well Prepared for Challenges with Mets," MLB.com, January 10, 2011, available at http://newyork.mets.mlb.com/news/article.jsp?ymd=20110108&content_id=16409604&vkey=news_mlb&c_id=mlb.

3. Quoted in "Baseball Reforms for Dominican Republic," interview transcript, *PRI's The World*, March 12, 2010, available at http://www.theworld.org/2010/03/baseball-reforms-for-dominican-republic.

4. Quoted in "MLB and Baseball Reform," DRSol.com, April 27, 2010.

5. Ibid.

6. Ibid.

7. "Baseball's Sheriff in High Noon Showdown with Dominican Desperados," *Dominican Today*, April 15, 2010.

8. Field notes, April 18, 2010.

9. See, e.g., Nick Cafardo, "Clean-up Crew Hard at Work: MLB Panel Tackles Dominican Issues?" *Boston Globe*, August 16, 2009.

10. Listindiario.com, March 10, 2010, available at http://www.listin.com.do/el-deporte/2010/3/10.

11. Astín Jacobo, interview by the author, August 18, 2010.

12. Ibid., May 11, 2010; ibid., June 1, 2011.

13. Renaldo Peralta, interview by the author, May 27, 2005.

14. Amaurys Nina, interview by the author, August 2010.

15. Interview by the author, August 18, 2010.

16. "Protesta y el miedo a las medidas del alderson" [Protest and fear for Alderson's measures], *Diario Libre*, April 15, 2010, available at http://en.kiosko.net/do/2010-04-15/np/do_diario_libre.html.

17. Quoted in Juan Mercado, "Sigue el tranque con MLB!" [Follow the dam with MLB], *El Día*, April 22, 2010, available at http://www.eldia.com.do/deportes.

18. Ramón Rodríguez, "Scouts en contra del draft en República Dominicana" [Scouts against the draft in the Dominican Republic], *Listin Diario*, April 15, 2010, available at http://listin.com.do/el-deporte/2010/4/15/138480/Scouts-en-contra-del-

draft-en-Republica-Dominicana; "Baseball's Sheriff in High Noon Showdown with Dominican Desperados"; Mario Emilio Guerrero, "En EUA ven con ojeriza la presencia masiva de latinos en GL" [The U.S. Dislikes the Massive Presence of Latinos in the Major Leagues], *Listin Diario*, April 18, 2010, available at http://www.listindiario.com .do/el-deporte/2010/4/17/138825/En-EUA-ven-con-ojeriza-la-presencia-masiva-de-latinos-en-GL.

19. Quoted in Christian Red, "MLB Commissioner Bud Selig Taps Sandy Alderson with the Difficult Task of Fixing Dominican Baseball," *New York Daily News*, June 5, 2010, available at http://www.nydailynews.com/sports/baseball/mlb-commissioner-bud-selig-taps-sandy-alderson-difficult-task-fixing-dominican-baseball-article-1.182147.

20. Jacobo interview, August 18, 2010.

21. Nathanael Pérez Neró, "Los buscones enfrentarán a Alderson" [The buscones confront Alderson], *Diario Libre*, April 8, 2010, available at http://www.diariolibre .com/noticias_det.php?id=240842&l=1.

22. Jacobo interview, August 18, 2010.

23. Ibid.

24. Quoted in Jesse Sanchez, "Alderson Meets with Dominican Officials: Says Country Will Remain Priority, Source of Talent for MLB," MLB.com, April 26, 2010, available at http://mlb.mlb.com/news/article.jsp?ymd=20100426&content_id= 9586714&vkey=news_mlb&fext=.jsp&c_id=mlb.

25. Field notes, August 26, 2010.

26. Astín Jacobo, interview by the author, August 19, 2010.

27. Ibid., June 2, 2011.

28. Field notes.

29. Ibid., June 16, 2011.

30. Ibid.

31. Astín Jacobo, interview by the author, October 2, 2010.

32. Ibid., June 1, 2011.

33. Amaurys Nina, interview by the author, August 18, 2010.

34. The firm, based in Santo Domingo, is made up of the sports agents Ulises Cabrera, Brian Mejia and Roberto Morales.

35. Jacobo interview, August 18, 2010.

36. Ibid.

37. Ibid.

38. Ibid.

39. Ibid.

40. Ibid.

41. Quoted in "Major League Baseball to Debut 'El Torneo Supremo,'" press release, March 24, 2011, available at http://mlb.mlb.com/news/press_releases/press_release .jsp?ymd=20110324&content_id=17095358&vkey=pr_mlb&fext=.jsp&c_id=mlb.

42. Ibid.

43. Jacobo interview, October 14, 2010.

44. Field notes, June 1, 2011.

45. Jacobo interview, August 18, 2011.

CONCLUSION

1. Robert K. Merton, "The Unanticipated Consequences of Purposive Social Action," *American Sociological Review* 1, no. 6 (1936): 894–904. The concept has a history dating back a few centuries. Economist Adam Smith's "invisible hand" was built on this notion, for instance.

2. Similar stories are told about the lives of such Hall of Fame baseball players as Stan Musial, Roberto Clemente, and Hank Aaron, all of whom played with makeshift bats, balls, and gloves.

3. Jesús Alou, interview by the author, May 20, 2012.

4. Rob Ruck, *The Tropic of Baseball: Baseball in the Dominican Republic* (Westport, CT: Meckler, 1991), 49.

5. Alan Klein, *Sugarball: The American Game, the Dominican Dream* (New Haven, CT: Yale University Press, 1991), 29.

6. Astín Jacobo Sr., interview by the author, July 31, 1989.

7. Ruck, *Tropic of Baseball*, 73–74.

8. Klein, *Sugarball*, 66–69.

9. Ibid., 47–48.

10. Ibid., 47-48.

11. Field notes, April 29, 2012.

12. Gilberto Reyes, interview by the author, August 19, 2006.

13. Marcos Bretón and José Luis Villegas, *Away Games: The Life and Times of a Latin Ball Player* (New York: Simon and Schuster, 1999), 28.

14. T. J. Quinn, "Concern over MLB Rule in Latin America: Rule Change Effectively Prevents Teams from Paying Signing Bonuses to Amateurs," ESPN.com, March 1, 2012, available at http://espn.go.com/espn/otl/story/_/page/MLB-rule-change/major-league-baseball-rule-change-free-agent-pay-causes-concern-dominican-republic-venezuela.

15. Andrew Keh, "New Deal Extends Baseball's Labor Tranquillity," *New York Times*, November 22, 2011, available at http://www.nytimes.com/2011/11/23/sports/baseball/new-deal-extends-baseballs-labor-tranquility.html?_r=0.

16. Ben Badler, "International Bonuses Rise in 2011," *Baseball America*, March 15, 2012, available at http://www.baseballamerica.com/today/prospects/international-affairs/2012/2613107.html.

17. Astín Jacobo, interview by the author, August 20, 2011.

18. Jan Aart Scholte, *Globalization: A Critical Introduction*, 2d ed. (New York: Palgrave Macmillan, 2005), 60.

19. Astín Jacobo, interview by the author, March 15, 2013.

20. Ibid., May 16, 2012.

21. Ibid., January 23, 2013.

22. Ibid., March 15, 2013.

Index

Academy system 13, 29; academy directors, 48; clustering at Boca Chica, 45, 51; and competition, 61; discipline of players in, 57–58; as educational institution, 48; habitus in, 56; leadership in, 60; and relations with local communities, 46; socialization of players in, 54, 56; as system, 33; trouble handled in, 60. *See also individual academies*

Alderson, Sandy, 14, 135–151, 162; and cheap Latin American signings, 73

Alfonso, Carlos, 50–51

Almonte, Danny, 130–132

Alou (Rojas), Felipe, 14, 39, 106–107, 108, 114, 155, 156, 160

Alou (Rojas), Jesús, 43–44, 46, 53–54, 72, 73, 79, 160; as academy director, 48, 49; and the education initiative, 63, 66; on language acquisition, 63

Alvarez Lugo, Carlos (Esmailyn Gonzalez), 123, 132

Anthropology of difference, 14

Aranguré, Jorge, Jr., 117

Arias and Goodman Baseball Academy, 86–87

Artiaga, Sal, 43, 62

Avila, Ralph, 17; administrative style of, 49, 51; and Campo Las Palmas, 62, 154; as Dodgers' point man, 123–124; and the

Dominican Summer League, 43; on early *buscones*, 72; as founder of the modern Dominican academy, 37, 40; and remediation, 40–41; and scouting, 39; on signing bonuses, 54; on television's impact, 158; on the working agreement between the Dodgers and the Tigres del Licey, 38

Away Games (Bretón and Villegas), 80

Aybar, Willy, 79, 117–121; Aybar/Soto case, 74, 118–119, 120

Badler, Ben 163

Bair, Jennifer, 24

Batista, Jean Carlos, 101–102

Boras, Scott, 86, 89, 133

Born to Play Academy, 85

Bourdieu, Pierre, 54, 115–116

Bowden, Jim, 132

Bretón, Marcos, 80, 179n43

Buscones, 13, 28, 52, 164; Dominican views of, 76; forcing bigger signings, 75; Samuel Herrera, 83; Ramon Martínez, 82; Edgar Mercedes, 85–86; negative depictions of, 75; non-Dominican, 86–87; origin of, 71–72; origin of the word, 70; proto-*buscones*, 73; relations among, 88–89; relationship of, to players, 29; role of, 69–70; Enrique Soto, 79–81; training their prospects, 54

Alan Klein is a Professor of Sociology-Anthropology at Northeastern University. He is the author of *Sugarball: The American Game, the Dominican Dream*; *Growing the Game: The Globalization of Major League Baseball*; and *Baseball on the Border: A Tale of Two Laredos*.